Nikon® D7000™
FOR
DUMMIES®

by Julie Adair King

WILEY

John Wiley & Sons, Inc.

Nikon® D7000™ For Dummies®

Published by
John Wiley & Sons, Inc.
111 River Street
Hoboken, NJ 07030-5774

www.wiley.com

Copyright © 2011 by John Wiley & Sons, Inc., Hoboken, New Jersey

Published by John Wiley & Sons, Inc., Hoboken, New Jersey

Published simultaneously in Canada

For general information on our other products and services, please contact our Customer Care Department within the U.S. at 877-762-2974, outside the U.S. at 317-572-3993, or fax 317-572-4002.

For technical support, please visit www.wiley.com/techsupport.

Wiley publishes in a variety of print and electronic formats and by print-on-demand. Some material included with standard print versions of this book may not be included in e-books or in print-on-demand. If this book refers to media such as a CD or DVD that is not included in the version you purchased, you may download this material at http://booksupport.wiley.com. For more information about Wiley products, visit www.wiley.com.

Library of Congress Control Number: 2010943058

ISBN: 978-1-118-01202-4 (pbk); ISBN 978-1-118-06357-6 (ebk); ISBN 978-1-118-06358-3 (ebk);

ISBN 978-1-118-06359-0 (ebk)

Manufactured in the United States of America

10 9 8 7 6 5 4 3 2

WILEY

About the Author

Julie Adair King is the author of many books about digital photography and imaging, including the best-selling *Digital Photography For Dummies*. Her most recent titles include a series of *For Dummies* guides to popular digital SLR cameras, including the *Canon EOS Rebel T2i/550D, T1i/500D, XSi/450D, XS/1000D,* and *XTi/400D,* and *Nikon D5000, D3100, D3000, D300s, D90, D60,* and *D40/D40x.* Other works include *Digital Photography Before & After Makeovers, Digital Photo Projects For Dummies, Julie King's Everyday Photoshop For Photographers, Julie King's Everyday Photoshop Elements,* and *Shoot Like a Pro!: Digital Photography Techniques.* When not writing, King teaches digital photography at such locations as the Palm Beach Photographic Centre. A graduate of Purdue University, she resides in Indianapolis, Indiana.

Author's Acknowledgments

I am deeply grateful for the chance to work once again with the wonderful publishing team at John Wiley and Sons. Kim Darosett, Jennifer Webb, Steve Hayes, Jen Riggs, and Sheree Montgomery are just some of the talented editors and designers who helped make this book possible. And finally, I am also indebted to technical editor Dave Hall, without whose insights and expertise this book would not have been the same.

Publisher's Acknowledgments

We're proud of this book; please send us your comments at http://dummies.custhelp.com. For other comments, please contact our Customer Care Department within the U.S. at 877-762-2974, outside the U.S. at 317-572-3993, or fax 317-572-4002.

Some of the people who helped bring this book to market include the following:

Acquisitions and Editorial

Project Editor: Kim Darosett

Executive Editor: Steven Hayes

Copy Editor: Jennifer Riggs

Technical Editor: David Hall

Editorial Manager: Leah Cameron

Editorial Assistant: Amanda Graham

Sr. Editorial Assistant: Cherie Case

Cartoons: Rich Tennant
(www.the5thwave.com)

Composition Services

Project Coordinator: Sheree Montgomery

Layout and Graphics: Claudia Bell, Carl Byers, Samantha K. Cherolis, Joyce Haughey

Proofreader: Melissa D. Buddendeck

Indexer: Sharon Shock

Publishing and Editorial for Technology Dummies

Richard Swadley, Vice President and Executive Group Publisher

Andy Cummings, Vice President and Publisher

Mary Bednarek, Executive Acquisitions Director

Mary C. Corder, Editorial Director

Publishing for Consumer Dummies

Kathleen Nebenhaus, Vice President and Executive Publisher

Composition Services

Debbie Stailey, Director of Composition Services

Contents at a Glance

Table of Contents

Introduction

*N*ikon. The name has been associated with top-flight photography equipment for generations. And the introduction of the D7000 has only enriched Nikon's well-deserved reputation, offering all the control a die-hard photography enthusiast could want while at the same time providing easy-to-use, point-and-shoot features for the beginner.

In fact, the D7000 offers so *many* features that sorting them all out can be more than a little confusing, especially if you're new to digital photography, SLR photography, or both. For starters, you may not even be sure what SLR means or how it affects your picture taking, let alone have a clue as to all the other techie terms you encounter in your camera manual — *resolution, aperture, white balance,* and so on. And if you're like many people, you may be so overwhelmed by all the controls on your camera that you haven't yet ventured beyond fully automatic picture-taking mode. Which is a shame because it's sort of like buying a Porsche and never actually taking it on the road.

Therein lies the point of *Nikon D7000 For Dummies.* Through this book, you can discover not just what each bell and whistle on your camera does, but also when, where, why, and how to put it to best use. Unlike many photography books, this one doesn't require any previous knowledge of photography or digital imaging to make sense of things, either. In classic *For Dummies* style, everything is explained in easy-to-understand language, with lots of illustrations to help clear up any confusion.

In short, what you have in your hands is the paperback version of an in-depth photography workshop tailored specifically to your Nikon picture-taking powerhouse.

A Quick Look at What's Ahead

This book is organized into four parts, each devoted to a different aspect of using your camera. Although chapters flow in a sequence that's designed to take you from absolute beginner to experienced user, I've also tried to make each chapter as self-standing as possible so that you can explore the topics that interest you in any order you please.

Here's a brief preview of what you can find in each part of the book:

➤ **Part I: Fast Track to Super Snaps:** Part I contains four chapters to help you get up and running. Chapter 1 offers a tour of the external controls on your camera, shows you how to navigate camera menus to access internal options, and walks you through initial camera setup. Chapter 2 explains basic picture-taking options, such as shutter-release mode and image quality settings, and Chapter 3 shows you how to use the camera's fully automatic exposure modes. Chapter 4 explains the ins and outs of using Live View, the feature that lets you compose pictures on the monitor, and also covers movie recording.

➤ **Part II: Working with Picture Files:** This part offers two chapters, both dedicated to after-the-shot topics. Chapter 5 explains how to review your pictures on the camera monitor, delete unwanted images, and protect your favorites from accidental erasure. Chapter 6 guides you through the process of downloading pictures to your computer, preparing photos for printing, and sharing images online.

➤ **Part III: Taking Creative Control:** Chapters in this part help you unleash the full creative power of your camera by moving into the advanced shooting modes (P, A, S, and M). Chapter 7 covers the critical topic of exposure, and Chapter 8 explains how to manipulate focus and color. Chapter 9 summarizes all the techniques explained in earlier chapters, providing a quick-reference guide to the camera settings and shooting strategies that produce the best results for portraits, action shots, landscape scenes, and close-ups.

➤ **Part IV: The Part of Tens:** In famous *For Dummies* tradition, the book concludes with two "top ten" lists containing additional bits of information and advice. Chapter 10 covers features found on the camera's Retouch menu, including tools that enable you to crop your photo, adjust color and exposure, and make other picture adjustments right in the camera. Chapter 11 wraps up the book by detailing some camera features that, although not found on most "Top Ten Reasons I Bought My Nikon D7000" lists, are nonetheless interesting, useful on occasion, or a bit of both.

Icons and Other Stuff to Note

If this isn't your first *For Dummies* book, you may be familiar with the large, round icons that decorate its margins. If not, here's your very own icon-decoder ring:

A Tip icon flags information that will save you time, effort, money, or some other valuable resource, including your sanity. Tips also point out techniques that help you get the best results from specific camera features.

When you see this icon, look alive. It indicates a potential danger zone that can result in much wailing and teeth-gnashing if ignored. In other words, this is stuff that you really don't want to learn the hard way.

Lots of information in this book is of a technical nature — digital photography is a technical animal, after all. But if I present a detail that is useful mainly for impressing your technology-geek friends, I mark it with this icon.

I apply this icon either to introduce information that is especially worth storing in your brain's long-term memory or to remind you of a fact that may have been displaced from that memory by some other pressing fact.

Additionally, I need to point out three additional details that will help you use this book:

- **Other margin art:** Replicas of some of your camera's buttons and onscreen symbols also appear in the margins of some paragraphs. I include these to provide a quick reminder of the appearance of the button or feature being discussed.

- **Software menu commands:** In sections that cover software, a series of words connected by an arrow indicates commands that you choose from the program menus. For example, if a step tells you to "Choose File➪Convert Files," click the File menu to unfurl it and then click the Convert Files command on the menu.

- **Camera firmware:** *Firmware* is the internal software that controls many of your camera's operations. The D7000 firmware consists of two parts, called A, B, and L. At the time this book was written, both A and B were version 1.00, and L was version 1.002.

  Occasionally, Nikon releases firmware updates, and it's a good idea to check out the Nikon Web site (www.nikon.com) periodically to find out whether any updates are available. (Chapter 1 tells you how to determine which firmware version your camera is running.) Firmware updates typically don't carry major feature changes — they're mostly used to solve technical glitches in existing features — but if you do download an update, be sure to read the accompanying description of what it accomplishes so that you can adapt my instructions as necessary.

eCheat Sheet

As a little added bonus, you can find an electronic version of the famous *For Dummies* Cheat Sheet at www.dummies.com/cheatsheet/nikond7000. The Cheat Sheet contains a quick-reference guide to all the buttons, dials, switches, and exposure modes on your D7000. Log on, print it out, and tuck it in your camera bag for times when you don't want to carry this book with you.

Practice, Be Patient, and Have Fun!

To wrap up this preamble, I want to stress that if you initially think that digital photography is too confusing or too technical for you, you're in very good company. *Everyone* finds this stuff a little mind-boggling at first. So take it slowly, experimenting with just one or two new camera settings or techniques at first. Then, each time you go on a photo outing, make it a point to add one or two more shooting skills to your repertoire.

I know that it's hard to believe when you're just starting out, but it really won't be long before everything starts to come together. With some time, patience, and practice, you'll soon wield your camera like a pro, dialing in the necessary settings to capture your creative vision almost instinctively.

So without further ado, I invite you to grab your camera, a cup of whatever it is you prefer to sip while you read, and start exploring the rest of this book. Your D7000 is the perfect partner for your photographic journey, and I thank you for allowing me, through this book, to serve as your tour guide.

Part I
Fast Track to Super Snaps

The 5th Wave   By Rich Tennant

"Well, well! Guess who just lost 9 pixels?"

In this part . . .

Making sense of all the controls on your D7000 isn't something you can do in an afternoon — heck, in a week, or maybe even a month. But that doesn't mean that you can't take great pictures today. By using your camera's point-and-shoot automatic modes, you can capture terrific images with very little effort. All you do is compose the scene, and the camera takes care of almost everything else.

This part shows you how to take best advantage of your camera's automatic features and also addresses some basic setup steps, such as adjusting the viewfinder to your eyesight and getting familiar with the camera menus, buttons, and other controls. In addition, chapters in this part explain how to obtain the very best picture quality, whether you shoot in an automatic or manual mode, and how to use your camera's Live View and movie-making features.

1

Getting the Lay of the Land

still remember the day that I bought my first *single-lens reflex* (SLR) film camera. I was excited to finally move up from my one-button, point-and-shoot camera, but I was a little anxious, too. My new pride and joy sported several unfamiliar buttons and dials, and the explanations in the camera manual clearly were written for someone with an engineering degree. And then there was the whole business of attaching the lens to the camera, an entirely new task for me. I saved up my pennies a long time for that camera — what if my inexperience caused me to damage the thing before I even shot my first pictures?

You may be feeling similarly insecure if your Nikon D7000 is your first SLR, although some of the buttons on the camera back may look familiar if you've previously used a digital point-and-shoot camera. If your D7000 is both your first SLR and first digital camera, you may be doubly intimidated.

Trust me, though, that your camera isn't nearly as complicated as its exterior makes it appear. With a little practice and the help of this chapter, which introduces you to each external control, you'll quickly become as comfortable with your camera's buttons and dials as you are with the ones on your car's dashboard. This chapter also guides you through the process of mounting and using an SLR lens, working with digital memory cards, navigating your camera's menus, and customizing basic camera operations.

Looking at Lenses

One of the biggest differences between a point-and-shoot camera and an SLR *(single-lens reflex)* camera is the lens. With an SLR, you can swap out lenses to suit different photographic needs, going from an extreme close-up lens to a super-long telephoto, for example. In addition, an SLR lens has a movable focusing ring that gives you the option of focusing manually instead of relying on the camera's autofocus mechanism.

Digital SLR lenses are incredibly complex pieces of optical equipment. I don't have room in this book to go into a lot of detail about the science of lenses, nor do I think that an in-depth knowledge of the subject is terribly important to your photographic success. But the next few sections share a couple of tidbits that may be of help when you're first getting acquainted with your lens, shopping for lenses, or trying to figure out whether the bag of old lenses you inherited from your Uncle Ted or found on eBay will work with your D7000.

Checking lens compatibility

You can mount a wide range of lenses on your D7000. But some lenses aren't fully compatible with all camera features. For example, with some lenses, you can't take advantage of the autofocusing system and must focus manually instead.

Your camera manual has a complete listing of all the lens types that can be mounted on the D7000 and explains what features are supported with each type. But for maximum compatibility, look for these types: Type D or G AF Nikkor, AF-S Nikkor, or AF-I Nikkor. (The latter is an older, expensive professional lens that is no longer sold but might be available on the resale market.)

All the aforementioned lens types (as well as some others) offer CPU (central processing unit) technology, which allows the lens to talk to the camera. This feature is critical to getting maximum performance from the autofocusing system, exposure metering system, and so on. That's not to say that you can't use a non-CPU lens; you just lose access to some camera features. The Non-CPU Lens Data option on the Setup menu helps you get the most functionality possible with a non-CPU lens; check out the section "Cruising the Setup menu," toward the end of this chapter, for details.

The information in this book assumes that you're using a CPU lens that supports all the camera's functions. If your lens doesn't meet that criteria, check the camera manual for specifics on what features are unavailable or need to be implemented differently.

Factoring in the crop factor

Every lens can be characterized by its *focal length,* which is measured in millimeters. Focal length determines the camera's angle of view, the apparent size and distance of objects in the scene, and *depth of field* (how much of the scene can be rendered in sharp focus).

According to photography tradition, a focal length of 50mm is described as a "normal" lens. Most point-and-shoot cameras feature this focal length, which is a medium-range lens that works well for the type of snapshots that users of those kinds of cameras are likely to shoot. A lens with a focal length under 35mm is characterized as a *wide-angle* lens because at that focal length, the camera has a wide angle of view and produces a large depth of field, making it good for landscape photography. A short focal length also has the effect of making objects seem smaller and farther away. At the other end of the spectrum, a lens with a focal length longer than 80mm is considered a *telephoto* lens and often referred to as a *long lens.* With a long lens, angle of view narrows, depth of field decreases, and faraway subjects appear closer and larger, which is ideal for wildlife and sports photographers.

It's important to know, however, that when you mount a lens on the D7000, the angle of view is different than the lens's stated focal length. This variation, which holds true for most digital cameras, occurs because of the difference in size between a 35mm film negative — the standard around which lens focal lengths are measured — and the size of an *image sensor,* which is the light-sensitive component of a digital camera.

With a D7000, the effective angle of view is equivalent to that produced by a focal length about 1.5 times the actual focal length. For example, a 50mm lens on the D7000 produces the same angle of view as a 75mm lens on a 35mm film camera. (50 × 1.5 = 75.)

The end result is the same as if you shot a photo with your film camera and then cropped away some of the perimeter. For this reason, the value used to calculate the effective angle of view is sometimes called a camera's *crop factor.* In Figure 1-1, the red outline indicates the image area that results from the 1.5 crop factor. (You may also see this value referred to as the *lens multiplier.*)

Although the area the lens can capture changes when you move a lens from a 35mm film camera to a digital body, depth of field isn't affected, nor is the spatial relationship between objects in the frame. So when lens shopping, gauge those two characteristics by looking at the stated lens focal length — no film-to-digital conversion math is required.

Figure 1-1: A lens mounted on a 35mm film camera captured this entire scene; when mounted on the D7000, it captured the smaller area indicated by the red frame.

Getting shake-free shots with Vibration Reduction (VR) lenses

Some Nikon lenses, including the 18–105mm lens sold as part of the D7000 kit, offer *Vibration Reduction.* This feature, indicated by the initials VR in the lens name, attempts to compensate for small amounts of camera shake that are common when photographers handhold their cameras and use a slow shutter speed, a lens with a long focal length, or both. That camera movement during the exposure can produce blurry images. Although Vibration Reduction can't work miracles, it enables most people to capture sharper handheld shots in many situations than they otherwise could.

You enable and disable Vibration Reduction via the VR switch on the lens, labeled in Figure 1-2. Here's what you need to know about taking best advantage of this feature:

Vibration Reduction switch

Figure 1-2: Turn on Vibration Reduction for sharper handheld shots, but turn off the feature when you use a tripod.

✓ **For handheld shooting, set the VR switch to the On position.** Vibration Reduction will engage whenever you press the shutter button halfway as well as just after you press the button all the way to take the picture. If you pay close attention, the image in the viewfinder may appear to be a little blurry immediately after you take the picture. That's a normal result of the Vibration Reduction operation and doesn't indicate a problem with your camera or focus.

✓ **With the kit lens, turn off Vibration Reduction when you mount the camera on a tripod.** When you use a tripod, Vibration Reduction can have detrimental effects because the system may try to adjust for movement that isn't actually occurring. This recommendation assumes that the tripod is "locked down" so that the camera is immovable.

You don't need to disable Vibration Reduction when you want to create motion effects by panning the camera, however. (*Panning* means to move the camera horizontally or vertically as you take the shot, a technique that blurs the background while keeping the subject sharply focused, creating a heightened sense of motion.) The Vibration Reduction system is smart enough to ignore panning movement and compensate only for movement in other directions.

✓ **For other lenses, check the lens manual to find out whether your lens offers a similar feature.** On non-Nikon lenses, Vibration Reduction may go by another name: *image stabilization, optical stabilization, anti-shake, vibration compensation,* and so on. In some cases, the manufacturers may recommend that you leave the system turned on or select a special setting when you use a tripod or pan the camera.

Additionally, some lenses enable you to engage different types of stabilization (the settings may be called Active/Normal or something similar); again, refer to the lens manual for specifics.

Chapter 8 offers more tips on achieving blur-free photos, and it also explains focal length and its impact on your pictures. See Chapter 7 for an explanation of shutter speed.

Attaching and removing lenses

Whatever lens you choose, follow these steps to attach it to the camera body:

1. **Turn off the camera.**

2. **Remove the cap that covers the lens mount on the front of the camera.**

3. **Remove the cap that covers the back of the lens.**

4. **Hold the lens in front of the camera so that the little white dot on the lens aligns with the matching dot on the camera body.**

   Official photography lingo uses the term *mounting index* instead of *little white dot.* Either way, you can see the markings in question in Figure 1-3.

The figure (and others in this book) shows you the 18–105mm AF-S lens that's sold as part of the D7000 kit. If you buy a lens from a manufacturer other than Nikon, your dot may be red or some other color, so check the lens instruction manual.

The AF in the lens name stands for *autofocus,* as you may have guessed. The S stands for *silent wave,* a Nikon autofocus technology.

Mounting index dots

Lens-release button

Figure 1-3: When attaching the lens, align the index markers as shown here.

5. **Keeping the dots aligned, position the lens on the camera's lens mount.**

6. **Turn the lens in a counter-clockwise direction until the lens clicks into place.**

   To put it another way, turn the lens toward the side of the camera that sports the shutter button, as indicated by the red arrow in the figure.

7. **On a CPU lens that has an aperture ring, set and lock the ring so the aperture is set at the highest f-stop number.**

   Check your lens manual to find out whether your lens sports an aperture ring and how to adjust it. To find out more about apertures and f-stops, see Chapter 7.

To detach a lens from the camera body, take these steps:

1. **Turn off the camera and locate the lens-release button, labeled in Figure 1-3.**

2. **Press the lens-release button while turning the lens clockwise (away from the shutter button) until the mounting index on the lens is aligned with the index on the camera body.**

   Again, the mounting indexes are the little guide dots labeled in Figure 1-3. When the dots line up, the lens detaches from the mount.

3. **Place the rear protective cap onto the back of the lens.**

   If you aren't putting another lens on the camera, cover the lens mount with the protective cap that came with your camera, too.

Always attach and remove lenses in a clean environment to reduce the risk of getting dust, dirt, and other contaminants inside the camera or lens. For added safety, point the camera body slightly down when performing this maneuver; doing so helps prevent any flotsam in the air from being drawn into the camera by gravity.

Changing the focusing method (auto or manual)

In addition to the lens-related features covered in the preceding sections, make note of the following controls, which you use to set the focusing method to manual or autofocusing:

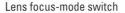

- ✔ **Lens focus-mode switch:** Assuming that your lens offers autofocusing as well as manual focusing, it likely has a switch that you use to choose between the two options. The switch might be labeled A/M (for auto/manual), as shown in Figure 1-4, or AF/MF. Some lenses offer a setting called AF/M (or something similar), which enables you to set initial focus using autofocusing and then refine focus manually. Check your lens manual for specifics, and check the Nikon manual to confirm that your lens can autofocus with the D7000.

- ✔ **Focus-mode selector:** Also shown in Figure 1-4, this switch sets the camera's internal focusing mechanism to manual focusing (M) or autofocusing (AF).

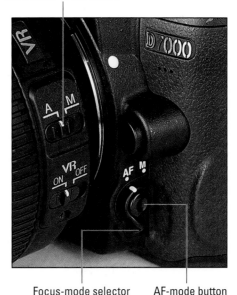

Lens focus-mode switch

Focus-mode selector   AF-mode button

Figure 1-4: Set the focus mode both on the camera body and the lens.

When you use autofocusing, pressing the AF-mode button at the center of the Focus-mode selector enables you to access two settings that tweak autofocus performance, the Autofocus mode and AF-area mode settings. Chapter 8 explains each. This button is your *only* way to access those settings — they're not available via menus as they are on other Nikon dSLRs.

Chapter 8 details how to take best advantage of the D7000's autofocusing system, including ways to select a specific focus point and choose when focus is locked on your subject. Manual focusing is fairly simple: Just twist the focus ring on the lens to bring your subject into focus. The placement and appearance of the focus ring depend on the lens; Figure 1-5 shows you the one on the kit lens. By the way, even when you focus manually, the camera provides some feedback to help you determine whether focus is set correctly. Look in the Chapter 8 section that's devoted to manual focusing for details.

Focal length mark

Zoom ring   Focus ring

Figure 1-5: On the 18–105mm kit lens, the manual-focusing ring is set near the back of the lens, as shown here.

If you have trouble focusing, you may be too close to your subject; every lens has a minimum focusing distance. You may also need to adjust the viewfinder to accommodate your eyesight; you can get help with the process a few paragraphs from here.

Zooming in and out

If you bought a zoom lens, it has a movable zoom ring. The location of the zoom ring on the D7000 kit lens is shown in Figure 1-5. To zoom in or out, just rotate that ring.

The numbers at the edge of the zoom ring, by the way, represent focal lengths. The number that's aligned with the white dot at the edge of the focus ring represents the current focal length. In Figure 1-5, for example, the focal length is 50mm.

Adjusting the Viewfinder Focus

Tucked behind the right side of the rubber eyepiece that surrounds the viewfinder is a tiny dial that enables you to adjust the focus of your viewfinder to accommodate your eyesight. Figure 1-6 offers a close-up look at the dial, which is officially known as the *diopter adjustment control.*

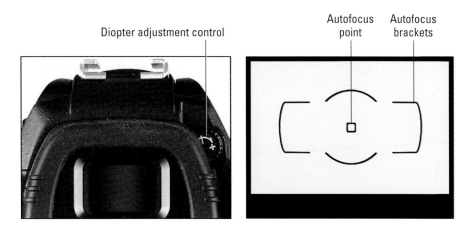

Diopter adjustment control   Autofocus point   Autofocus brackets

Figure 1-6: Rotate this little dial to adjust the viewfinder focus to your eyesight.

If you don't take this step, scenes that appear out of focus through the viewfinder may actually be sharply focused through the lens, and vice versa. Here's how to make the necessary adjustment:

1. **Remove the lens cap from the front of the lens.**

2. **Look through the viewfinder and concentrate on the autofocus point and brackets, labeled on the right side of Figure 1-6.**

   These markings relate to autofocusing, which you can read more about in Chapters 3 and 8. Depending on your selected focus options, you may see only the brackets and not the autofocus point.

3. **Rotate the diopter adjustment dial until the viewfinder markings appear to be in focus.**

The Nikon manual warns you not to poke yourself in the eye as you perform this maneuver. This warning seems so obvious that I laugh every time I read it — which makes me feel doubly stupid the next time I poke myself in the eye as I perform this maneuver.

Ordering from Camera Menus

You access many of your camera's features via internal menus, which, conveniently enough, appear when you press the Menu button. Features are grouped into six main menus, described briefly in Table 1-1.

Table 1-1		D7000 Menus
Symbol	*Open This Menu . . .*	*To Access These Functions*
▶	Playback	Viewing, deleting, and protecting pictures
📷	Shooting	Basic photography settings
✏️	Custom Setting	Advanced photography options and some basic camera options
🔧	Setup	Additional basic camera options
🖌️	Retouch	Built-in photo retouching options
📑📄	My Menu/Recent Settings	Your custom menu or 20 most recently used menu options

After you press the Menu button, you see on the camera monitor a screen similar to the one shown in Figure 1-7. Along the left side of the screen, you see the icons shown in Table 1-1, each representing one of the available menus. The icon that's highlighted or appears in color is the active menu; options on that menu automatically appear to the right of the column of icons. In the figure, the Shooting menu is active, for example.

I explain all the menu options elsewhere in the book; for now, just familiarize yourself with the process of navigating menus and selecting options therein. The Multi Selector, shown on the right in Figure 1-7, is the key to the game.

Press the edges of the Multi Selector to navigate up, down, left, and right through the menus.

Menu icons   Multi Selector

Figure 1-7: Use the Multi Selector to navigate menus.

In this book, the instruction "Press the Multi Selector left" means to press the left edge of the control. "Press the Multi Selector right" means to press the right edge, and so on.

Here's a bit more detail about navigating menus:

- **Select a menu.** Press the Multi Selector left to jump to the column containing the menu icons. Then press up or down to highlight the menu you want to display. Finally, press right to jump over to the options on the menu.

- **Select and adjust a function on the current menu.** Again, use the Multi Selector to scroll up or down the list of options to highlight the feature you want to adjust and then press OK (the button at the center of the Multi Selector). Settings available for the selected item then appear. For example, if you select the Image Quality item from the Shooting menu, as shown on the left in Figure 1-8, and press OK, the available Image Quality options appear, as shown on the right in the figure. Repeat the old up-and-down scroll routine until the choice you prefer is highlighted. Then press OK to return to the previous screen.

    In some cases, you may see a right-pointing arrowhead instead of OK next to an option. That's your cue to press the Multi Selector right to display a submenu or other list of options (although pressing OK usually works just as well).

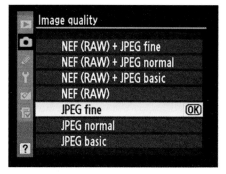

Figure 1-8: Select the option you prefer and press OK to return to the active menu.

✓ **Create a custom menu or view your 20 most recently adjusted menu items.** The sixth menu is actually two menus bundled into one: My Menu and Recent Settings, both shown in Figure 1-9. The menu icon changes depending on which of these two functions is active; Table 1-1 shows both icons. Each menu contains a Choose Tab option; select this option and press OK to shift between the two menus.

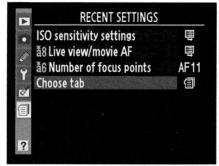

Figure 1-9: The My Menu screen lets you design a custom menu; the Recent Settings menu offers quick access to the last 20 menu options you selected.

Here's what the two menus offer:

- *My Menu:* Through this screen, you can create a custom menu that contains your favorite options. Chapter 11 details the steps.

- *Recent Settings:* This screen lists the 20 menu items you ordered most recently. So to adjust those settings, you don't have to wade through all the other menus looking for them — just head to the Recent Settings menu instead.

To remove an item from the Recent Settings menu, highlight the item and press the Delete button. Press again to confirm your decision and go forward with trashing the item.

 In addition to creating a custom menu, you can store two collections of menu settings as custom exposure modes, which you then select via the U1 and U2 settings on the Mode dial. Chapter 11 shows you how.

Decoding the Displays

Your D7000 gives you three ways to monitor the most critical picture-taking settings:

✔ **Control panel:** The LCD panel on top of the camera offers an array of shooting data, as shown on the left in Figure 1-10. The data that appears depends on what camera features you're currently using.

 You can illuminate the panel temporarily by rotating the On/Off switch past the On position to the little light bulb marker, shown on the right in the figure, and then releasing the switch.

Battery status   Illuminate Control panel

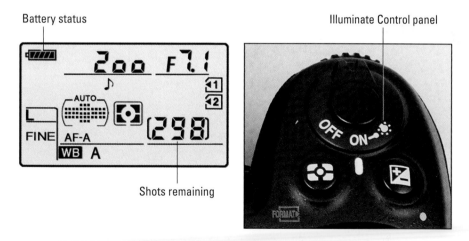

Shots remaining

Figure 1-10: Rotate the On/Off switch to the light bulb position to illuminate the Control panel.

 ✔ **Information display:** If your eyesight is like mine, making out the tiny type on the Control panel can be difficult. Fortunately, you can press the Info button to display the Information screen on the monitor. As shown in Figure 1-11, this screen displays the current shooting settings at a size that's a little easier on the eyes. See the section "Customizing shooting and display options" for information on how to adjust the display colors. Like the Control panel, the Information screen data varies depending on what shooting settings are currently in force.

The Information screen has a hidden power, too: After the screen is displayed, you can press Info again to activate the control strip at the bottom, as shown on the left in Figure 1-12. You then can quickly adjust any of the settings on the two rows of the strip. Use the Multi Selector to highlight a setting — a little *tooltip* (text label) appears to identify it — and then press OK. The camera then zips you directly to the menu containing the available settings, as shown on the right in the figure. Make your choice and press OK again to exit the menu. You can then adjust another setting or press Info one more time to turn off the display.

Figure 1-11: Press the Info button to view picture-taking settings on the monitor.

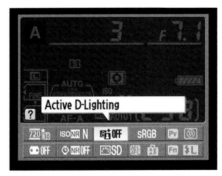
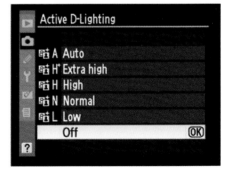

Figure 1-12: Press the Info button while the Information screen is displayed to gain quick access to the settings at the bottom of the screen.

✔ **Viewfinder:** You can view some camera settings in the viewfinder as well, as shown in Figure 1-13. As with the other displays, the viewfinder information that appears depends on what action you're currently undertaking.

If what you see in Figures 1-10 through 1-13 looks like a confusing mess, don't worry. Much of the display information relates to options that won't mean anything to you until you make your way through later chapters. But do make note of the following two key points of data that are helpful from the get-go:

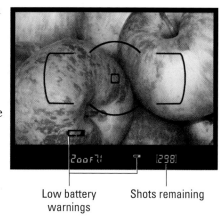

Low battery warnings   Shots remaining

Figure 1-13: You also can view some camera information at the bottom of the viewfinder.

- **Battery status indicator:** A full battery icon like the one in Figures 1-10 and 1-11 shows that the battery is fully charged; if the icon appears empty, go look for your battery charger.

  When the battery gets seriously low, the viewfinder displays not one, but two warning symbols, as shown in Figure 1-13. You can disable the larger warning symbol; see the section "Customizing shooting and display options" later in this chapter for details.

- **Shots remaining:** Labeled in Figures 1-10, 1-11, and 1-13, this value indicates how many additional pictures you can store on the current memory card (or cards, if you put one in each of the camera's two card slots).

  The value is presented a little differently if the card can hold more than 999 pictures. The initial K appears next to the value to indicate that the first value represents the picture count in thousands. For example, 1.0K means that you can store 1,000 more pictures (*K* being a universally accepted symbol indicating 1,000 units). The number is then rounded down to the nearest hundred. So if the number of shots remaining is, say, 1,230 more pictures, the value reads as 1.2K.

Working with Memory Cards

Instead of recording images on film, digital cameras store pictures on *memory cards*. Your D7000 uses a specific type of memory card — an *SD card* (for *Secure Digital*).

Most SD cards sold today carry the designation SDHC (for *High Capacity*) or SDXC (for *eXtended Capacity*), depending on how many gigabytes (GB) of data they hold. SDHC cards hold from 4GB to 32GB of data; the SDXC moniker is assigned to cards with capacities greater than 32GB. You also can use an Eye-Fi SD card, which enables you to send pictures to your computer over a wireless network. (Because of space limitations, I don't cover Eye-Fi connectivity in this book; if you want more information about these cards, you can find it online at www.eye.fi.)

To enable you to shoot oodles of pictures without having to swap out memory cards, the D7000 has two memory-card slots. Flip back the cover on the right side of the camera, as shown in Figure 1-14, to reveal the slots. The next section explains some details you need to know when you use two cards at a time, but first, here are some general guidelines for using SD cards:

Slot 1

Memory card access light   Slot 2

Figure 1-14: Insert cards with the labels facing the back of the camera.

> ✔ **Inserting a card:** Always turn off the camera before inserting or removing memory cards to avoid potential damage to the card and the camera. Place the card in the slot with the label facing the back of the camera, as shown in Figure 1-14. Push the card into the slot until it clicks into place; the memory card access light (labeled in the figure) blinks for a second to let you know the card is inserted properly.

> ✔ **Formatting a card:** The first time you use a new memory card or insert a card that's been used in other devices (such as an MP3 player),

you should *format* it. To find out why, see the cleverly named section "Formatting cards," a little later in this chapter.

✔ **Removing a card:** After making sure that the memory card access light is off, indicating that the camera has finished recording your most recent photo, turn off the camera. Open the memory card door, depress the memory card slightly until you hear a little click, and then let go. The card pops halfway out of the slot, enabling you to grab it by the tail and remove it.

When both memory card slots are empty, the symbol [-E-] blinks in the shots remaining area of the viewfinder, Control panel, and Information screen. A little card symbol also blinks in the image area of the view-finder; see "Customizing shooting and display options" later in this chapter to find out how to disable this alert (although I'm not sure why you would). If you do have a card in the camera and you get these messages, try taking it out and reinserting it.

Don't touch!   Lock switch

✔ **Handling cards:** Don't touch the gold contacts on the back of the card. (See the left card in Figure 1-15.) When cards aren't in use, store them in the protective cases they came in or in a memory card wallet. Keep cards away from extreme heat and cold as well.

✔ **Locking cards:** The tiny switch on the side of the card, labeled *Lock switch* in Figure 1-15, enables you to lock your card, which prevents any data from being erased or recorded to the card. Press the switch toward the bottom of the card to lock the card contents; press it toward the top of the card to unlock the data.

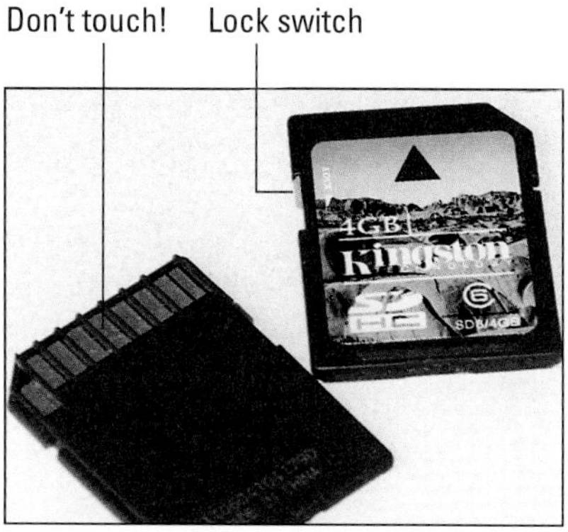

Figure 1-15: Avoid touching the gold contacts on the card.

You also can protect individual images on a card from accidental erasure by using the camera's Protect feature, which I cover in Chapter 5.

Using two cards at the same time

When you install two memory cards, you specify how you want the camera to feed picture files to each card. By default, the camera fills up the card in Slot 1 first and then puts additional files on the card in Slot 2. But you have other options; to explore them, open the Shooting menu and select Role Played by Card in Slot 2, as shown on the left in Figure 1-16. Press OK to access your choices, which work as follows:

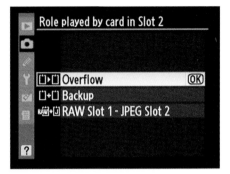

Figure 1-16: This option tells the camera how to make use of the card in Slot 2.

- **Overflow:** This setting is the default; again, the camera fills up the card in Slot 1 (the top slot) and then automatically switches to the other card.

- **Backup:** The camera records each picture to both cards. This option gives you some extra security — should one card fail, you have a backup on the other card.

- **Raw Slot 1 - JPEG Slot 2:** This setting relates to the Image Quality option, which Chapter 2 explains. If you select an Image Quality setting that records the photo both in the Raw (NEF) format and the JPEG format, the camera stores the Raw files on the card in Slot 1 and the JPEG files on the card in Slot 2. If you change to an Image Quality setting that captures only a single file type, the camera sends a copy of the JPEG file to each card.

A couple other critical points about using two cards:

- **Monitoring card use in the Information display:** You can tell which secondary slot function is in force by looking at the Image Quality readout of the Information screen, highlighted on the left in Figure 1-17. The little card symbols tell you what's going where. In the figure, the symbols show that the camera is set up to send Raw files to the card in Slot 1 and the JPEG versions to the card in Slot 2. (*Fine* represents one of three available settings for JPEG files, as covered in Chapter 2.) If you see the same file data for each card — for example, the word Raw appears in both cards — the Backup option is selected. And if the file type label appears in only one card, with the other card appearing empty, the Overflow option is selected.

- **Monitoring card use in the Control panel:** Symbols representing each card also appear in the Control panel, as shown on the right in Figure 1-17. Otherwise, only the symbol for the single installed card appears. A blinking card symbol indicates that the card is full. You can't glean anything about the primary and secondary card functions from this display, however.

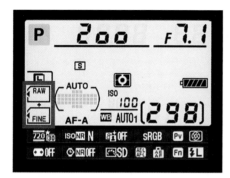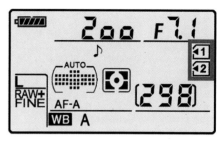

Figure 1-17: These symbols represent your memory cards.

✓ **Determining how many more shots you can take:** When you set the second card to the Backup or Raw/JPEG option, the shots remaining value (298, in Figure 1-17) is based on whichever card contains the least amount of free space. When either card is out of space, you can't take any more pictures. For the Overflow option, the value tells you the shots remaining for the card in Slot 1 until you fill that card and then indicates the amount of free space on the second card.

✓ **Selecting a card to store movie files:** Movie recording throws a small wrench in the card configuration system. No matter what setting you chose for the Role Played by Card in Slot 2 menu option, movie files always go on the card in Slot 1 by default. But if Card 2 has more empty space, you may want to send your movie files to it so that you can record a longer movie — the longer the movie, the bigger the movie file. Simply choosing Overflow doesn't work because the camera can't put part of the file on one card and the rest on the other.

To change the movie-storage setup, select Movie Settings on the Shooting menu and press OK. Then set the Destination option to Card 2. See Chapter 4 for complete details about movie recording.

✓ **Copying pictures from one card to another:** You can take this step by choosing the Copy Image(s) option on the Playback menu. For details, see Chapter 6.

Formatting cards

The first time you use a new memory card or insert a card that's been used in other devices, such as MP3 players or phones, you should *format* it. Formatting ensures that the card is properly prepared to record your pictures. Formatting after you download pictures to your computer is also a good idea. However, don't use your computer's file-management tools to format the card; the camera is better equipped to do the job.

Formatting erases *everything* on your memory card. So before formatting, be sure that you have copied any pictures or other data to your computer.

You can format a card in two ways:

✔ **Choose the Format Memory Card command from the Setup menu, as shown in Figure 1-18.** When you select the command, you're asked to select which card you want to format. After taking that step, you see a screen where you need to confirm your decision to format the card. Highlight Yes and press OK to go forward.

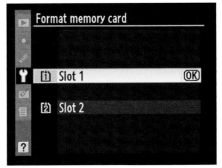

Figure 1-18: Formatting removes all data from the memory card.

✔ **Simultaneously press and hold the Metering Mode and Delete buttons.** See the little red Format labels next to the buttons? They're reminders that you use these buttons to quickly format a memory card. Hold the buttons down for about two seconds, until you see the letters *For* blink in the Control panel on top of the camera.

After you press the buttons, the Control panel also displays the icon for the card that will be formatted if you go forward. If you have two cards installed in the camera, you can switch to the other card by rotating the Main command dial. You also see the shots remaining value, which indicates how many pictures you can fit on the memory card at the current Image Quality and Image Size settings. (If the card contains any pictures, the number will grow after you complete formatting because those images will be erased.)

While the display is blinking, press and release both buttons again. When formatting is complete, the *For* message disappears, and the Control panel display returns to normal.

If you insert a memory card and see the letters *For* blink in the Control panel or viewfinder, you must format the card before you can do anything else.

Exploring External Camera Controls

Scattered across your camera's exterior are a number of buttons, dials, and switches that you use to change picture-taking settings, review and edit your photos, and perform various other operations. In later chapters, I discuss all your camera's functions in detail and provide the exact steps to follow to access them. This section provides just a basic road map to the external controls plus a quick introduction to each.

One note before you move on: Many of the buttons perform multiple functions and so have multiple "official" names. I think that's a little confusing, so I always refer to each button by the first moniker you see in the lists here.

Topside controls

Your virtual tour begins with the bird's-eye view shown in Figure 1-19. There are a number of controls of note here:

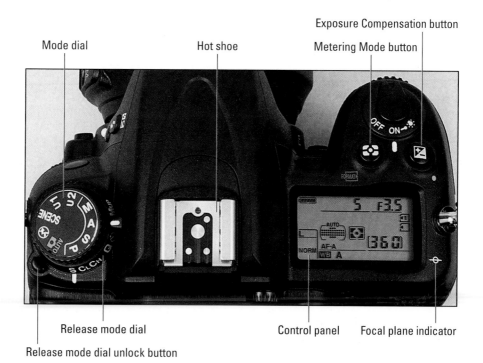

Figure 1-19: Press and hold the Release mode dial unlock button before rotating the dial.

✔ **Control panel:** You can view many picture-taking settings on this LCD panel. See the earlier section "Decoding the Displays," in this chapter, for more info.

✔ **On/Off switch and shutter button:** Okay, I'm pretty sure you already figured this combo button out. But remember that you can illuminate the Control panel by rotating the On/Off switch past the On position to the little light bulb icon. Moving the switch to that position also activates the exposure meters. After you release the switch, the panel backlight and meters remain active for about six seconds or until you take a picture. You can also turn off the panel light by rotating the switch to the light bulb position again.

Through options on the Custom Setting menu, you can change the delay time for the meter shutoff and also choose to display the Information screen along with lighting up the Control panel when you move the switch to the light bulb position. See the section "Reviewing Basic Setup Options," toward the end of this chapter, for details.

✔ **Exposure Compensation button:** When working in the camera's three semi-automatic exposure modes (P, S, and A), you can apply an exposure-adjustment feature called Exposure Compensation by pressing this button while rotating the Main command dial (the one on the back of the camera; refer to Figure 1-20). Chapter 7 explains. You also press this button along with the Qual button to reset the main picture-taking settings to their default options; see the end of this chapter for details. (The green dot by each button reminds you of their shared function.)

✔ **Metering Mode button:** Press this button while rotating the Main command dial to select an exposure *metering mode,* which determines what part of the frame the camera considers when calculating exposure. Chapter 7 has details.

The little red Format label above the button reminds you that you can press this button together with the Delete button — which also sports the label — to quickly format a memory card. See the earlier section "Formatting cards," for details.

✔ **Mode dial:** With this dial, labeled in Figure 1-19, you set the camera to a fully automatic, semi-automatic, or manual exposure mode. You also can set up and select two of your own modes, U1 and U2 (*U* for *user.*) Chapter 3 details the fully automatic modes; Chapter 7 explains the semi-automatic and manual modes (P, S, A, and M); and Chapter 11 shows you how to create your custom modes.

✔ **Release mode dial:** You use this dial, set directly under the Mode dial, to switch from normal shooting, where you take one picture with each press of the shutter button, to one of the camera's other Release modes, including Self-Timer mode. A letter representing the selected mode appears at the bottom of the dial. For example, in Figure 1-19, the S (Single Frame) mode is selected. See Chapter 2 for a look at all your options.

To rotate the dial, you must press and hold the little lock-release button labeled in Figure 1-19.

✔ **Flash hot shoe:** A *hot shoe* is a connection for attaching an external flash head. The contacts on the shoe are covered by a little black insert when the camera ships from the factory; to attach your flash, remove the cover, as shown in Figure 1-19.

Should you ever need to know the exact distance between your subject and the camera, the *focal plane indicator* labeled in Figure 1-19 is key. This mark indicates the plane at which light coming through the lens is focused onto the negative in a film camera or the image sensor in a digital camera. Basing your measurement on this mark produces a more accurate camera-to-subject distance than using the end of the lens or some other external point on the camera body as your reference point.

Back-of-the-body controls

Traveling over the top of the camera to its back side, shown in Figure 1-20, you encounter the following controls:

Figure 1-20: Rotate the Live View switch to the right and release it to switch between viewfinder and Live View shooting.

✓ **Main command dial:** After you activate certain camera features, you rotate this dial, labeled in Figure 1-20, to select a specific setting. For example, to choose a White Balance setting, you press the WB button as you rotate the Main command dial. (Chapter 8 explains white balancing.)

✓ **AE-L/AF-L button:** When you're taking pictures in some automatic modes, you can lock focus and exposure settings by holding down this button. Chapter 7 explains why you may want to do so.

If you don't use the button's normal function often, you can assign another job to it. Instructions in this book assume that you stick with the default button function, but if you want to explore your options, see Chapter 11.

✓ **Live View switch:** Rotate the switch to the right and release it to turn the Live View feature on and off. As soon as you turn Live View on, the scene in front of the lens appears on the monitor, and you no longer can see anything through the viewfinder. You then can compose a still photo using the monitor or begin recording a movie. Chapter 4 details Live View photography and movie recording.

✓ **Movie-record button:** After shifting to Live View mode, press this button to start recording a movie using the default recording settings. (See Chapter 4 to find out how to adjust the settings.) Press again to stop recording.

✓ **Multi Selector/OK button:** This dual-natured control, labeled in Figure 1-20, plays a role in many camera functions. You press the outer edges of the Multi Selector left, right, up, or down to navigate camera menus and access certain other options. At the center of the control is the OK button, which you press to finalize a menu selection or other camera adjustment.

✓ **Focus Selector Lock switch:** Just beneath the Multi Selector, this switch relates to the camera's autofocusing system. When the switch is set to the position shown in Figure 1-20, you can use the Multi Selector to tell the camera to base focus on a specific focusing point. Setting the switch to the L position locks in the selected point. See Chapter 8 for details on all this focusing stuff.

✓ **Info button:** Press this button to display the Information screen on the camera monitor. See the earlier section "Decoding the Displays" for details.

✓ **Playback button:** Press this button to switch the camera into picture review mode. Chapter 5 details picture playback.

✓ **Delete button:** Sporting a trash can icon, the universal symbol for delete, this button enables you to erase pictures. Chapter 5 has specifics.

✔ **Menu button:** Press this button to access menus of camera options. See the earlier section "Ordering from Camera Menus," in this chapter, for help using menus.

✔ **WB/Help/Protect button:** This button serves several purposes:

- *White balance control:* For picture-taking purposes, the button's main function is to access white balance options, a topic you can explore in Chapter 8.

- *Help:* You also can press this button to display helpful information about certain menu options. See "Asking Your Camera for Help," later in this chapter, for details.

- *Protect:* In playback mode, pressing the button locks the picture file — hence the little key symbol that appears on the button face — so that it isn't erased if you use the picture-delete functions. (The picture *is* erased if you format the memory card, however.) See Chapter 5 for details.

✔ **ISO/Playback Zoom Out/Thumbnail button:** In picture-taking mode, pressing this button accesses the ISO setting, which controls the camera's sensitivity to light. Chapter 7 has details.

In playback mode, pressing the button enables you display multiple image thumbnails on the screen and to reduce the magnification of the currently displayed photo. See Chapter 5 for a complete rundown of picture playback options.

✔ **Qual (Quality)/Playback Zoom In button:** In playback mode, pressing this button magnifies the currently displayed image and also reduces the number of thumbnails displayed at a time. Note the plus sign in the middle of the magnifying glass — plus for zoom in.

In picture-taking mode, pressing the button gives you fast access to the Image Quality and Image Size options, both of which you can explore in Chapter 2. And the green dot just below the button reminds you that you can press the button along with the similarly marked Exposure Compensation button to restore some camera options to their default settings, as outlined at the end of this chapter.

As for the monitor, I show it in this book without its protective plastic cover. But when the camera isn't in use, it's a good idea to keep the cover on to protect the screen from scratches and other damage.

Also note two more backside features: When you play movies that contain sound, the audio comes wafting from the cluster of tiny holes labeled Speaker in Figure 1-20. And if you use the optional wireless remote control, the rear infrared sensor picks up the signal from the remote's transmitter. (See Figure 1-21 for a look at the front infrared sensor.)

Front-left controls

On the front-left side of the camera body, as shown in Figure 1-21, you find the following:

- ✔ **Flash/Flash Compensation:** Pressing this button pops up the camera's built-in flash (except in automatic shooting modes, in which the camera decides whether the flash is needed). By holding the button down and rotating the Main command dial, you can adjust the Flash mode (normal, red-eye reduction, and so on). In advanced exposure modes (P, S, A, and M), you also can adjust the flash power by pressing the button and rotating the Sub-command dial. (That's the dial on the front of the camera, just below the shutter button.) See Chapter 7 for all things flash related.

- ✔ **BKT (Bracket) button:** This button is key to enabling automatic *bracketing,* a feature that simplifies the job of recording the same subject at various exposure, flash, and white balance settings. Chapter 7 details flash and exposure bracketing; Chapter 8 discusses white balancing.

- ✔ **Lens-release button:** You press this button before removing the lens from your camera. See the first part of this chapter for help with mounting and removing lenses.

- ✔ **Focus-mode selector:** This switch sets the camera to manual or auto-focusing. See the earlier section "Changing the focusing method (auto or manual)" for the short story; see Chapter 8 for complete focusing details.

Microphone

Front infrared receiver

Flash button

Lens-release button

AF-mode button

Focus-mode selector

Figure 1-21: Press the Flash button to pop up the built-in flash.

✔ **Microphone:** See the three little holes right below the D7000 label? They lead to the camera's internal microphone, included for capturing sound when you record movies. You also can attach an external microphone to the camera for better sound; see the upcoming Figure 1-23 for a look at the microphone jack and head to Chapter 4 for a primer in the art of movie making.

✔ **Front infrared receiver:** Here's the second of two receivers that can pull in the signal from the optional wireless remote control unit. Figure 1-20 shows you where to aim the remote transmitter if you're standing behind the camera.

Front-right controls

Figure 1-22 offers a look at the front-right side of the camera, shown with the lens detached to make the following controls a little easier to spot:

✔ **Sub-command dial:** This dial is the counterpart to the Main command dial on the back of the camera. As with the Main dial, you rotate this one to select certain settings, usually in conjunction with pressing another button.

✔ **AF-assist lamp:** In dim lighting, a beam of light sometimes shoots out from this little lamp to help the camera's autofocus system find its target. In general, leaving the AF-assist option enabled is a good idea, but if you're shooting at an event where the light from the lamp may be distracting, you can disable it through the Built-In AF-Assist Illuminator option on the Custom Setting menu. Chapter 8 explains autofocus features.

The lamp also lights before the shutter is released in Self-Timer mode and before the flash fires in red-eye reduction flash mode. Chapter 2 offers more information about both of these features.

Figure 1-22: You can set the Fn (Function) and Depth-of-Field Preview buttons to perform a variety of operations.

✔ **Depth-of-Field Preview button:** By pressing this button, you can see how different aperture settings affect *depth of field,* or the zone of sharp focus in your image. Chapter 7 explains aperture settings, and Chapter 8 delves into depth of field. Chapter 11 shows you how to assign a different function to the button if you don't care to preview depth of field.

✏ **Function (Fn) button:** By default, pressing this button locks the flash exposure value, an option Nikon calls *FV Lock.* Chapter 7 explains.

As with the Depth-of-Field Preview button, you can change the operation that's accomplished by pressing the button. Again, see Chapter 11 for the scoop.

Hidden connections

Hidden under little covers on the left side of the camera, you find the following inputs for connecting the camera to various devices, as shown in Figure 1-23.

✏ **A/V and HDMI jacks:** Use these to connect your camera to a television through a regular audio/video cable or high-def (HDMI) cable. The camera comes with the standard A/V cable; the HDMI cable is sold separately. Chapter 5 offers more details.

Audio/Video out   USB port   HDMI mini-pin connector

Microphone jack   Accessory terminal

Figure 1-23: You can plug in an external flash cord, remote control, or GPS unit here.

✏ **USB port:** One way to download images to your computer is to connect the camera and computer via the USB cable provided in the camera box. The tiny end of the cable goes into this port. Chapter 6 explains the downloading process.

✏ **Stereo mini-pin microphone jack:** If you're not happy with the audio quality provided by the internal microphone, you can plug in an external microphone here. The jack accepts a 3.5mm microphone plug. See Chapter 4 for all things movie related.

✏ **Accessory terminal:** Here's where you attach the optional Nikon GP-1 GPS (Global Positioning System) unit and the MC-DC2 wired remote control. I don't cover these optional devices, so refer to the manuals that ship with them or the Nikon Web site to find out more.

If you turn the camera over, you find a tripod socket, which enables you to mount the camera on a tripod that uses a ¼-inch screw, plus the battery chamber. The other little rubber cover is related to the optional MB-D11 battery pack; you remove the cover when attaching the battery pack. Connections for attaching an optional AC power adapter live inside the regular-battery chamber; the camera manual provides specifics on running the camera on AC power.

Asking Your Camera for Help

Programmed into your camera's internal software is a handy information help line — a great tool for times when you forget the purpose of a particular feature or want a little picture-taking guidance.

If you see a small question mark in the lower-left corner of a menu, press and hold the WB button to display information about the current shooting mode or selected menu option. (The little question mark symbol on the button reminds you of this function.) For example, Figure 1-24 shows the help screen associated with the Active D-Lighting setting. If you need to scroll the screen to view all the help text, keep the button depressed and scroll by using the Multi Selector. Release the button to close the help screen.

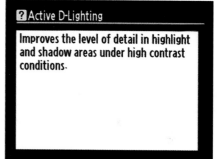

Figure 1-24: Press and hold the WB button to display onscreen help.

Reviewing Basic Setup Options

Your camera offers scads of options for customizing its performance. Later chapters explain settings related to actual picture taking, such as those that affect flash behavior and autofocusing. The rest of this chapter details options related to initial camera setup, such as setting the date and time, adjusting monitor brightness, and the like.

Cruising the Setup menu

Start your camera customization by opening the Setup menu, which offers the following options:

  ✔ **Format Memory Card:** Page 1 of the Setup menu, as shown in Figure 1-25, starts with this command, which wipes all data off the card and ensures that it's properly set up to record pictures. For quicker results,

you can use the two-button
formatting process outlined in
the earlier section "Formatting
cards."

✔ **Save User Settings:** Use this
option to set up custom exposure
modes (U1 and U2 on the Mode
dial). Chapter 11 shows you how
to take advantage of this feature.

✔ **Reset User Settings:** To wipe out
your custom exposure modes,
select this option.

✔ **LCD Brightness:** This option
enables you to make the camera

Figure 1-25: Visit the Setup menu to start
customizing your camera.

monitor brighter or darker. But if you take this step, what you see on the
display may not be an accurate rendition of your image. Crank up the
monitor brightness, for example, and an underexposed photo may look
just fine. So I recommend sticking with the default setting (0).

✔ **Clean Image Sensor:** Your D7000 has an internal cleaning system designed
to keep a filter that's fitted onto the *image sensor* — that's the part of the
camera that actually captures the image — free of dust and dirt. By choosing the Clean Image Sensor command, you can perform a cleaning at any
time. Just choose the command, press OK, select Clean Now, and press
OK again. You also can tell the camera to perform automatic cleaning
every time you turn the camera on or off, only at startup, only at shutdown, or never; to do so, select Clean at Startup/Shutdown instead of
Clean Now. Then press the Multi Selector right, highlight the cleaning
option you prefer, and press OK.

✔ **Lock Mirror Up for Cleaning:** This feature is necessary when cleaning the
camera image sensor (or technically, the aforementioned filter) — an operation that I don't recommend that you tackle yourself because you can easily
damage the camera if you don't know what you're doing. If you *are* comfortable with the process, be sure that the camera battery is charged before
you start; the menu option disappears when the battery is low.

When you shoot long-exposure images, mirror lockup helps avoid
camera shake that can blur the photo. But to use that technique, set
the Release mode dial to the Mirror Up setting and follow the shooting
steps provided in Chapter 2. Use the Setup menu's mirror-up option for
camera cleaning only.

✔ **Video Mode and HDMI:** These options relate to viewing your images
and movies on a television, a topic I cover in Chapter 5. The Video Mode
setting also affects movie-recording options, covered in Chapter 4.

✔ **Flicker Reduction:** The second page of the Setup menu leads off with
this option, as shown in Figure 1-26. Changing the setting may reduce
flickering or banding of the Live View display when you're working in an

area lit by fluorescent or mercury-vapor lamps. You're supposed to choose the setting that matches the electrical current in the room — but there are only two settings, so just experiment to see which one produces the best display.

Figure 1-26: Changing the Flicker Reduction settings may improve the quality of the Live View display in areas lit by fluorescent or mercury-vapor lamps.

↙ **Time Zone and Date:** When you turn on your camera for the first time, it displays this option and asks you to set the current date and time. Keeping the date/time accurate is important because that information is recorded as part of the image file. In your photo browser, you can then see when you shot an image and, equally handy, search for images by the date they were taken.

On a related note: If you see the message "Clock" blinking in the Control panel and you've already set the date and time, the internal battery that keeps the clock running is depleted. Simply charging the main camera battery and then putting that battery back in the camera sets the clock ticking again, but you need to reset the camera time and date.

↙ **Language:** This option determines the language of text on the camera monitor.

↙ **Image Comment:** See Chapter 11 to find out about this feature, which enables you to add text comments into a picture file.

↙ **Auto Image Rotation:** This option is one of two that determines whether pictures are rotated to the correct orientation (horizontal or vertical) in playback mode. Chapter 5 has details.

↙ **Image Dust Off Ref Photo:** This feature enables you to record an image that serves as a point of reference for the automatic dust-removal filter available in Nikon Capture NX 2. I don't cover this accessory software, which must be purchased separately, in this book.

↙ **Battery Info:** Select this option to view detailed information about your battery, as shown in Figure 1-27. The Bat Meter data shows you the current power remaining as a percentage value, and the Pic Meter value tells you how many times you've pressed and released the shutter button since the last time you charged the battery. The final readout, Battery Age, lets you know how much more life you can expect out of the battery before it can no longer be recharged. When the display moves toward the right end of the little meter, it's time to buy a new battery.

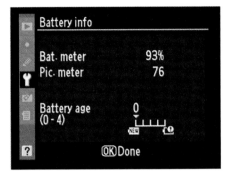

Figure 1-27: You can check the health of your battery via the Battery Info menu item.

The screen in Figure 1-27 shows the display as it appears when you use the regular camera battery. If you attach the optional battery pack, see its manual and the camera manual to find out how to interpret the data that's reported.

✓ **Wireless Transmitter:** If you purchase the optional WT-4 wireless transmitter to connect your camera to a wireless network, you can set up the connection through this menu option. As with other optional accessories, I must refer you to the product manuals for details, as the publisher absolutely refuses to let me turn this book into a 10-inch-thick tome.

✓ **Copyright Information:** Scroll to the final page of the Setup menu, shown in Figure 1-28, to access this option, which enables you to add a hidden copyright notice to your photo files. The copyright data can then be read in some photo software, including the free browser software that ships with your camera (Nikon ViewNX 2). Chapter 11 has details.

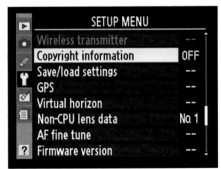

Figure 1-28: The final page of the Setup menu offers these options.

✓ **Save/Load Settings:** This option is a variation of the Save User Settings feature. With Save User Settings, you store settings that you can recall by setting the Mode dial to U1 or U2. The Save/Load Settings feature creates a data file that records the major menu settings and stores the file on your memory card. (The camera manual contains a list of the settings that are preserved.) If you later want to use those settings again, just choose the Save/Load Settings menu option again.

This option is especially useful in a work situation where several photographers share the same camera — if you don't like your co-worker's settings, you can quickly load your own onto the camera.

Be aware of two important details:

- *The settings file is always stored on the memory card in Slot 1.* If that card is full, the camera displays an error message when you try to save your settings. (See the earlier section "Using two cards at the same time," in this chapter, for information about memory cards.)

- *The settings filename is NCSETUP7.* Don't change the filename, or you can't reload the settings later.

✔ **GPS:** If you purchase the optional Nikon GPS tracking unit for your camera, this menu item holds settings related to its operation. This book doesn't cover this accessory, but the camera manual provides some help to get you started.

✔ **Virtual Horizon:** Here's a cool aid for shooting pictures that require your camera to be level with the horizon. When you select this option, as shown on the left in Figure 1-29, and then press OK, you see a screen with a built-in level, as shown on the right. When the camera is level to the horizon, the arrow at the top of the display turns green, as shown in the figure. (If the entire display is gray, without the little degree markers, the camera is tilted too far forward or backward for the system to do its thing.) Unfortunately, the display shows only on the monitor and not in the viewfinder, so it's mostly of use setting up your camera on a tripod. However, you can display an alignment grid in the viewfinder, an option covered a little later in this chapter. You also can set the Fn or Depth-of-Field Preview button to display a level indicator in the viewfinder; Chapter 11 offers details. During Live View shooting, you can enable a display option that superimposes the Virtual Horizon tool over the live image on the monitor. Chapter 4 had details on that feature.

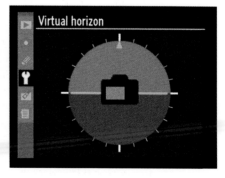

Figure 1-29: The Virtual Horizon display helps you make sure the camera is level.

✔ **Non-CPU Lens Data:** A CPU lens is equipped with technology that enables it to transmit certain data about the lens to the camera. That data helps the camera's autofocusing and exposure systems work correctly. When you use a non-CPU lens, you lose access to certain D7000 features. (Your manual spells them out.) But you can gain back a little of the lost functionality by "registering" your lens through this Setup menu option. You simply assign the lens a number — you can register up to nine non-CPU lenses — and then enter the maximum aperture and focal length of each lens.

The rest of this book assumes that you're instead working with a CPU lens that supports all the camera's features. Again, though, your camera manual offers additional help if you want to go the non-CPU route.

✔ **AF Fine Tune:** If your focus always seems slightly off when you use autofocusing, you may be able to improve the situation through this feature. It enables you to create a custom focusing adjustment for up to 12 lens types, telling the camera to set the focus point just a tad in front of or behind where it normally would. Nikon recommends *not* using this feature unless it's absolutely necessary, and even then, you may want to get some expert assistance.

✔ **Eye-Fi Upload:** Your camera can work with some Eye-Fi memory cards, which enable you to send your pictures over a wireless network to your computer. If you do put one of the cards in the camera, this option appears on the Setup menu and contains settings for making the transfer. When no Eye-Fi card is installed, the option doesn't appear, as in Figure 1-28.

Unfortunately, Eye-Fi cards are more expensive than regular cards. But if you do use the cards and you find yourself in a situation where wireless devices are not allowed, choose Disable from the Eye-Fi Upload menu to shut off the signal. For the whole story on Eye-Fi, including help with setting up your wireless transfers, visit the company's Web site at www.eye.fi.

✔ **Firmware Version:** Select this option and press OK to view what version of the camera firmware, or internal software, your camera is running. You see three separate firmware items, A, B, and L. (Don't worry what the letters mean — they simply refer to different operational aspects of the camera.) At the time this book was written, both A and B were in version 1.00, and L was version 1.002.

Keeping your camera firmware up to date is important, so visit the Nikon Web site (www.nikon.com) regularly to find out whether your camera sports the latest version. You can find detailed instructions on how to download and install any firmware updates on the site.

Browsing the Custom Setting menu

Displaying the Custom Setting menu, whose icon is a little pencil, takes you to the left screen shown in Figure 1-30. Here you can access six submenus that carry the labels A through F. Each of the submenus holds clusters of options related to a specific aspect of the camera's operation. Highlight a submenu and press OK to get to those actions, as shown on the right.

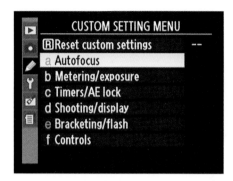 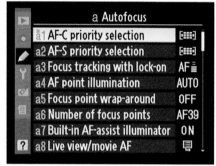

Figure 1-30: Select one of the six submenus and press OK to access the available options.

A few important points about this menu:

✔ After you jump to the first submenu, you can simply scroll up and down the list to view options from other submenus. You don't have to keep going back to the first screen in Figure 1-30, selecting the submenu, pressing OK, and so on.

✔ An asterisk above a letter, as in the highlighted option on the right in Figure 1-30, indicates that you selected a setting other than the default setting. See the last section of this chapter to find out how to restore the camera defaults.

✔ In the Nikon manual, instructions sometimes reference these settings by a menu letter and number. For example, "Custom Setting a1" refers to the first option on the Autofocus submenu. I try to be more specific in this book, however, so I use the actual setting names. (Really, everyone has enough numbers to remember, don't you think?)

✔ Notice that those option letter/number labels are assigned colors to indicate their submenu categories: Autofocus options are red, metering/exposure options are yellow, and so forth.

With those clarifications out of the way, the following sections describe only the customization options related to basic camera operations. Turn to the index for help locating information about other Custom Setting options.

Adjusting automatic monitor-shutdown timing

To help save battery power, your camera automatically shuts off the monitor after a period of inactivity. You can specify how long you want the camera to wait before taking that step through the Monitor Off Delay option, found on the Timers/AE Lock portion of the Custom Setting menu and shown in Figure 1-31. You can specify the auto-off timing for picture playback, menu displays, the Information display, and the Live View display. Additionally, you can adjust the length of time the camera displays a picture immediately after you press the shutter button, known as the Image Review period. Chapter 5 talks more about viewing your photos.

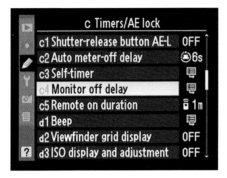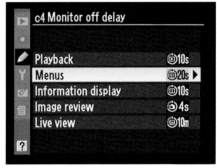

Figure 1-31: Visit the Timers/AE Lock submenu to adjust the timing of automatic monitor shut-off.

Customizing shooting and display options

Head for the Shooting/Display section of the Custom Setting menu, shown in Figure 1-32, to tweak various aspects of how the camera communicates with you, as well as to control a couple of basic shooting functions. Later chapters discuss options related to picture-taking; the following affect the basic camera interface:

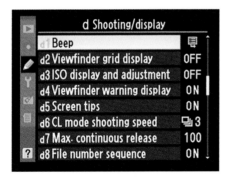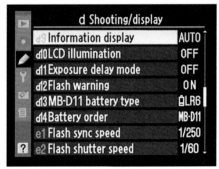

Figure 1-32: Sick of hearing your camera? Turn it off with the Beep option.

~ **Beep:** By default, your camera beeps at you after certain operations, such as after it sets focus when you use certain autofocusing settings. If you're doing top-secret surveillance work and need the camera to hush up, set this option to Off. You also can vary the volume and pitch of the beep. (Sorry, no fancy ring tones available.) On the Information and Control panel displays, a little musical note icon appears when the beep is enabled.

Also check out Chapter 2 for information about the Quiet Shutter mode, which tamps down camera noise even further.

✔ **Viewfinder Grid Display:** You can display tiny gridlines in the viewfinder, as shown in Figure 1-33, by setting this option to On. The gridlines are a great help when you need to ensure the alignment of objects in your photo — for example, to make sure that the horizon is level in a landscape. The Virtual Horizon feature discussed earlier in the chapter is an alternative.

Figure 1-33: The viewfinder grid is another aid for ensuring that the horizon is level in the frame.

✔ **Viewfinder Warning Display:** By default, you see two low-battery warnings in the viewfinder when your battery is about to give out. (Refer to Figure 1-13, earlier in this chapter.) If you don't want to see the larger of the two warnings — it can be annoying if you know your battery's low but you have to keep shooting as long as possible anyway — turn off this option. The tiny battery-recharge nag remains in the lower part of the viewfinder regardless. When this option is enabled, a tiny memory-card symbol flashes in the viewfinder when no card is inserted in the camera. And if you set the Picture Control option to Monochrome, a small B/W (for black and white) symbol appears. Chapter 8 explains Picture Controls.

✔ **Screen Tips:** If you don't want to see the little help labels that appear when you adjust settings via the Information display, turn this option to Off. For a look at what I'm talking about, revisit Figure 1-24.

✔ **File Number Sequence:** This option controls how the camera names your picture files. If you set this option to Off, the camera restarts file numbering at 0001 every time you format your memory card or insert a new memory card. Numbering is also restarted if you create custom folders (an advanced option covered in Chapter 11). Needless to say, this setup can cause problems over time, creating a scenario where you wind up with multiple images that have the same filename — not on the current memory card, but when you download images to your computer. So I strongly encourage you to stick with the default setting, On. Note that when you get to picture number 9999, file numbering is still reset to 0001, however. The camera automatically creates a new folder to hold for your next 9999 images.

As for the Reset option, it tells the camera to look at the largest file number on the current card (or in the selected folder) and then assign the next highest number to your next picture. If the card or selected folder is empty, numbering starts at 0001. Then the camera behaves as if you selected the On setting.

Should you snap enough pictures to reach folder 999, and that folder contains either 999 pictures or a photo that has the file number 9999, the camera will refuse to take another photo until you choose that Reset option and either format the memory card or insert a brand new one.

✔ **Information Display:** Normally, the camera tries to make the data on the display easier to read by automatically shifting from black text on a light background to light text on a black background, depending on the ambient light. If you prefer one display style over the other, visit this menu item and change the setting from Auto to Manual. You can then select either Dark on Light (for dark lettering on a light background) or Light on Dark (for light lettering on a dark background).

In this book, I show the Information screen using the Dark on Light display because it reproduces better in print.

✔ **LCD Illumination:** This setting affects a backlight that can be turned on to illuminate the Control panel. When the option is set to Off, as it is by default, you can illuminate the panel briefly by rotating the On/Off switch past the On setting, to the little light bulb marking. The backlight turns off automatically a few seconds after you release the switch.

If you instead set the LCD Illumination option to On, the backlight comes on automatically anytime the exposure meters are activated (which happens when you press the shutter button halfway). Obviously, this option consumes more battery power than simply using the On/Off switch to light up the panel when you really need it.

✔ **MB-D11 Battery Type and Battery Order:** You don't need to worry about these options unless you buy the optional MB-D11 battery adapter that enables you to power your camera with AA batteries. If you go that route, select the MB-D80 Battery Type option to specify which type of AAs you're using. (Be sure to read the manual for a list of which AA batteries are acceptable, as well as some other details about using them.) Then use the Battery Order option to tell the camera whether you want it to draw power from the battery pack or the regular camera battery when you have both installed. The Control panel displays the letters BP when the battery pack is the current power source.

Customizing controls

On the Controls section of the Custom Setting menu, you find options that enable you to change the function or behavior of some of the camera's buttons and dials. Chapter 11 talks about most of these options — I purposely put this information at the back of the book in hopes that you'd leave things at their default settings until you've fully explored all the other chapters. If you change the settings, instructions you find along the way won't work.

There are a few Controls options, though, that I suggest you check out now:

✔ **On/Off Light Switch:** Normally, rotating the On/Off switch past the On
position to the light bulb symbol illuminates the Control panel. But
if you set the option highlighted on the left in Figure 1-34 to the setting shown on the right, rotating the switch activates the Information
screen as well as the Control panel. (The menu and manual use the
light bulb symbol instead of the text name I've given it here.) You may
find this maneuver easier than pressing the Info button to light up the
Information display. The downside is that you use power to light up
the Control panel when what you really want to see is the Info display. I
leave it up to you to make the call.

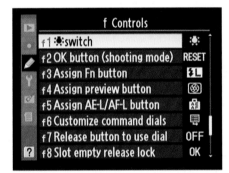
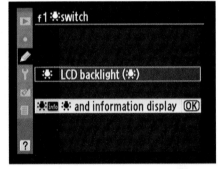

Figure 1-34: Select this setting if you want to use the On/Off switch to activate the Information
screen as well as the Control panel light.

✔ **Slot Empty Release Lock:** This setting determines whether the shutter release is disabled when no memory card is in the camera. At the
default setting, OK, you can take a temporary picture, which appears
in the monitor with the word Demo but isn't recorded anywhere. (The
feature is provided mainly for use in camera stores, enabling sales-
people to demonstrate the camera without having to keep a memory
card installed.) I suggest that you change the setting to Release Locked
unless you're starting a little camera shop in your garage and want to
demonstrate the camera to your neighbors.

Restoring default settings

Should you ever want to return your camera to its original, out-of-the-box
state, the camera manual contains a complete list of all the default settings.

You can also partially restore default settings by taking these steps:

- **Reset all Shooting Menu options:** Open the Shooting menu, choose Reset Shooting Menu, and press OK.

- **Reset all Custom Setting Menu options:** Choose the Reset Custom Settings option at the top of the Custom Setting menu.

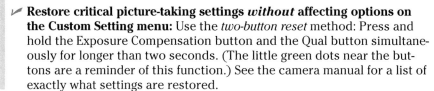

- **Restore critical picture-taking settings *without* affecting options on the Custom Setting menu:** Use the *two-button reset* method: Press and hold the Exposure Compensation button and the Qual button simultaneously for longer than two seconds. (The little green dots near the buttons are a reminder of this function.) See the camera manual for a list of exactly what settings are restored.

2

Choosing Basic Picture Settings

*E*very camera manufacturer strives to provide a good *out-of-box* experience — that is, to ensure that your initial encounter with the camera is a happy one. To that end, the camera's default settings are carefully selected to make it as easy as possible for you to take a good picture the first time you press the shutter button. On the D7000, the default settings are designed to let you take a picture the same way you do with most automatic, point-and-shoot cameras: You compose the shot, press the shutter button halfway to focus, and then press the button the rest of the way to record the image.

Although you can get a nice picture using the default settings in many cases, they're not designed to produce the optimal results in every shooting situation. Rather, they're established as a one-size-fits-all approach. You may be able to use the defaults to take a decent portrait, for example, but probably need to tweak a few settings to capture action. Adjusting a few options can help turn that decent portrait into a stunning one, too.

So that you can start fine-tuning camera settings to your subject, this chapter explains the most basic picture-taking options, such as the exposure mode, shutter-release mode, and the image size and quality. They're not the most exciting options to explore (don't think I didn't notice you stifling a yawn), but they make a big difference in how easily you can capture the photo you have in mind. You also need to understand this core group of camera settings to take best advantage of the advanced color, focus, and exposure controls covered in Part III of the book.

Choosing an Exposure Mode

The first picture-taking setting to consider is the exposure mode, which you select via the Mode dial, as shown in Figure 2-1. Your choice determines how much control you have over two critical exposure settings — aperture and shutter speed — as well as many other options, including those related to color and flash photography.

Your exposure mode choices break down as follows:

✔ **Fully automatic exposure modes:** For people who haven't yet explored photography concepts like aperture and shutter speed — or who just aren't interested in "going there" — the D7000 offers the following point-and-shoot modes, all detailed in Chapter 3:

• *Auto:* The camera analyzes the scene in front of the lens and tries to select the most appropriate camera settings to capture the image. In dim lighting, the built-in flash may fire.

• *Auto Flash Off:* This mode, represented by the icon labeled in Figure 2-1, works just like Auto but disables the flash.

• *Scene modes:* Set the dial to Scene to access automatic modes geared to capturing specific types of shots: portraits, landscapes, child photos, and such.

Because these modes are designed to make picture-taking simple, they prevent you from accessing many of the camera's features. You can't use the White Balance control, for example, to tweak picture colors. Options that are off limits appear dimmed in the camera menus. (You do have control over all the settings discussed in this chapter.)

✔ **Semi-automatic modes:** To take more creative control but still get some exposure assistance from the camera, choose one of these modes:

Auto Flash Off

Figure 2-1: The Mode dial setting determines how much input you have over exposure, color, and other picture options.

- *P (programmed autoexposure):* The camera selects the aperture and shutter speed necessary to ensure a good exposure. But you can choose from different combinations of the two to vary the creative results. For example, shutter speed affects whether moving objects appear blurry or sharp. So you might use a fast shutter speed to freeze action, or you might go the other direction, choosing a shutter speed slow enough to blur the action, creating a heightened sense of motion.

- *S (shutter-priority autoexposure):* You select the shutter speed, and the camera selects the proper aperture to properly expose the image. This mode is ideal for capturing sports or other moving subjects because it gives you direct control over shutter speed.

- *A (aperture-priority autoexposure):* In this mode, you choose the aperture, and the camera automatically chooses a shutter speed to properly expose the image. Because aperture affects *depth of field,* or the distance over which objects in a scene remain in sharp focus, this setting is great for portraits because you can select an aperture that results in a soft, blurry background, putting the emphasis on your subject. For landscape shots, on the other hand, you might choose an aperture that keeps the entire scene sharply focused so that both near and distant objects have equal visual weight.

All three semi-automatic modes give you complete access to all the camera's features. So even if you're not ready to explore aperture and shutter speed yet, go ahead and set the mode dial to P if you need to access a setting that's off limits in the fully automated modes. The camera then operates pretty much as it does in Auto mode but without limiting your ability to control picture settings if you need to do so.

When you're ready to dig into exposure issues and try out these exposure modes, head for Chapter 7.

✔ **Manual:** In this mode, also detailed in Chapter 7, you select both the aperture and shutter speed. But the camera still offers an assist by displaying an exposure meter to help you dial in the right settings. You have complete control over all other picture settings, too.

✔ **U1 and U2:** These two settings represent the pair of custom exposure modes that you can create by following the steps laid out in Chapter 11. (The *U* stands for *user.*) They give you a quick way to immediately switch to all the picture settings you prefer for a specific type of shot. For example, you might store the options you like to use for indoor portraits as U1, and store settings for sports shots as U2.

One very important and often misunderstood aspect about the exposure modes: Although the Mode dial setting determines your access to exposure and color controls as well as to some other advanced camera features, it has no bearing on your *focusing* choices. You can choose from manual focusing or autofocusing in any mode, assuming that your lens offers autofocusing. (Chapter 1 shows you how to set the lens to manual or autofocusing.)

Choosing the Shutter-Release Mode

Chapter 7 explains the *shutter,* which is the thing inside the camera that controls when light is allowed to enter through the lens, strike the image sensor, and create a picture — *expose the image,* in technical terms. The shutter opens when you press the shutter button and closes after the image is exposed. Photo lingo uses the term *shutter release* to refer to the action of the shutter opening.

By default, the D7000 is set to capture one image each time you press the shutter button. But you have a variety of other shutter-release options. You can delay the shutter release for a few seconds after the button is pressed, for example, or set the camera to record a continuous burst of images as long as you hold down the shutter button.

The primary point of control for shutter release is the Release mode dial, shown in Figure 2-2. To change the setting, press and hold the little black Release mode dial unlock button (labeled in Figure 2-2) while rotating the dial. The letter displayed next to the white marker represents the selected setting. For example, in Figure 2-2, the S is aligned with the marker, showing that the Single Frame mode is selected. The Information display shows you the current mode as well, as shown in Figure 2-3.

Current release mode   Release mode dial

Release mode dial unlock button

Figure 2-2: You can choose from a variety of Release modes.

Upcoming sections explain the various Release modes and introduce you to a few menu options that also affect the shutter release. Before I shoo you off to those paragraphs, though, I want to point out one possible shutter-release problem: When you set the Autofocus mode to AF-S (an option that I cover in Chapter 8), by default, the camera insists on achieving focus before it opens the shutter. You can keep pressing the shutter button all day, and the camera just ignores you if it can't set focus. You adjust this behavior through Custom Setting menu item A2, which has the oh-so-friendly name AF-S Priority Selection. Chapter 8 explains more about this option.

Release mode

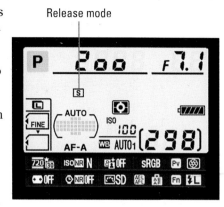

Figure 2-3: This symbol represents the current Release mode.

Single Frame and Quiet modes

S At the default Release mode setting, Single Frame, you get one picture each time you press the shutter button. In other words, this is normal-photography mode. The only other thing you need to know is that you must press the shutter button in two stages for autoexposure and autofocusing to work correctly: Press the button halfway; pause to let the camera set focus and exposure, and then press the rest of the way to take the picture.

Q Quiet Shutter mode works just like Single Frame mode but makes less noise as it goes about its business. Designed for situations when you want the camera to be as silent as possible, this mode disables the beep that the autofocus systems may sound when it achieves focus. Using this mode also decreases the internal may sound the camera makes from the time you fully depress the shutter button to the time you lift your finger off it.

Continuous (burst mode) shooting

Setting the Release mode dial to Continuous Low or Continuous High enables *burst mode* or *continuous capture* shooting. At both settings, the camera records a continuous series of images for as long as you hold down the shutter button, making it easier to capture fast-paced action.

Here's how the two modes differ:

CL

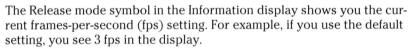

✔ **Continuous Low:** At the default setting, Continuous Low mode can capture a maximum of three frames per second. But you can set the maximum capture number as high as five frames per second and as low as one frame per second.

Why would you want to capture fewer than the maximum number of shots? Well, frankly, unless you're shooting something that's moving at a really fast pace, not too much is going to change between frames when you shoot at five frames per second. So when you set the burst rate that high, you typically wind up with lots of shots that show the exact same thing, wasting space on your memory card. I keep this value set to the default, three, and then if I want a higher burst rate, I use the Continuous High setting, explained next.

To adjust the maximum capture setting for the Continuous Low mode, scroll through the Custom Setting menu to find the CL Mode Shooting Speed (menu item d6), as shown on the left in Figure 2-4. Press OK to display your options, as shown on the right.

The Release mode symbol in the Information display shows you the current frames-per-second (fps) setting. For example, if you use the default setting, you see 3 fps in the display.

CH

✔ **Continuous High:** This mode works just like Continuous Low except that it records up to six frames per second. You can't adjust the frame rate for this mode.

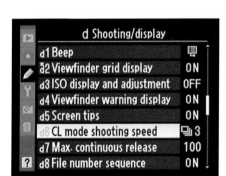 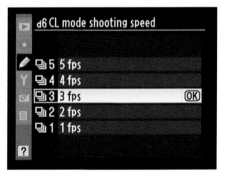

Figure 2-4: You can specify the maximum frames-per-second rate for Continuous Low Release mode.

For both modes, you can limit the maximum number of shots the camera takes with each press of the shutter button. Again, the idea behind this feature is simply to prevent firing off lots of wasted frames. Make the adjustment via the

Max Continuous Release option, found just below the CL Mode Shooting Speed option, as shown in Figure 2-5.

A few other critical details about these two release modes:

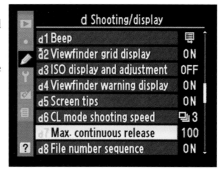

Figure 2-5: This option limits the number of shots recorded with each press of the shutter button in the Continuous Low and Continuous High modes.

- **You can't use flash**. Continuous mode doesn't work with flash because the time that the flash needs to recycle between shots slows down the capture rate too much.

- **Images are stored temporarily in the memory buffer**. The camera has a little bit of internal memory — a *buffer* — where it stores picture data until it has time to record them to the memory card. The number of pictures the buffer can hold depends on certain camera settings, such as resolution and file type (JPEG or Raw). The viewfinder displays an estimate of how many pictures will fit in the buffer; see the sidebar "What does [r 24] in the viewfinder mean?" later in this chapter, for details.

After shooting a burst of images, wait for the memory card access light on the back of the camera to go out before turning off the camera. That's your signal that the camera has successfully moved all data from the buffer to the memory card. Turning off the camera before that happens may corrupt the image file.

- **Your mileage may vary.** The maximum number of frames per second is an approximation. The actual number of frames you can capture depends on a number of factors, including your shutter speed. At a slow shutter speed, the camera may not be able to reach the maximum frame rate. (See Chapter 7 for an explanation of shutter speed.) Additionally, although you can capture as many as 100 frames in a single burst, the frame rate can drop if the buffer gets full.

Self-timer shooting

You're no doubt familiar with this release mode, which delays the shutter release for a few seconds after you press the shutter button, giving you time to dash into the picture. Here's how it works on the D7000: After you press the shutter button, the autofocus-assist illuminator on the front of the camera starts to blink, and the camera emits a series of beeps (assuming that you didn't disable its voice, a setting I cover in Chapter 1). A few seconds later, the camera captures the image.

By default, the camera waits ten seconds after you press the shutter button and then records a single image. But you can tweak the delay time and capture as many as nine shots at a time. Set your self-timer preferences through the Self-Timer option on the Custom Setting menu, as shown in Figure 2-6. Here's what you need to know about the three self-timer settings:

- ✔ **Self-Timer Delay:** Choose a delay time of 2, 5, 10, or 20 seconds.

- ✔ **Number of Shots:** Specify how many frames you want to capture with each press of the shutter button; the maximum is nine frames.

- ✔ **Interval between Shots:** If you choose to record multiple shots, this setting determines how long the camera waits between each one. You can set the delay to a half second (the default setting), one second, two seconds, or three seconds.

You also can record a timed series of shots by using the Interval Timer Shooting option on the Shooting menu; see the upcoming section "Automatic time-lapse photography" for details.

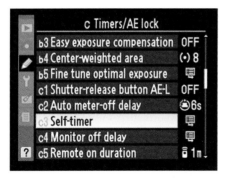
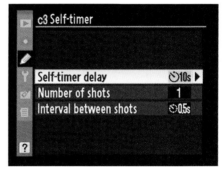

Figure 2-6: You can adjust the self-timer capture delay via the Custom Setting menu.

When you use Self-Timer mode or trigger the shutter release with a remote control — that is, any time you take a shot without your eye to the viewfinder — you should remove the little rubber cup that surrounds the viewfinder and then insert the viewfinder cover that shipped with your camera. (Dig around in the accessories box — the cover is a tiny black piece of plastic, about the size of the viewfinder.) Otherwise, light may seep into the camera through the viewfinder and affect exposure. You can also simply use the camera strap or something else to cover the viewfinder in a pinch.

Remote Control mode

 Select this Release mode setting when you use the optional Nikon ML-L3 wireless remote-control unit. By default, the camera releases the shutter two seconds after you press the remote control button. To adjust that timing, hunt down the Remote Control Mode option on the Shooting menu, as shown in Figure 2-7. Choose from these options:

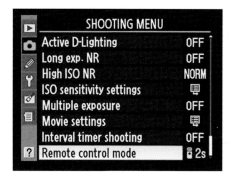

Figure 2-7: Set preferences for remote-control shutter release via this menu option.

 ✔ **Delayed Remote:** Results in a two-second delay.

 ✔ **Quick-Response Remote:** The shutter opens immediately.

 ✔ **Remote Mirror-Up:** As Its name implies, this setting enables you to use the remote for mirror-up shooting, a technique explained next.

Mirror lockup and exposure delay

One component of the optical system of a dSLR camera is a tiny mirror that moves every time you press the shutter button. The small vibration caused by the action of the mirror can result in slight blurring of the image when you use a very slow shutter speed, shoot with a long telephoto lens, or take extreme close-up shots.

MUP To cope with that issue, many cameras offer mirror-lockup shooting, which delays opening the shutter until after the mirror movement is complete. On the D7000, enable this feature by setting the Release mode to Mirror Up (or, if you're using a remote control, by selecting the Remote Mirror-Up setting, as just explained).

Mirror lockup shooting requires that you press the shutter button twice to take the picture. Follow these steps:

1. **After framing and focusing, press the shutter button all the way down to lock up the mirror.**

   At this point, you can no longer see anything through the viewfinder. Don't panic — that's normal. The mirror's function is to enable you to see in the viewfinder the scene that the lens will capture, and mirror lockup prevents it from serving that purpose.

2. **To record the shot, let up on the shutter button and then press it all the way down again.**

   If you don't take the shot within about 30 seconds, the camera will record a picture for you automatically.

Remember that you still need to worry about moving the camera itself during the shot — even with the mirror locked up, the slightest jostle of the camera can cause blurring. In other words, situations that call for mirror lockup also call for a tripod. With the kit lens, turn off Vibration Reduction as well; with other lenses, check the manufacturer's recommendations about this issue.

Adding a remote-control shutter-release further ensures a shake-free shot — even the action of pressing the shutter button can move the camera enough to cause some slight blurring. Or you can just wait the 30 seconds needed for the camera to take the picture automatically, if your subject permits.

As an alternative to mirror lockup, you can use the Single Frame, Quiet Shutter, Self-Timer, or Remote Control Release modes and enable the Exposure Delay feature. Look for the setting in the Shooting/Display section of the Custom Setting menu. If you set the option to On, as shown in Figure 2-8, the camera waits about one second after the mirror is raised to record the image, ensuring that the mirror movement is complete before the image is recorded. (Just don't forget you enabled the feature, or you'll drive yourself batty trying to figure out why the camera isn't

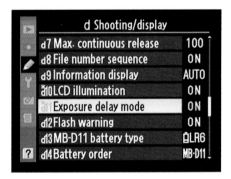

Figure 2-8: Enabling Exposure Delay is another way to make sure that mirror vibrations don't cause blurring.

responding to your shutter-button finger. I say this from experience . . .)

What does [r 24] in the viewfinder mean?

When you look in your viewfinder to frame a shot, the initial value shown in brackets at the right end of the viewfinder display indicates the number of additional pictures that can fit on your memory card. For example, in the left viewfinder image below, the value shows that the card can hold 203 more images.

As soon as you press the shutter button halfway, which kicks the autofocus and exposure mechanisms into action, that value changes to instead show you how many pictures can fit in the camera's *memory buffer.* In the right image

here, for example, the r 24 value tells you that 24 pictures can fit in the buffer.

So what's the *buffer?* It's a temporary storage tank where the camera stores picture data until it has time to fully record that data onto the camera memory card. This system exists so that you can take a continuous series of pictures without waiting between shots until each image is fully written to the memory card. When the buffer is full, the camera automatically disables the shutter button until it catches up on its recording work.

`2ₒₒ F5.6` `ISO AUTO [203]`   `2ₒₒ F5.6` `ISO AUTO [r 24]`

Automatic time-lapse photography

The Self-Timer Release mode enables you to take up to nine pictures with one press of the shutter button, timing the frames at intervals of a half-second to three seconds. If you want to record more frames or enjoy more flexibility over the interval between images, bail out of Self-Timer mode and instead enable Interval Timer Shooting.

With Interval Timer Shooting, you can record a whole memory-card full of images and space the shots minutes or even hours apart. This feature enables you to capture a subject as it changes over time — a technique commonly known as *time-lapse photography.* Here's how to do it:

1. **Set the Release mode to any setting but Self-Timer or Remote Control.**

   Those modes aren't compatible with interval-timing shooting.

2. **Display the Shooting menu, highlight Interval Timer Shooting, as shown on the left in Figure 2-9, and press OK.**

   The screen on the right in Figure 2-9 appears.

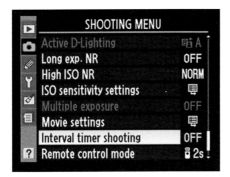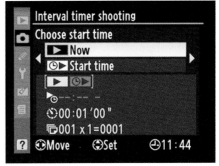

Figure 2-9: The Interval Timer Shooting feature enables you to do time-lapse photography.

3. To begin setting up your capture session, highlight Now or Start Time.

- *If you want to start the captures right away,* highlight Now.

- *To set a later start time for the captures,* highlight Start Time.

4. Press the Multi Selector right to display the capture-setup screen.

If you selected Start Time in Step 3, the screen looks like the one in Figure 2-10. If you selected Now, the Start Time option is dimmed, and the Interval option is highlighted instead.

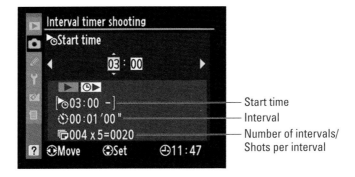

Figure 2-10: Press the Multi Selector right or left to cycle through the setup options; press up or down to change the highlighted value.

5. Set up your recording session.

You get three options: Start Time, Interval (time between shots), and Number of Intervals and Number of Shots per Interval (determines total number of shots recorded). The current settings for each option appear in the bottom half of the screen, as labeled in Figure 2-10.

At the top of the screen, little value boxes appear. The highlighted box is the active option and relates to the setting that's highlighted at the bottom of the screen. For example, in the figure, the hour box for the Start Time setting is active. Press the Multi Selector right or left to cycle through the value boxes; to change the value in a box, press the Multi Selector up or down.

A few notes about your options:

- The Interval and Start Time options are based on a 24-hour clock. (The current time appears in the bottom-right corner of the screen and is based upon the date/time information you entered when setting up the camera.)

- For the Interval option, the left column box is for the hour setting; the middle, minutes; and the right, seconds. Make sure that the value you enter is longer than the shutter speed you plan to use.

- For the Start Time option, you can set the hour and minute values only. Again, the Start Time option is available only if you selected Start Time in Step 3.

- The Number of Intervals value multiplied by the Number of Shots per interval determines how many pictures will be recorded.

6. Press the Multi Selector right until you see the screen shown in Figure 2-11.

7. Highlight On and press OK.

If you selected Now as your interval-capture starting option, the first shot is recorded about three seconds later. If you set a delayed start time, the camera displays a "Timer Active" message for a few seconds, and then the monitor turns off.

A few final factoids:

Figure 2-11: When you see this screen, highlight On and press OK to begin timed interval shooting.

✔ **Monitoring the shot progress:** The letters INTVL blink in the Control panel while an interval sequence is in progress. Before each shot is captured, the display changes to show the number of intervals remaining and the number of shots remaining in the current interval. The first value appears in the space usually occupied by the shutter speed; the second takes the place of the f-stop setting. You also can view the values at any time by pressing the shutter button halfway.

- **Interrupting interval shooting:** Between shots, bring up the Interval Timing menu screen, highlight Pause, and press OK. To resume the interval shooting, highlight Restart and press OK. To cancel interval timing altogether, select Off and press OK. You can also interrupt the interval sequence by turning off the camera — which also gives you the chance to install an empty memory card, if the current ones are full. When you turn on the camera again, choose Restart and press OK to continue shooting.

- **Bracketing:** You can apply automatic bracketing during interval shooting. See Chapter 7 to find out what bracketing is all about.

- **Autofocusing:** If you're using autofocusing, be sure that the camera can focus on your subject. It will initiate focusing before each shot.

- **Exposure Delay:** You can enable the Exposure Delay feature, outlined earlier in this chapter, for interval shooting. But be sure that the interval between shots is long enough to account for the delay.

- **Between shots:** You can view pictures in Playback mode or adjust menu settings between shots. The monitor goes dark about four seconds before the next shot is taken.

Choosing the Right Quality Settings

Almost every review of the D7000 contains glowing reports about the camera's top-notch picture quality. As you've no doubt discovered, those claims are true: This baby can create large, beautiful images. What you may *not* have discovered is that Nikon's default Image Quality setting isn't the highest that the D7000 offers. Why, you ask, would Nikon do such a thing? Why not set up the camera to produce the best images right out of the box? The answer is that using the top setting has some downsides. Nikon's default choice represents a compromise between avoiding those disadvantages while still producing images that will please most photographers.

Whether that compromise is right for you, however, depends on your photographic needs. To help you decide, the rest of this chapter explains the Image Quality setting, along with the Image Size setting, which is also critical to the quality of images that you print. Just in case you're having quality problems related to other issues, though, the next section provides a handy quality-defect diagnosis guide.

Diagnosing quality problems

When I say *picture quality,* I'm not talking about the composition, exposure, or other traditional characteristics of a photograph. Instead, I'm referring to how finely the image is rendered in the digital sense.

Figure 2-12 illustrates the concept: The first example is a high-quality image, with clear details and smooth color transitions. The other examples show five common digital-image defects.

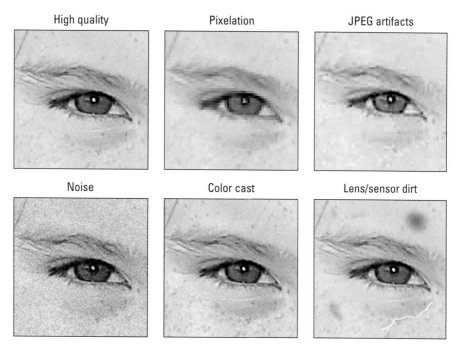

Figure 2-12: Refer to this symptom guide to determine the cause of poor image quality.

Each of these defects is related to a different issue, and only one is affected by the Image Quality setting on your D7000. So if you aren't happy with your image quality, first compare your photos to those in the figure to properly diagnose the problem. Then try these remedies:

✏ **Pixelation:** When an image doesn't have enough *pixels* (the colored tiles used to create digital images), details aren't clear, and curved and diagonal lines appear jagged. The fix is to increase image resolution, which you do via the Image Size control. See the next section, "Considering image size: How many pixels are enough?" for details.

✏ **JPEG artifacts:** The "parquet tile" texture and random color defects that mar the third image in Figure 2-12 can occur in photos captured in the JPEG *(jay-peg)* file format, which is why these flaws are referred to as

JPEG artifacts. This is the defect related to the Image Quality setting; see "Understanding Image Quality options (JPEG or Raw)," later in this chapter, to find out more.

✔ **Noise:** This defect gives your image a speckled look, as shown in the lower-left example in Figure 2-12. Noise can occur with very long exposure times or when you choose a high ISO Sensitivity setting on your camera. You can explore both issues in Chapter 7.

✔ **Color cast:** If your colors are seriously out of whack, as shown in the lower-middle example in the figure, try adjusting the camera's White Balance setting. Chapter 8 covers this control and other color issues.

✔ **Lens/sensor dirt:** A dirty lens is the first possible cause of the kind of defects you see in the last example in the figure. If cleaning your lens doesn't solve the problem, dust or dirt may have made its way onto the camera's image sensor.

Your D7000 offers an automated, internal sensor-cleaning mechanism. By default, this automatic cleaning happens every time you turn the camera on or off. You also can request a cleaning session at any time via the Clean Image Sensor command on the Setup menu. (Chapter 1 has details on this menu option.) But if you frequently change lenses in a dirty environment, the internal cleaning mechanism may not be adequate, in which case a manual sensor cleaning is necessary. You can do this job yourself, but . . . I don't recommend it. Image sensors are pretty delicate beings, and you can easily damage them or other parts of your camera if you aren't careful. Instead, find a local camera store that offers this service. In my area (central Indiana), sensor cleaning costs between $30–$50.

When diagnosing image problems, you may want to open the photos in ViewNX 2 or some other photo software and zoom in for a close-up inspection. Some defects, especially pixelation and JPEG artifacts, have a similar appearance until you see them at a magnified view. (See Part II for information about using ViewNX 2.)

I should also tell you that I used a little digital enhancement to exaggerate the flaws in my example images to make the symptoms easier to see. With the exception of an unwanted color cast or a big blob of lens or sensor dirt, these defects may not even be noticeable unless you print or view your image at a very large size. And the subject matter of your image may camouflage some flaws; most people probably wouldn't detect a little JPEG artifacting in a photograph of a densely wooded forest, for example.

In other words, don't consider Figure 2-12 as an indication that your D7000 is suspect in the image quality department. First, *any* digital camera can produce these defects under the right circumstances. Second, by following the guidelines in this chapter and the others mentioned in the preceding list, you can resolve any quality issues that you may encounter.

Considering image size: How many pixels are enough?

Like other digital devices, your D7000 creates pictures out of *pixels,* which is short for *picture elements.* You can see some pixels close up in the right example of Figure 2-13, which shows a greatly magnified view of the eye area in the left image.

Figure 2-13: Pixels are the building blocks of digital photos.

You can specify the pixel count of your images, also known as the *resolution,* in two ways:

QUAL

 ✔ **Qual button + Sub-command dial:** Hold down the Qual (Quality) button while rotating the Sub-command dial to cycle through the available settings. You can monitor the setting in the Control panel and Information display, in the areas highlighted in Figure 2-14.

 ✔ **Shooting menu:** Select the Image Size option and press OK to access the available settings, as shown in Figure 2-15.

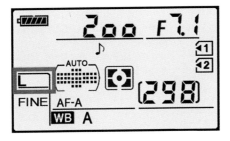 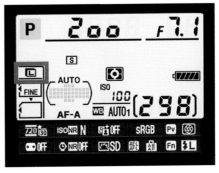

Figure 2-14: The current setting appears in the Control panel and Information display.

 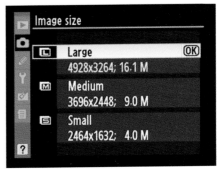

Figure 2-15: You can view the pixel count for each setting in the Shooting menu.

Either way, you can choose from three settings: Large, Medium, and Small. You can view the resulting resolution value for each setting if you adjust the option via the Shooting menu, as shown on the right in Figure 2-15.

The first pair of numbers shown for each setting represents the image *pixel dimensions* — that is, the number of horizontal pixels and the number of vertical pixels. The second value indicates the approximate total resolution, which you get by multiplying the two pixel dimension values. This number is usually stated in megapixels, abbreviated M on the menu screen (but typically abbreviated as MP in other resources, including this book). One megapixel equals 1 million pixels.

Note, however, that if you select Raw (NEF) as your file format, all images are captured at the Large setting. The upcoming section "Understanding Image Quality options (JPEG or Raw)" explains file formats.

So how many pixels are enough? To make the call, you need to understand the three ways that pixel count affects your pictures:

- **Print size:** Pixel count determines the size at which you can produce a high-quality print. If you don't have enough pixels, your prints may exhibit the defects you see in the pixelation example in Figure 2-12, or worse, you may be able to see the individual pixels, as in the right example in Figure 2-13. Depending on your photo printer, you typically need anywhere from 200 to 300 pixels per linear inch, or *ppi,* of the print. To produce an 8 x 10 print at 200 ppi, for example, you need a pixel count of 1600 x 2000, or just less than 2 megapixels.

Even though many photo-editing programs enable you to add pixels to an existing image, doing so isn't a good idea. For reasons I won't bore you with, adding pixels — known as *upsampling* — doesn't enable you to successfully enlarge your photo. In fact, upsampling typically makes matters worse. The printing discussion in Chapter 6 includes some example images that illustrate this issue.

- **Screen display size:** Resolution doesn't affect the quality of images viewed on a monitor, television, or other screen device the way it does for printed photos. Instead, resolution determines the *size* at which the image appears. This issue is one of the most misunderstood aspects of digital photography, so I explain it thoroughly in Chapter 6. For now, just know that you need *way* fewer pixels for onscreen photos than you do for printed photos. In fact, even the Small resolution setting on your camera creates a picture too big to be viewed in its entirety in most e-mail programs.

- **File size:** Every additional pixel increases the amount of data required to create a digital picture file. So a higher-resolution image has a larger file size than a low-resolution image.

Large files present several problems:

- You can store fewer images on your memory card, on your computer's hard drive, and on removable storage media such as a CD-ROM.

- When you share photos online, larger files take longer to upload and download.

- When you edit your photos in your photo software, your computer needs more resources and time to process large files.

As you can see, resolution is a bit of a sticky wicket. What if you aren't sure how large you want to print your images? What if you want to print your photos *and* share them online?

I take the better-safe-than-sorry route, which leads to the following recommendations about which Image Size setting to use:

- **Always shoot at a resolution suitable for print.** You then can create a low-resolution copy of the image in your photo editor for use online. In fact, your camera offers a built-in resizing option; Chapter 6 shows you how to use it.

- **For everyday images, Medium is a good choice.** I find the Large setting (16.1 MP) to be overkill for most casual shooting, which means that you're creating huge files for no good reason. Keep in mind that even at the Small setting, your pixel count (2464 x 1632) is more than enough to produce an 8-x-10-inch print at 200 ppi.

- **Choose Large for an image that you plan to crop, print very large, or both.** The benefit of maxing out resolution is that you have the flexibility to crop your photo and still generate a decent-sized print of the remaining image. Figures 2-16 and 2-17 offer an example. When I was shooting this photo, I couldn't get any closer to the bee — okay, didn't *want* to get closer to the bee — than the first picture shows. But because I had the resolution cranked up to Large, I could later crop the shot to the composition you see in Figure 2-17 and still produce a great print. In fact, I could've printed the cropped image at a much larger size than fits here.

Figure 2-16: I couldn't get close enough to fill the frame with the subject, so I captured this image at the Large resolution setting.

Figure 2-17: A high-resolution original enabled me to crop the photo tightly and still have enough pixels to produce a quality print.

Understanding Image Quality options (JPEG or Raw)

If I had my druthers, the Image Quality option would instead be called File Type because that's what the setting controls.

Here's the deal: The file type, sometimes known as a file *format,* determines how your picture data is recorded and stored. Your choice does impact picture quality, but so do other factors, as outlined at the beginning of this chapter. In addition, your choice of file type has ramifications beyond picture quality.

At any rate, your D7000 offers two file types: JPEG and Camera Raw, or just Raw for short. You also can choose to record two copies of each picture, one in the Raw format and one in the JPEG format.

You can view the current format in the Control panel and Information display, as shown in Figure 2-18. For JPEG, the displays indicate the JPEG quality level — Fine, Normal, or Basic. (The next section explains these three options.)

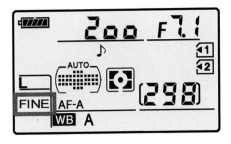
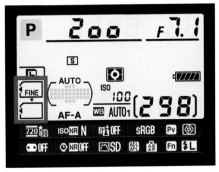

Figure 2-18: The current Image Quality setting appears here.

In the Information display, the icons used for the Quality setting depend on whether you're using one or two memory cards and how you told the camera to use the card in Slot 2 (done through the Role Played by Card in Slot 2 option on the Shooting menu). In Figure 2-18, the symbol shows that two cards are installed, and that the Overflow setting is selected for Slot 2. See the Chapter 1 section related to using two memory cards at the same time for information on how to decode this aspect of the display.

The rest of this chapter explains the pros and cons of each file format to help you decide which one works best for the types of pictures you take. If you already have your mind made up, you can select the format you want to use in two ways:

QUAL

- ✓ **Qual button + Main command dial:** Hold down the Qual (Quality) button while rotating the Main command dial to cycle through all the format options.

  Be sure to spin the Main command dial: Rotating the Sub-command dial while pressing the Qual button adjusts the Image Size (resolution) setting.

- ✓ **Shooting menu:** You also can set the Image Quality option via the Shooting menu, as shown in Figure 2-19.

  The menu also contains two additional options related to the Quality setting: JPEG Compression and NEF (Raw) Recording. Look for details about these features in the upcoming discussions of each format.

JPEG: The imaging (and Web) standard

Pronounced *jay-peg,* the JPEG format is the default setting on your D7000, as it is for most digital cameras. The next two sections tell you what you need to know about JPEG.

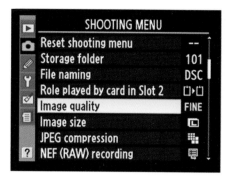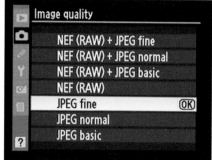

Figure 2-19: The Shooting menu enables you to select the Image Quality setting plus a few related options.

JPEG pros and cons

JPEG has become the de facto digital-camera file format for two main reasons:

- ✔ **Immediate usability:** All Web browsers and e-mail programs can display JPEG files, so you can share your pictures online immediately after you shoot them. The same can't be said for Raw (NEF) files, which must be converted to JPEG for online use. You also can print and edit JPEG files immediately, whether you want to use your own software or have pictures printed at a retail site. You can view and print Raw files using Nikon ViewNX 2, the software that comes with your camera, but many third-party photo programs can't open Raw images — and retail printing sites typically don't accept Raw files either. You can read more about the conversion process in the upcoming section "Raw (NEF): The purist's choice."

- ✔ **Small files:** JPEG files are much smaller than Raw files. And smaller files consume less room on your camera memory card and in your computer's storage tank.

The downside — you knew there had to be one — is that JPEG creates smaller files by applying *lossy compression*. This process actually throws away some image data. Too much compression leads to the defects you see in the JPEG artifacts example in Figure 2-12.

Fortunately, your camera enables you to specify how much compression you're willing to accept, as outlined next.

Customizing your JPEG capture settings

You have two levels of control over the quality of your JPEG images:

- **Fine, Normal, or Basic:** When you select the file type, whether through the Shooting menu or by using the Qual button with the Main command dial, you can choose from three JPEG settings, each of which produces a different level of compression.

  - *JPEG Fine:* At this setting, the compression ratio is 1:4 — that is, the file is four times smaller than it'd otherwise be. In plain English, that means that very little compression is applied, so you shouldn't see many compression artifacts, if any.

  - JPEG Normal: Switch to Normal, and the compression ratio rises to 1:8. The chance of seeing some artifacting increases as well. This setting is the default option.

  - *JPEG Basic:* Shift to this setting, and the compression ratio jumps to 1:16. That's a substantial amount of compression and brings with it a lot more risk of artifacting.

- **Compression priority:** The size of the file produced at any of the three quality levels varies from picture to picture depending on the subject matter. The difference occurs because a picture with lots of detail and a wide color palette can't be as easily compressed as one with large areas of flat color and a limited color spectrum.

  By default, the camera applies compression with a goal of producing consistent file sizes, which means that highly detailed photos can take a larger quality hit from compression. But through the JPEG Compression option on the Shooting menu, shown in Figure 2-20, you can tell the camera to instead give priority to producing optimum picture quality when applying compression. To go that route, choose the Optimal Quality setting, as shown in the figure. For the default option, choose Size Priority.

  Note that the compression ratios just mentioned for the Fine, Normal, and Basic options assume that you use the Size Priority option. The ratios will vary from picture to picture, as will the picture file sizes, if you select Optimal Quality.

Even if you choose the Size Priority option and combine it with JPEG Basic — thereby producing the lowest-quality JPEG results — you don't get anywhere near the level of artifacting that you see in my example in Figure 2-12, however. Again, that example is exaggerated to help you be able to recognize artifacting defects and understand how they differ from other image quality issues. In fact, if you keep your image print or display size small, you aren't likely to notice a great deal of quality difference between the compression settings. It's only when you greatly enlarge a photo that the differences become apparent.

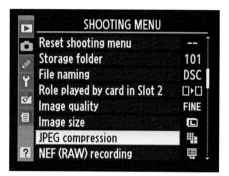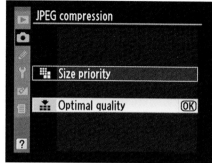

Figure 2-20: Set the JPEG Compression option to Optimal Quality to get the best-looking JPEG pictures.

Nikon chose the Normal and Size Priority options as the default JPEG settings — in other words, a notch down from the top quality settings. For my money, though, the file-size benefit you gain from dropping the quality down from Fine to Normal and using the Size Priority option instead of Optimal Quality isn't worth even a little quality loss, especially with the price of camera memory cards getting lower every day. You never know when a casual snapshot is going to turn out to be so great that you want to print or display it large enough that even minor quality loss becomes a concern. And of all the defects that you can correct in a photo editor, artifacting is one of the hardest to remove. So if I shoot in the JPEG format, I stick with Fine and set the JPEG Compression option to Optimal Quality.

I suggest that you do your own test shots, however, carefully inspect the results in your photo editor, and make your own judgment about what level of artifacting you can accept. Artifacting is often much easier to spot when you view images onscreen. It's difficult to reproduce artifacting here in print because the print process obscures some of the tiny defects caused by compression.

If you don't want *any* risk of artifacting, bypass JPEG altogether and change the file type to Raw (NEF), explained next.

Raw (NEF): The purist's choice

The second picture file type you can create is Camera Raw, or just *Raw* (as in uncooked) for short.

Each manufacturer has its own flavor of Raw. Nikon's is *NEF* (for Nikon Electronic Format), so you see the three-letter extension NEF at the end of Raw filenames.

Raw pros and cons

Raw is popular with advanced, very demanding photographers for these reasons:

- ✓ **Greater creative control:** With JPEG, internal camera software tweaks your images, making adjustments to color, exposure, and sharpness as needed to produce the results that Nikon believes its customers prefer. With Raw, the camera simply records the original, unprocessed image data. The photographer then uses a tool known as a *Raw converter* to produce the actual image, making decisions about color, exposure, and so on at that point.

- ✓ **Higher bit depth:** *Bit depth* is a measure of how many distinct color values an image file can contain. When you choose JPEG as the Image Quality setting, your pictures contain 8 bits each for the red, blue, and green color components, or *channels,* that make up a digital image, for a total of 24 bits. That translates to roughly 16.7 million possible colors.

  Choosing the Raw setting delivers a higher bit count. You can set the camera to collect 12 bits per channel or 14 bits per channel. (More about that option and some other Raw-related options momentarily.)

  Although jumping from 8 to 14 bits sounds like a huge difference, you may not really ever notice any impact on your photos — that 8-bit palette of 16.7 million values is more than enough for superb images. Where having the extra bits can come in handy is if you really need to adjust exposure, contrast, or color after the shot in your photo-editing program. In cases where you apply extreme adjustments, having the extra original bits sometimes helps avoid a problem known as *banding* or *posterization,* which creates abrupt color breaks where you should see smooth, seamless transitions. (A higher bit depth doesn't always prevent the problem, however, so don't expect miracles.)

- ✓ **Better picture quality:** Raw doesn't apply the destructive, lossy compression associated with JPEG, so you don't run the risk of the artifacting that can occur with JPEG. On the D7000, you can apply two alternative types of compression to reduce Raw file sizes slightly, but neither impact image quality to the extent of JPEG compression. Or you can turn off compression altogether.

As with most things in life, Raw isn't without its disadvantages, however. To wit:

✔ **You can't do much with your pictures until you process them in a Raw converter.** You can't share them online, for example, or put them into a text document or multimedia presentation. You can print them immediately if you use Nikon ViewNX 2, but most other photo programs require you to convert the Raw files to a standard format such as JPEG or TIFF (a popular format for images destined for professional printing) first.

✔ **To get the full benefit of Raw, you need software other than Nikon ViewNX 2.** The ViewNX software that ships free with your camera does have a command that enables you to convert Raw files to JPEG or to TIFF. However, this free tool gives you limited control over how your original data is translated in terms of color, exposure, and other characteristics — which defeats one of the primary purposes of shooting Raw.

A different Nikon program, Nikon Capture NX 2, offers a sophisticated Raw converter, but it costs about $180. You can get a look at Capture NX 2 as well as some competing programs in Chapter 6.

Of course, the D7000 also offers an in-camera Raw converter, which I also cover in Chapter 6. But although it's convenient, this tool isn't the easiest to use because you must rely on the small camera monitor when making judgments about color, exposure, sharpness, and so on. The in-camera tool also doesn't offer the complete cadre of features available in Capture NX 2 and other converter software utilities.

✔ **Raw files are larger than JPEGs.** The type of file compression that you can enable for Raw files doesn't degrade image quality to the degree you get with JPEG compression, but the tradeoff is a larger file. In addition, Raw files are always captured at the maximum resolution available on the camera, even if you don't really need all those pixels. For both reasons, Raw files are significantly larger than JPEGs, so they take up more room on your memory card and on your computer's hard drive or other picture-storage device.

Whether the upside of Raw outweighs the down is a decision that you need to ponder based on your photographic needs, your schedule, and your computer-comfort level. If you do decide to try Raw shooting, the next section explains a few Raw setup options.

Customizing your Raw capture settings

If you opt for Raw, you can control three aspects of how your pictures are captured:

✔ **Raw only or Raw+JPEG:** You can choose to capture the picture in the Raw format or create two files for each shot, one in the Raw format and another in the JPEG format, as shown in Figure 2-21. The figure shows the list of options that appears when you change the Image Quality setting through the Shooting menu; you can select from the same settings when you adjust the option by pressing the Qual button and rotating the Main command dial.

For Raw+JPEG, you can specify whether you want the JPEG version captured at the Fine, Normal, or Basic quality level, and you can set the resolution of the JPEG file through the Image Size option, explained earlier in this chapter. Again, the Image Size setting doesn't affect the Raw file; the camera always captures the file at the maximum resolution.

Figure 2-21: You can create two files for each picture, one in the Raw format and a second in the JPEG format.

I often choose the Raw+JPEG Fine option when I'm shooting pictures I want to share right away with people who don't have software for viewing Raw files. I upload the JPEGs to a photo-sharing site where everyone can view them and order prints, and then I process the Raw versions of my favorite images for my own use when I have time. Having the JPEG version also enables you to display your photos on a DVD player or TV that has a slot for an SD memory card — most can't display Raw files but can handle JPEGs. Ditto for portable media players and digital photo frames.

✓ **Raw bit depth:** You can specify whether you want a 12-bit Raw file or a 14-bit Raw file. More bits mean a bigger file but a larger spectrum of possible colors, as explained in the preceding section. You make the call through the NEF (Raw) Recording option on the Shooting menu, as shown in Figure 2-22. The default setting is 14 bits.

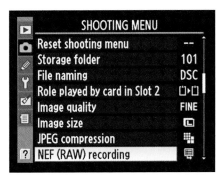
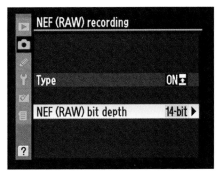

Figure 2-22: Set the file bit depth through this Shooting menu option.

✔ **Raw compression:** By default, the camera applies *lossless compression* to Raw files. As its name implies, this type of compression results in no visible loss of image quality and yet still reduces file sizes by about 20 to 40 percent. In addition, the compression is *reversible,* meaning that any quality loss that does occur through the compression process is reversed at the time you process your Raw images. Technically, some original data may be altered, but you're unlikely to notice the difference in your pictures.

You can change to a setting that delivers a greater degree of file-size savings if you prefer. Again, select the (NEF) Raw Recording option on the Shooting menu, but this time choose Type, as shown on the left in Figure 2-23, and press OK to display the screen shown on the right. Selecting the Compressed setting instead of Lossless Compressed shrinks files by about 40 to 55 percent. Nikon promises that this setting has "almost no effect" on image quality. But the compression in this case is not reversible, so if you do experience some quality loss, there's no going back.

Together, the choices you make for these three settings make a big difference in the size of your picture files and, thus, your memory card capacity. A 12-bit file captured at the Compressed setting, for example, has a file size of 13.6MB. If you ratchet up the Raw settings to combine the 14-bit file with the Lossless Compressed setting, a single picture file consumes about 19.4MB. And if you choose Raw+JPEG capture, well, just add the size of the JPEG file into the equation. If you choose the 14-bit and Lossless Compressed settings for the Raw file and create the second file as a JPEG Fine at the highest resolution, for example, the combined size of the Raw plus JPEG files is (gulp) 27.2MB (19.4MB for the Raw file plus 7.8MB for the Large/Fine JPEG when the Size Priority setting is selected for the JPEG Compression option).

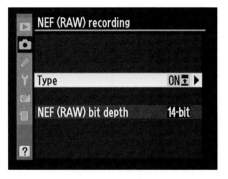
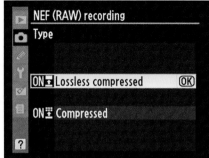

Figure 2-23: To keep Raw file compression to a minimum, select the Lossless Compressed option.

Most photographers, I think, will be perfectly happy with the settings that produce the smaller Raw files (12-bit, Compressed). And frankly, I doubt that too many people could perceive much difference between a photo captured at that setting and a 14-bit, Lossless Compressed picture. But if you're using your camera for commercial photography — whether you shoot weddings, do high-end studio work, or shoot fine-art photography for sale — you may feel more comfortable knowing that you're capturing files at the absolute maximum quality and bit depth. The higher bit depth also may make sense if you're shooting in really difficult lighting because, again, it gives you the potential of capturing a broader range of colors and tones.

If you choose to create both a Raw and JPEG file, note a couple of things:

✔ If you're using only one memory card, you see the JPEG version of the photo during playback. However, the Image Quality data that appears with the photo reflects your capture setting (Raw+Basic, for example). The size value relates to the JPEG version; Raw files are always captured at the Large size. To use the in-camera Raw processing option on the Retouch menu, display the JPEG image and then proceed as outlined in Chapter 6.

✔ If both the JPEG and Raw files are stored on the same memory card, deleting the JPEG image also deletes the Raw copy. See Chapter 1 to find out how you can send the two versions to separate memory cards instead. If you go that route, deleting one file doesn't delete the other. (Either way, after you transfer the two files to your computer, deleting one doesn't affect the other.)

✔ If two memory cards are installed, you can choose to send the Raw files to one card and the JPEG files to another by setting the Role Played by Card in Slot 2 option on the Shooting menu to Raw Slot 1 - JPEG Slot 2 setting.

Chapter 5 explains more about viewing and deleting photos. Chapter 1 explains how to configure a two-memory-card setup.

3

Taking Great Pictures, Automatically

*A*re you old enough to remember the Certs television commercials from the 1960s and '70s? "It's a candy mint!" declared one actor. "It's a breath mint!" argued another. Then a narrator declared the debate a tie and spoke the famous catchphrase: "It's two, two, two mints in one!"

Well, that's sort of how I see the Nikon D7000. On one hand, it provides a full range of powerful controls, offering just about every feature a serious photographer could want. On the other, it offers automated photography modes that enable people with absolutely no experience to capture beautiful images. "It's a sophisticated photographic tool!" "It's as easy as 'point and shoot!'" "It's two, two, two cameras in one!"

Now, my guess is that you bought this book for help with your camera's advanced side so that's what other chapters cover. This chapter, however, is devoted to your camera's easiest shooting modes, showing you how to get the best results in your camera's fully automatic modes, including Auto, Portrait mode, Sports mode, Landscape mode, and all the other Scene modes.

Note: Information in this chapter assumes that you're using the viewfinder to compose your pictures. Things work a little differently in Live View mode, which enables you to use the monitor instead of the viewfinder, so Chapter 4 concentrates on that shooting option.

Setting Up for Automatic Success

Your D7000 offers a variety of fully automatic exposure modes, which you access via the Mode dial, shown in Figure 3-1. Your choices include Auto, which is a general purpose, point-and-shoot type of option; Auto Flash Off, which does the same thing as Auto but without flash; and Scene, which gives you access to more than a dozen additional automatic modes that are geared to shooting specific types of pictures.

Auto Flash Off

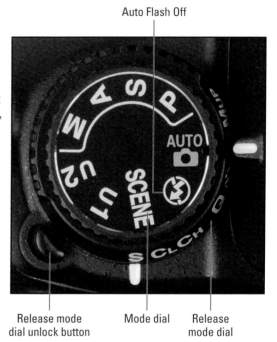

Even in these automatic modes, you have a few ways to control the camera's behavior. You can adjust the following settings:

Release mode   Mode dial   Release
dial unlock button   mode dial

Figure 3-1: For almost-automatic photography, use the Auto, Auto Flash Off, or Scene modes.

- **Release mode:** This setting, fully detailed in Chapter 2, determines the number of images that are recorded with each press of the shutter button and the timing of each shot. Choose the Release mode via the dial that's directly under the Mode dial, as labeled in Figure 3-1. (Don't forget to press the little dial unlock button before moving the dial.)

  For normal shooting, set the dial to the S (Single Frame) position, as shown in the figure; at this setting, the camera captures one image each time you press the shutter button. When shooting action, consider changing to Continuous Low or Continuous High, which record a burst of images as long as you hold down the shutter button. Just remember that you can't use flash in either of the Continuous modes.

✔ **Focusing:** You can enjoy auto-focusing, if your lens supports it, or focus manually. On the D7000 kit lens, select the setting via the switch labeled in Figure 3-2. Then also set the Focus-mode selector switch on the camera body to AF for autofocus or M for manual focusing.

✔ **Vibration Reduction (VR):** When enabled, this feature helps produce sharper images by compensating for camera movement that can occur when you handhold the camera. On the kit lens, turn Vibration Reduction on or off via the VR switch labeled in Figure 3-2. Select On for handheld photography; set the switch to Off when you mount the camera on a tripod. See Chapter 1 for additional details.

Lens focus-mode switch

Vibration Reduction switch   Focus-mode selector

Figure 3-2: You can choose automatic or manual focusing in any exposure mode (if your lens supports autofocusing).

✔ **Flash:** In Auto exposure mode, as well as in many of the Scene modes, the camera automatically raises and fires the built-in flash in dim lighting. But in most cases, you can alter the behavior of the flash through the Flash mode setting.

Chapter 7 provides complete details about Flash modes and other flash settings, but here's a quick intro:

• *Checking the current Flash mode:* Symbols representing the current Flash mode appear in the Information display and Control panel. For example, in Figure 3-3, the symbols show that the flash is set to Auto, meaning that the camera will automatically fire the flash if it thinks the ambient lighting is insufficient.

The *TTL* label that appears with the icon in the left screen in Figure 3-3 stands for *through-the-lens,* which refers to the way that the camera measures the ambient light when it calculates how much flash power is needed.

• *Changing the Flash mode:* Press the Flash button and rotate the Main command dial.

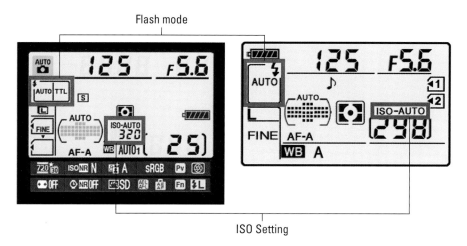

Figure 3-3: These symbols show the current Flash mode and ISO Sensitivity setting.

- *Disable flash:* Select the Flash Off mode, represented in the displays by the symbol shown in the margin here.

- *Use red-eye reduction flash:* Look for the Flash mode accompanied by the little eye icon, as shown here. In this mode, the camera still controls whether the flash fires, but if it does see the need for flash, it emits a brief burst of light before the actual flash fires — the idea being that the prelight will constrict the subject's pupils, which helps reduce the chances of red-eye. Warn your subject to wait until after the final flash to stop smiling.

  Note that some Scene modes use a variation of red-eye reduction, combining that feature with a slow shutter speed. In that case, you see the little eye icon plus the word Slow. It's important to use a tripod and ask your subject to remain still during the exposure to avoid a blurry picture. And the Night Portrait Scene mode combines a slow shutter with the normal Auto flash mode, so the word Slow appears with the normal flash symbol. Again, use a tripod for good results.

- *Locking the flash power (FV Lock):* Some automatic modes let you use this feature; it's a little complicated, though, so I save it for Chapter 7.

✓ **Image Quality and Image Size:** By default, pictures are recorded at the Large Image Size setting, producing a 16.1 MP (megapixel) image, and the Normal Image Quality setting, which creates a JPEG picture file with a moderate amount of compression. Chapter 2 explains both options and offers advice on when you may want to stray from the default settings.

✔ **Exposure:** You have access to one exposure-adjustment option, ISO Sensitivity, which determines how much light is needed to properly expose the image. At the default setting, Auto, the camera adjusts the ISO Sensitivity as needed. Stick with Auto for now; when you're ready to fully delve into this setting and the other exposure controls, Chapter 7 awaits. You can adjust the setting through the Shooting menu or by pressing the ISO button while rotating the Main command dial. The current setting appears in the displays in the areas labeled in Figure 3-3. (In the Information display, the camera also shows you the specific ISO value it plans to use when taking the picture — 320, in Figure 3-3.)

✔ **Advanced Shooting menu options:** You also can control the following more advanced Shooting menu options:

- *Auto Distortion Control:* This feature attempts to correct for the slight distortion that can occur when you shoot with wide-angle or extreme telephoto lenses. Leave this one set to its default, Off, until you explore the details in Chapter 8.

- *Color Space:* Again, stick with the default setting, sRGB, until you delve into the advanced color issues covered in Chapter 8.

- *Long Exposure Noise Reduction and High ISO Noise Reduction:* These features try to compensate for image defects that can occur when you use a long exposure time or high ISO setting. Chapter 7 explains the pros and cons of enabling them. For now, leave the Long Exposure NR setting turned to its default, Off, and leave the High ISO NR setting at Normal.

If you're not up to sorting through any of these choices, in fact, just leave them all at their default settings and skip to the next section to get step-by-step help with taking your first pictures. After all, the defaults are chosen because they're the best solutions for most shooting scenarios. See the end of Chapter 1 to find out how to restore the default Shooting menu options.

As Easy as It Gets: Auto and Auto Flash Off

When you set the Mode dial to the Auto or Auto Flash Off setting (refer to Figure 3-1), the camera analyzes the scene in front of the lens and selects the picture-taking options that it thinks will best capture the image. All you need to do is compose the scene and press the shutter button. The only difference between the two modes is that Auto Flash Off disables flash, as its name implies, providing an easy way to ensure that you don't break the rules when shooting in locations that don't permit flash: museums, churches, and so on.

The following steps walk you through the process of taking a picture in both modes. Remember that these steps assume that you're using the viewfinder, which is the best option in most cases. Chapter 4 explains why and shows you how to take pictures in Live View mode.

1. **Set the Mode dial to Auto or Auto Flash Off.**

2. **Set the focusing method (auto or manual), Release mode, and other basic settings as outlined in the preceding section.**

3. **Look for the focus markings in the viewfinder.**

   The markings vary depending on whether you set the camera to auto or manual focusing:

   • *Autofocus*: At the default autofocus settings, you see a pair of brackets that indicate the area covered by the camera's 39 autofocus points, as shown in Figure 3-4.

   • *Manual focus:* You see the brackets along with a single rectangle. The rectangle, labeled in the figure, represents the active focus point. By default, the center focus point is selected.

4. **Frame the image so that your subject appears within the autofocus brackets (for autofocusing) or focus point (manual focusing).**

   If necessary, you can reposition the focus point by pressing the Multi Selector.

5. **To focus manually, rotate the focus ring on the lens.**

   On the kit lens, remember to move the lens switch from A to M before turning the focusing ring to avoid damaging the lens. If you use another lens, check the lens manual for instructions.

6. **Press and hold the shutter button halfway down.**

   At this point, the following occurs:

   • *Exposure metering begins.* The autoexposure meter analyzes the light and selects initial aperture (f-stop) and shutter speed settings, which are two critical exposure controls. These two settings appear in the viewfinder; in Figure 3-5, the shutter speed is 1/250 second, and the f-stop is f/7.1. (Chapter 7 explains these two options in detail.) The autoexposure meter continues monitoring the light up

Autofocus brackets   Focus point

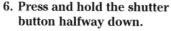

Figure 3-4: Position your subject within the area surrounded by the autofocus brackets or, if focusing manually, under the focus point.

to the time you take the picture, however, so the f-stop and shutter speed values may change if the lighting conditions change.

- *In Auto exposure mode, the built-in flash may pop up if the camera thinks additional light is needed.* You can set the Flash mode to auto (normal) or red-eye reduction mode. Or, if you prefer, you can disable the flash by changing the Flash mode to Off, as explained in the preceding section. (Or just move the Mode dial to the Auto Flash Off exposure setting.)

- *If autofocusing is enabled, the camera's autofocus system begins to do its thing.* In dim light, a little lamp located on the front of the camera, just to the left of the shutter button, may shoot out a beam of light. That lamp, called the *autofocus-assist illuminator,* or *AF-assist lamp* for short, helps the camera measure the distance between your subject and the lens so that it can better establish focus.

7. Check the focus indicators in the viewfinder.

Again, the camera provides focusing feedback differently depending on whether you're using autofocusing or handling the focus chores yourself:

- *Autofocusing:* When the camera has established focus, one or more focus points appear and flash red for a split second. Then just a single black focus point remains to show you the final focusing area selected by the camera. In the display at the bottom of the viewfinder, the round focus indicator, labeled in Figure 3-5, lights to give you further notice that focus has been achieved. You also hear a tiny beep, assuming that you didn't disable that feature via the Beep option on the Custom Setting menu.

- *Manual focus:* You see the green focus indicator in the viewfinder when the camera thinks that the object under your selected focus point is in focus.

For both auto and manual focusing, a little triangle to the right or left of the focus indicator means that focus isn't yet spot on. If the triangle is to the left of the dot, as shown on the left in Figure 3-6, focus is set in front of the subject; if the triangle is to the right, focus is set behind the subject. And if both triangles blink, the autofocus system is stymied, so switch to manual focus. (Make sure to adjust the viewfinder to your eyesight, as covered in Chapter 1, so that you get an accurate depiction of focus.)

Focus indicator

Figure 3-5: The green light indicates that the camera has locked focus on the objects under the selected focus point.

8. Press the shutter button the rest of the way down to record the image.

When the recording process is finished, the picture appears briefly on the camera monitor. If the picture doesn't appear or you want to take a longer look at the image, see Chapter 5, which covers picture playback.

Focus in front of subject   Focus behind subject

Figure 3-6: A triangle next to the focus indicator announces a focusing problem.

I need to add a few important points about working in the Auto and Auto Flash Off exposure modes:

- **Exposure:** In dim lighting, the camera may need to use a very high ISO setting or very slow shutter speed when flash is disabled. Unfortunately, a high ISO can create *noise,* a defect that makes your picture look grainy. And a slow shutter speed can produce blur if either the camera or subject moves during the exposure. If you spot either problem, enable flash or add some other light source. See Chapter 7 for details about both issues as well as other tips for dealing with exposure problems.

- **Autofocusing:** Autofocusing behavior is determined by two settings, the AF-area mode and the Autofocus mode, both explained fully in Chapter 8. By default, the camera uses these settings:

  - *AF-area mode:* The Auto Area option is selected, which means that the camera selects which autofocus point to use when establishing focus.

  - *Autofocus mode:* The default setting is AF-A, which stands for *auto-servo autofocus.* If the subject isn't moving, focus remains locked as long as you hold the shutter button halfway down. But if the camera detects motion, it continually adjusts focus up to the time you press the button fully to record the picture. (In this situation, the focus-achieved beep doesn't sound, and the focus indicator light may blink on and off as the camera adjusts focus.) To ensure that focus is correct, you must keep your subject within the area of the viewfinder covered by the focusing brackets.

In some cases, no amount of fiddling with the autofocus settings will help your camera lock focus where you intend. Some subjects just give autofocusing systems fits: Highly reflective objects, subjects behind fence bars, and scenes in which little contrast exists between the subject and the background are just a few potential problem areas. Again, the solution is to set the lens to manual focusing and handle the focusing job yourself.

I purposely didn't include an example of a photo taken in Auto or Auto Flash Off modes because, frankly, the results that these settings create vary widely depending on how well the camera detects whether you're trying to shoot a portrait, landscape, action shot, or whatever, as well as on lighting conditions. But the bottom line is that both take a one-size-fits-all approach that may or may not take best advantage of your camera's capabilities. So if you want to more consistently take great pictures instead of merely good ones, I encourage you to explore the exposure, focus, and color information found in Part III so that you can abandon this mode in favor of modes that put more photographic decisions in your hands. At the very least, step up to one of the Scene modes, detailed next.

Taking Advantage of Scene Modes

In Auto and Auto Flash Off exposure modes, the camera tries to figure out what type of picture you want to take by assessing what it sees through the lens. If you don't want to rely on the camera to make that judgment, your D7000 offers *Scene modes,* which are designed to automatically capture specific scenes in ways that are traditionally considered best from a creative standpoint. For example, most people prefer portraits that have softly focused backgrounds. So in Portrait mode, the camera selects settings that can produce that type of background.

Usually, Scene modes also apply color, exposure, contrast, and sharpness adjustments to the picture according to the traditional characteristics of the scene type. Landscape mode typically results in more vibrant colors, especially in the blue-green range, for example, whereas Portrait mode typically produces a softer image with more natural tones.

To access the Scene modes, set the Mode dial to Scene, as shown in Figure 3-7. The following section explains how to select a scene type; following that, you can get brief information about each one.

Figure 3-7: Set the Mode dial to Scene to experiment with automatic exposure modes based on different types of photographic scenes.

Scene modes in focus (or not)

When you focus the lens, either in autofocus or manual focus mode, you determine only the point of sharpest focus. The distance to which that sharp-focus zone extends from that point — what photographers call the *depth of field* — depends in part on the *aperture setting*, or *f-stop,* which is an exposure control. Some of the D7000's Scene modes are designed to choose aperture settings that deliver a certain depth of field.

The Portrait, Child, and Close Up settings, for example, try to use a wide aperture setting (low f-stop number) because doing so shortens the depth of field, rendering backgrounds softly focused — an artistic choice that most people prefer for those types of shots. On the flip side, the Landscape mode tries to use a small aperture (high f-stop number), which produces a large depth of field, keeping both foreground and background objects sharp.

However, the range of apertures the camera can select varies depending on the light. In dim lighting, an open aperture is needed to properly expose the picture, and in bright light, a small aperture may be required to avoid overexposing the picture. Additionally, the range of available aperture settings varies from lens to lens. So how much depth of field any Scene mode produces varies from shot to shot.

Another exposure-related control, *shutter speed,* also plays a focus role when you photograph moving objects. Moving objects appear blurry at slow shutter speeds; at fast shutter speeds, they appear sharply focused. In Sports mode, the camera tries to select a shutter speed fast enough to freeze action, but in dim lighting, that may not be possible: The less light, the slower the shutter speed needed to expose the photo. That means that even in Sports mode, a moving subject may appear blurry. Additionally, some Scene modes, such as Night Landscape and Candlelight, purposely choose a slow shutter speed in order to cope with the dark settings. For these modes, it's critical to use a tripod because any camera movement during the exposure can also blur the image.

To fully understand these issues — and to control focus and depth of field to a greater extent than the automated exposure modes allow — visit Chapters 7 and 8.

Before I shoo you off to either section, though, I want to offer a little advice: The Scene modes are a great way to start taking control over your pictures, and if nothing else, they encourage you to think about the characteristics that go into different types of photos. But don't expect miracles, especially if the lighting conditions or subject matter is challenging. The nearby sidebar "Scene modes in focus (or not)" provides some background information to explain why this is so.

There's also the whole notion of creative input to consider. Sure, most formal portraits feature a blurred background. But maybe you want to keep the background in focus because the setting is important to the story you're trying to tell — think of a shot of newlyweds standing in the front yard of their very first home, for example. The details of the yard and home likely will be just as important to the couple when they look back on that photo in years to come.

Long story short: Experiment with the Scene modes while you're discovering more about photography. But if you're not happy with your results, don't just keep trying over and over with the same Scene mode — you're not going to achieve anything different. Instead, head for Part III of this book, where you can find out how to master the advanced exposure modes and take full control over your pictures.

Selecting a Scene mode

To experiment with Scene modes, follow these steps:

1. **Set the Mode dial to Scene.**

2. **Rotate the Main command dial one notch.**

   An icon representing the current Scene mode appears in the upper-left corner of the Information display, as shown on the left in Figure 3-8. The next section describes each Scene mode.

3. **Rotate the Main command dial again to choose a different scene.**

   As soon as you rotate the dial, the display changes to show a roulette wheel of scene types, as shown on the right in Figure 3-8. Keep spinning the dial to cycle through all the options. An example photo appears to give you an idea of what the selected mode produces.

Current Scene mode

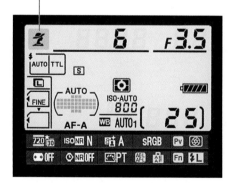 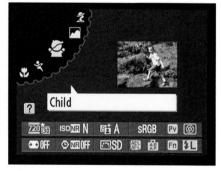

Figure 3-8: Rotate the Main command dial to cycle through the available scene types.

4. **When you find a Scene mode you like, stop rotating the Main command dial.**

    The camera sets itself up to take the picture, and the icon on the Information display reflects your Scene mode choice.

5. **Frame, focus, and shoot.**

    From here on in, everything works as it does for the Auto and Auto Flash Off exposure modes with the exception of your Flash mode choices and the default autofocusing behavior, which vary depending on the scene type you select.

Checking out the Scene (s)

Your camera offers a whopping 19 Scene modes, each designed to produce a specific result in terms of lighting, color, and focus. Again, because I presume that most people buying this book are more interested in the camera's more advanced options, I don't want to spend pages detailing each mode. So the following list provides just a quick overview and offers some tips and warnings to help you get the best results.

Before you start exploring the Scene choices, note these two general pointers:

✔ **Flash:** For modes that permit flash, you may be able to select a different Flash mode; press the Flash button while rotating the Main command dial to cycle through the available settings. Chapter 7 offers complete details on flash photography.

✔ **Autofocus:** For most Scene modes, the default autofocusing settings work as they do when you use the Auto mode; see the earlier section "As Easy as It Gets: Auto and Auto Flash Off" for details.

The following modes, however, don't use the Auto AF-area mode, in which the camera looks at all focus points within the focus-area brackets and then selects the focus point for you. Instead, they use these settings:

• *Close Up, Candlelight, Food, Silhouette, High Key, and Low Key*: These modes use Single Point AF-area mode. By default, focus is based on a single focus point at the center of the frame. You can use the Multi Selector to move the point to a different position if necessary.

• *Sports and Pet Portrait*: In these modes, the camera sets the AF-area mode to 39-point Dynamic Area. You start by selecting a single focus point, but if the subject leaves that point, the camera looks to other points for focusing information.

Chapter 8 shows you how to make best use of all these focusing options and how to adjust them to suit your subject.

And now without further ado, here's a review of all bazillion Scene modes, listed in the order you encounter them when you spin the command dial:

- ✔ **Portrait:** Choose this mode to produce the classic portrait look, with the subject set against a softly focused background, as shown in Figure 3-9. Colors are adjusted to produce natural-looking skin tones.

- ✔ **Landscape:** In the time-honored tradition of landscape photography, this mode produces crisp images with vivid blues and greens to create that bold, vacation-magazine look (see Figure 3-10). The camera also tries to select a high f-stop setting to extend depth of field, which keeps both foreground and background objects as sharp as possible. Flash is disabled.

- ✔ **Child:** A variation of Portrait mode, Child mode also aims for a blurry background and natural skin tones. Colors of clothing and other objects, however, are rendered more vividly. (I'm not a huge fan of this mode — I don't want background objects or clothing to take the eye away from the face of my subject.)

Portrait mode

Landscape mode

Figure 3-9: Portrait mode produces soft backgrounds to help emphasize your subject.

Figure 3-10: Landscape mode features bold colors and a large zone of sharp focus (depth of field).

✔ **Sports:** Select this mode to have a better chance of capturing a moving target without blur, as I did for my romping furboy in Figure 3-12. To accomplish this outcome, the camera selects a fast shutter speed, if possible. But remember that in dim lighting, it may need to use a slow shutter speed to expose the image — which typically means a shutter speed too low to freeze action. Flash is disabled. Note that in bright lighting, the Pet Portrait mode would produce similar results to what you see in Figure 3-11; that mode is also geared to using a fast shutter speed when possible.

Sports mode

Figure 3-11: Try Sports mode to capture action.

✔ **Close Up:** As with Portrait and Child mode, the camera selects an aperture designed to produce short depth of field, which helps keep background objects from competing for attention with your main subject, as shown in Figure 3-12.

✔ **Night Landscape:** This setting uses a slow shutter speed to capture nighttime city scenes, such as the one in Figure 3-13. Because of the long exposure time, use a tripod to avoid camera shake, which can blur the picture. Note that even when the camera remains perfectly still, any moving objects in the scene appear blurry, as does the fountain water in this example. This mode also is designed to reduce noise and avoid unnatural colors, both of which are common problems in night landscape shots. (See Chapter 7 for more information about noise; refer to Chapter 8 for help with color issues.) Flash is disabled.

✔ **Night Portrait:** This mode is designed to deliver a better-looking flash portrait at night (or in any dimly lit environment). It does so by constraining you to using Auto Slow-Sync, Auto Slow-Sync with Red-Eye Reduction, or Off Flash modes. In the first two Flash modes, the camera selects a shutter speed that results in a long exposure time. That slow shutter speed enables the camera to rely more on ambient light and less on the flash to expose the picture, which produces softer, more even lighting. If you disable flash, an even slower shutter speed is used.

Figure 3-12: Close Up mode helps emphasize the subject by throwing the background out of focus.

I cover the issue of long-exposure and slow-sync flash photography in detail in Chapter 7. For now, the critical thing to know is that the slower shutter speed means that you probably need a tripod. Your subjects also must stay perfectly still during the exposure.

✔ **Party/Indoor:** This mode is designed to capture indoor scenes that are lit by room lighting as well as the flash, using settings that

Figure 3-13: To capture this kind of after-dark photo, use Night Landscape mode and a tripod.

produce a nice balance between the two light sources. If the lighting is very dim, the camera may use a slow shutter speed, so use a tripod to avoid blurring.

- **Beach/Snow:** Use this mode when you're photographing a scene with lots of bright areas, such as sand or snow, which can fool the camera's autoexposure system into underexposing the image. Flash is disabled.

- **Dusk/Dawn:** Use this mode to better capture the colors of the sky when shooting landscapes just before the sun rises, or just after the sun sets. Flash is disabled. I recommend using a tripod when using this mode as well because the shutter speed the camera selects may be very slow.

- **Sunset:** Use this mode when photographing sunsets or sunrises and the sun is in the picture; the camera chooses settings designed to preserve the brilliant colors seen at those times of day. And, yep, you guessed it: A tripod produces a better chance of a sharp shot because the light will be dim and the camera will need to use a slow shutter speed.

When photographing sunsets, don't stare at the sun directly through your viewfinder because this can permanently damage your vision, especially when you're using a telephoto lens.

- **Pet Portrait:** Despite its name, this mode is just like Sports mode — meaning, you can use it to photograph any moving subject, not just pets — except that in dim lighting, the flash fires unless you set the Flash mode to Off. Note that if flash is required, the camera can raise the shutter speed no higher than 1/250 second, by default, which may not be fast enough to capture a really speedy animal. See Chapter 7 for details about flash and shutter speed.

- **Candlelight:** Use this mode when shooting subjects lit by candlelight. Flash is disabled, and because the ambient light will be dim, the shutter speed will likely be slow. Again, mount your camera on a tripod to avoid a blurry photo.

- **Autumn Colors:** This mode yields pictures with saturated reds and yellows of autumn leaves. The built-in flash is disabled. Mount your camera on a tripod in low-light situations.

- **Blossom:** Use this mode when you're photographing a field of blooming flowers. Flash is disabled; again, use a tripod when photographing in low-light situations.

- **Food:** This mode increases color saturation to render food more vividly. An important note about flash: Unlike other Scene modes, Food mode requires you to raise the built-in flash yourself if you want to add flash. To do so, press the Flash button. The flash pops up and sets itself to Fill Flash mode, which fires the flash regardless of the ambient light. To go flash free, just close the flash unit. You can't adjust the Flash mode.

✔ **Silhouette:** Use this mode when the sun is behind your subject(s), and you want the subjects to render as silhouettes. Flash is disabled; use a tripod in dim lighting.

✔ **Low Key:** Use this mode when you're shooting dark scenes and you want a somber look. Highlights are rendered properly, but shadows and dark areas of the image are black. Flash is disabled; use a tripod for sharp, blur-free shots.

✔ **High Key:** Experiment with using this mode for an interesting effect when photographing bright objects in bright light — crystal on a lace doily, for example. Flash is disabled.

Do you need high-speed memory cards?

Memory cards are categorized not just by their storage capacity, but also by their data-transfer speed. SD cards (the type used by your D7000) fall into one of four *speed classes:* Class 2, Class 4, Class 6, and Class 10, with the number indicating the minimum number of *megabytes* (units of computer data) that can be transferred per second. A Class 2 card, for example, has a minimum transfer speed of 2 megabytes, or MB, per second. Of course, with the speed increase comes a price increase, which leads to the question: Do you really have a need for speed?

The answer is "maybe." If you shoot a lot of movies with the D7000, I recommend a Class 6 or 10 card, as does Nikon — the faster data-transfer rate helps ensure smooth movie-recording and playback performance. For still photography, users who shoot at the highest resolution or prefer the Raw (NEF) file format may also gain from high-speed cards; both options increase file size and, thus, the time needed to store the picture on the card. (See Chapter 2 for details.)

As for picture downloading, how long it takes files to shuffle from card to computer depends not just on card speed but also on the capabilities of your computer and, if you use a memory card reader to download files, on the speed of that device. (Chapter 5 covers the file-downloading process.)

Long story short, if you want to push your camera to its performance limits, a high-speed card is worth the expense, especially for video recording. But if you're primarily interested in still photography or you already own slower-speed cards, try using them first — you may find that they're more than adequate for most shooting scenarios.

4

Exploring Live View Photography and Movie Making

In This Chapter

▷ Getting acquainted with Live View mode

▷ Customizing the Live View display

▷ Exploring Live View and movie autofocusing options

▷ Taking pictures in Live View mode

▷ Recording, playing, and trimming movies

*L*ike many newer dSLR cameras, the D7000 offers *Live View,* a feature that enables you to use the monitor instead of the viewfinder to compose photos. Turning on Live View is also the first step in recording a movie; using the viewfinder isn't possible when you shoot movies.

In many respects, taking a picture in Live View mode is no different from regular, through-the-viewfinder photography. But a few critical steps, including focusing, work very differently when you switch on Live View. So the first part of this chapter explains everything you need to know about Live View focusing as well as other aspects of the Live View system — including precautions to take to keep the camera from overheating. Following that, you can find details on taking still photos in Live View mode and shooting, viewing, and editing movies.

Using Your Monitor as a Viewfinder

The basics of taking advantage of Live View are pretty simple:

✔ **Switching to Live View:** Rotate the little lever on the Live View switch to the right and release it. Figure 4-1 shows you where to find the control. As soon as you take this step, you hear a sort of clicking sound as the internal mirror that normally sends the image from the lens to the viewfinder flips up, permitting the Live View preview to start. Then the scene in front of the lens appears on the monitor, and you no longer can see anything in the viewfinder. The Information screen, too, is no longer available; instead, critical settings appear superimposed over the live scene on the monitor.

✔ **Shooting photos:** Things work pretty much the same as for viewfinder photography — frame, focus, and press the shutter button. The main difference relates to autofocusing; see the upcoming section "Exploring Your Focusing Options" for details.

✔ **Recording movies:** Press the red movie-record button to start and stop recording. Your focusing options are the same as for still photography in Live View mode.

✔ **Choosing camera settings and viewing photos:** Press the Menu button to access menu settings or press the Playback button to view pictures or movies, as you normally do. You also can adjust settings via the usual external buttons, with the exception of the Qual button: In Live View mode, the button magnifies the display, so it can't be used to access the Image Size and Image Quality settings. Instead, set both options via the Shooting menu.

In Live View, you can control the same settings as for regular viewfinder photography. For movie recording, you have fewer choices; see the section "Shooting Digital Movies" for details.

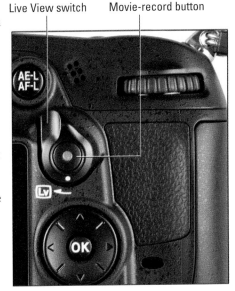

Live View switch   Movie-record button

Figure 4-1: Use this switch to toggle Live View on and off; press the red button to start and stop movie recording.

To return from the playback or menu screens to the Live View display, press the shutter button halfway and release it. Or press the Playback or Menu button again. (You need to press the Menu button twice; the first press activates the strip of menu icons.)

✔ **Exiting Live View mode:** Rotate the Live View switch a second time.

As you may have guessed from the fact that I devoted a whole chapter to the topic of Live View and movie recording, these points comprise just the start of the story, however. The next two sections provide some additional general information that applies to both still photography and movie recording; later sections get into the nitty-gritty of taking pictures in Live View mode and using the movie functions.

Live View safety tips

Whether your goal is a still image or a movie, be aware of the following tips and warnings any time you enable Live View:

✔ **Cover the viewfinder to prevent light from seeping into the camera and affecting exposure.** The camera ships with a little cover designed just for this purpose. To install it, first remove the little rubber eyecup that surrounds the viewfinder; just slide the eyecup up and out of the little groove that holds it in place. Then slide the cover down into the groove and over the viewfinder. (Orient the cover so that the *Nikon* label faces the viewfinder.)

Countdown warning

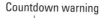

Figure 4-2: This timer appears to alert you to impending monitor shutdown.

✔ **By default, the monitor turns off after ten minutes of inactivity.** When only 30 seconds remain before monitor shutoff, a little countdown timer appears in the upper-left corner of the screen, as shown in Figure 4-2.

You can adjust the shutdown timing via the Monitor Off Delay option on the Timers/AE Lock section of the Custom Settings menu, shown on the left in Figure 4-3. Choose the Live View option, as shown on the right, and press OK to reveal the screen where you can change the setting. Options range from 5 to 30 minutes.

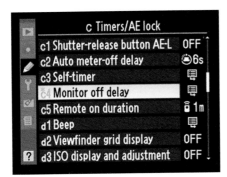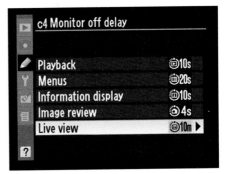

Figure 4-3: Adjust the delay time for automatic monitor shutdown via this menu option.

✔ **Using Live View for an extended period can harm your pictures and the camera.** When you work in Live View mode, the camera's innards heat up more than usual, and that extra heat can create the right electronic conditions for *noise*, a defect that gives your pictures a speckled look. Chapter 7 contains an illustration of this defect, which also is caused by long exposure times and high ISO Sensitivity settings.

Perhaps more importantly, the increased temperatures can damage the camera itself. For that reason, Live View is automatically disabled if the camera detects a critical heat level. In extremely warm environments, you may not be able to use Live View mode for very long before the system shuts down.

When the camera is 30 seconds or less from shutting down your Live View session to avoid overheating, the countdown timer shown in Figure 4-2 appears to let you know how many seconds you have left before the camera turns itself off. The warning doesn't appear during picture playback or when menus are active, however.

✔ **Aiming the lens at the sun or other bright lights also can damage the camera.** Of course, you can cause problems doing this even during normal shooting, but the possibilities increase when you use Live View. You not only can harm the camera's internal components but also the monitor.

✔ **Some lights may interfere with the Live View display.** The operating frequency of some types of lights, including fluorescent and mercury-vapor lamps, can create electronic interference that causes the monitor display to flicker or exhibit odd color banding. Changing the Flicker Reduction option on the Setup menu may resolve this issue. You're supposed to match the setting to the frequency of the electrical current being used by the lights, but if you're not sure what that frequency is and an electrical engineer isn't handy, just try changing the setting and see which one works best. You can choose from two options, 50 Hz and 60 Hz; see Figure 4-4. (In the U.S. and Canada, the standard frequency is 60 Hz, and in Europe, it's 50 Hz.)

Either way, the interference affects only the monitor display; the flicker or banding doesn't show in your pictures or movies.

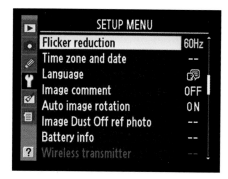

SETUP MENU	
Flicker reduction	60Hz
Time zone and date	--
Language	🗺
Image comment	OFF
Auto image rotation	ON
Image Dust Off ref photo	--
Battery info	--
Wireless transmitter	--

Figure 4-4: To reduce display flickering that can occur when you shoot by fluorescent light, try changing the Flicker Reduction setting.

- **Live View puts additional strain on the camera battery.** The monitor is a big consumer of battery juice, so keep an eye on the battery level icon to avoid running out of power at a critical moment.

- **The risk of camera shake during handheld shots is increased.** When you use the viewfinder, you can help steady the camera by bracing it against your face. But with Live View, you have to hold the camera away from your body to view the monitor, making it harder to keep the camera absolutely still. As Chapter 7 explains, any camera movement during the exposure can blur the shot, so using a tripod is the best course of action for Live View photography. If you do handhold the camera, enabling Vibration Reduction can help compensate for a bit of camera shake; Chapter 1 discusses this feature in more detail.

- **The display can be difficult to see clearly in bright sunlight.** If you've ever used a point-and-shoot camera that doesn't have a viewfinder, you're probably well aware of this problem. Although the D7000 monitor is of high quality, the display still can wash out in bright light, making it hard to see small details in the scene.

Because of these complications, I don't use Live View for still photography very often. Rather, I think of it as a special-purpose tool geared to situations where framing with the viewfinder is cumbersome. I find Live View most helpful for still-life, tabletop photography, especially in cases that require a lot of careful arrangement of the scene.

For example, I have a shooting table that's about waist high. Normally, I put my camera on a tripod, come up with an initial layout of the objects I want to photograph, set up my lights, and then check the scene through the viewfinder. Then there's a period of refining the object placement, the lighting, and so on. If I'm shooting from a high angle, requiring the camera to be positioned above the table and pointing downward, I have to stand on my tiptoes or get a stepladder to check things through the viewfinder between each compositional or lighting change. At lower angles, where the camera is tabletop height or below, I have to either bend over or kneel to look through the viewfinder, causing no end of later aches and pains to back and knees. With Live View, I can alleviate much of that bothersome routine (and pain) because I can usually see how things look in the monitor no matter what the camera position.

Customizing the Live View display

Whether you're using Live View for still photography or movie-making, you can choose from the following display styles, each of which adds different types of information to the screen. Press the Info button to cycle through the styles.

- **Show Photo Indicators:** By default, the display uses this mode, which reveals the shooting data shown on the left in Figure 4-5. Only options related to still photography appear. Later sections of this chapter detail what each of the little symbols indicates.

- **Show Movie Indicators:** Press Info to display only settings related to movie recording, as shown on the right in Figure 4-5. The later section "Shooting Digital Movies" explains the data that appears in this display.

- **Hide Indicators:** To declutter the screen a little, press the Info button to cycle from the default display to this mode, which presents only the information shown in Figure 4-6.

Figure 4-5: Press the Info button to shift from a display showing photography settings only (left) to movie settings only (right).

In this display mode, as well in the two described next, you may see four tiny horizontal markers near the corners of the image display area. They appear to show you how much of the vertical image area will not be included in the recorded movie if you set the movie resolution, or frame size, to a setting that produces a 16:9 frame aspect ratio. (The only setting that doesn't produce this ratio is 640 x 424, which captures the same aspect ratio as a still photo, 3:2.) I labeled one of the markers in Figure 4-6.

Movie frame height marker

Figure 4-6: Press Info again to hide everything but the settings at the bottom of the screen.

In the Show Movie Indicators view, the shaded bars at the top and bottom of the image display area serve the same purpose, as shown on the right side of Figure 4-5. The later section "Choosing the video type and quality" explains movie resolution options.

✔ **Framing Grid:** Press Info again to shift to this display, shown on the left of Figure 4-7. It offers the same framing grid that's available for the viewfinder. The grid is helpful when you need to precisely align objects in your photo.

✔ **Virtual Horizon:** You also can display the Virtual Horizon indicator, as shown on the right in Figure 4-7. This tool works the same way as the one you can enable through the Setup menu, introduced in Chapter 1. When the camera is level, the little green triangle appears, as shown in the figure.

WB In addition to these options, you can adjust the monitor brightness by pressing and holding the WB button to display the little brightness scale on the right side of the screen, as shown in Figure 4-8. While holding the button, press the Multi Selector up and down to adjust the brightness. The strip of reminder icons along the bottom of the screen (highlighted in the figure) is there to jog your memory of what buttons accomplish this function. (When you shoot in the P, S, A, or M exposure modes, rotating the Main command dial while pressing the button changes the White Balance setting, which appears highlighted in the upper-right corner of the screen.)

Figure 4-7: The Framing Grid (left) and Virtual Horizon (right) displays are helpful for shots that require precise alignment of objects in the scene or of the camera itself.

If you connect your camera to an HDMI (High-Definition Multimedia Interface) device, you no longer see the live scene on your camera monitor. Instead, the view appears on your video display. In that scenario, the arrangement of the shooting information on the screen may appear slightly different than in the examples in this chapter. Also note that if you connect the camera to an HDMI-CEC device, you may need to adjust an option on the Setup menu. Select HDMI, press OK, and turn off the Device Control option. Otherwise, you can't record a movie or take a picture in Live View mode. See the Chapter 5 section related to connecting the camera to a television for more HD details.

Brightness scale

Figure 4-8: Press the WB button and then press the Multi Selector up or down to adjust monitor brightness when Live View is enabled.

Exploring Your Focusing Options

As with viewfinder photography, you can opt for autofocusing or manual focusing during Live View shooting, assuming that your lens supports both. If you use the kit lens, set the switch on the lens to the A position for auto-focusing and to the M position to focus manually. (With other lenses, check

the lens instruction manual for help.)
Also set the Focus-mode selector on
the camera to AF for autofocusing
and M for manual focusing. Figure
4-9 offers a reminder of where to find
these two switches.

It's important to understand that the
camera typically taks longer to autofocus in Live View mode than it does
during viewfinder photography. So
if you need fast focusing response,
take the camera out of Live View
mode. If you do stay in Live View
mode, you control autofocusing performance through these two options:

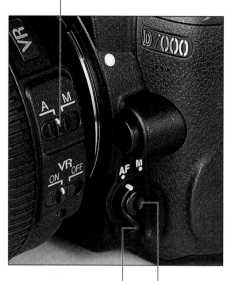

Lens focus-mode switch

Focus-mode selector   AF mode button

Figure 4-9: These controls set the major focusing options.

- ✔ **Autofocus mode:** For still
  photography, this setting
  determines when autofocusing
  begins. For movies, it determines whether the camera locks
  focus or continuously adjusts
  focusing during the recording.

- ✔ **AF-area mode:** With this option,
  you specify what part of the frame the autofocus system should consider when establishing focus.

You can quickly adjust both settings by pressing the AF mode button, labeled
in Figure 4-9, while rotating a command dial. Rotate the Main command dial
to change the Autofocus mode; rotate the Sub-command dial to change the
AF-area mode.

You also control autofocusing during regular photography through the
Autofocus mode and AF-area mode — and you adjust the settings in the same
way, combining the AF mode button with the command dials. But the settings
available for Live View are different from those provided for viewfinder photography. See the next two sections to explore the Live View offerings; visit
Chapter 8 for information about the Autofocus mode and AF-area mode settings available for viewfinder photography.

Choosing an Autofocus mode: AF-S or AF-F?

In Live View mode, you can choose from two Autofocus modes, AF-S or AF-F.
The settings work as follows:

✔ **AF-S (single-servo autofocus):** The camera sets and locks focus when you depress the shutter button halfway. (This autofocus setting is one of the few that works the same during Live View shooting as it does during viewfinder photography.) Generally speaking, AF-S works best for focusing on still subjects. For movie recording, you can lift your finger off the shutter button after focus is locked; the camera continues to use the established focusing distance throughout the entire recording unless you press the shutter button halfway to set and lock focus again.

✔ **AF-F (full-time servo autofocus):** If you choose this setting, autofocusing begins immediately — you don't need to press the shutter button halfway. Focusing is continuously adjusted until you *do* press the shutter button halfway, at which point it is locked as long as you keep your finger on the button.

The main purpose of AF-F is to enable continuous focus adjustment throughout a movie recording. To use this option, keep your finger off the shutter button altogether: Just switch the camera to the AF-F mode, wait for it to find its focus point, and the press the movie-record button to start recording. Focus is adjusted as needed if your subject moves through the frame or you pan the camera. If you decide to lock focus, you can depress the shutter button halfway, as usual. As soon as you release the button, continuous autofocusing begins again.

Unfortunately, there's a downside that makes AF-F less than ideal. If you shoot a movie with sound recording enabled, the camera's internal microphone picks up the sound of the autofocus motor as it adjusts focus. So if pristine audio is your goal, use AF-S mode and lock focus before you begin recording, or abandon autofocus altogether and focus manually. As another option, you can attach an external microphone to the camera and place it far enough away that it doesn't pick up the camera sounds. See the section "Reviewing other movie settings" for more details.

For still photography, focus is locked at the point you press the shutter button halfway, just as with AF-S mode. The only difference between the two modes is that AF-F mode finds a focusing target and keeps adjusting it until you press the shutter button halfway. You might find this option helpful when you're not sure where a moving subject will be at the time you want to snap the picture: As your subject moves or you pan the camera to keep the subject in the frame, autofocus is adjusted so that when the moment comes to take the shot, you just press halfway, pause, and take the picture. (That said, I prefer the continuous autofocusing options available for viewfinder photography for this kind of shot — I find them easier and more reliable than the Live View AF-F option.)

At any rate, to select the Autofocus mode setting, use either of these techniques:

- ⌐ **AF mode button + Main command dial:** Press and hold the button, labeled in Figure 4-9, to highlight the Autofocus mode, as shown in Figure 4-10. (The icon appears in the same spot in the other Live View display styles.) Keep the button pressed as you rotate the Main command dial.

- ⌐ **Live View/Movie AF menu option:** You also can access the setting via this menu option, found on the Autofocus section of the Custom Setting menu, as shown in Figure 4-11.

Autofocus mode

Figure 4-10: To adjust the Autofocus mode, press the AF mode button while rotating the Main command dial.

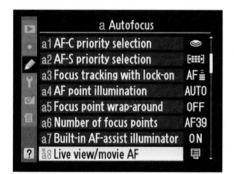
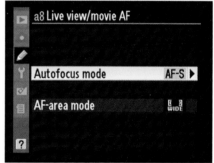

Figure 4-11: You also can access the Autofocus and AF-area mode settings via this Custom Setting menu option.

Selecting an autofocus target (AF-area mode)

Through the AF-area mode, you give the camera's autofocusing system instructions on what part of the frame contains your subject so that it can more easily set the focusing distance correctly.

You can view the current AF-area mode setting at the top of the monitor when you use the Photo Information and Movie Information display styles. Figure 4-12 reminds you where to look for the icon that represents the setting — it's right next to the Autofocus mode icon. In other display modes, press the AF mode button, labeled in Figure 4-9, to temporarily view the icon.

AF-area mode

You use almost the same techniques to change this setting as you do to adjust the Autofocus mode option:

Figure 4-12: Rotate the Sub-command dial while pressing the AF mode button to change the AF-area mode setting.

- ✔ **AF mode button + Sub-command dial:** Press the button while rotating the Sub-command dial to cycle through the available settings. Remember, rotating the Main command dial adjusts the Autofocus mode setting instead.

- ✔ **Live View/Movie AF menu option:** Refer to Figure 4-11 for a look at this option; again, it's found in the Autofocus section of the Custom Setting menu.

As with the Autofocus mode, the Live View AF-area mode options are different than the ones available for viewfinder photography, which I detail in Chapter 8. For Live View photography and movie recording, you can choose from the following settings:

- ✔ **Face Priority:** Designed for portrait shooting, this mode attempts to hunt down and focus on faces. Face Detection typically works only when your subjects are facing the camera, however. If the camera can't detect a face, it focuses on whatever is at the center of the frame.

- ✔ **Wide Area:** In this mode, you use the Multi Selector to move a little rectangular focusing frame around the screen to specify your desired focusing spot. (The red rectangle you see in Figure 4-12 is the Wide Area focusing frame.)

- ✔ **Normal Area:** This mode works the same way as Wide Area autofocusing but uses a smaller focusing frame. The idea is to enable you to base focus on a very specific area. With such a small focusing frame, however, you can easily miss your focus target when handholding the camera. If you move the camera slightly as you're setting focus and the focusing frame shifts off your subject as a result, focus will be incorrect. So for best results, use a tripod in this mode.

✓ **Subject Tracking:** This mode tracks a subject as it moves through the frame and is designed for focusing on a moving subject. But note that Subject Tracking isn't always as successful as you might hope. For a subject that occupies only a small part of the frame — say, a butterfly flitting through a garden — autofocus may lose its way. Ditto for subjects moving at a face pace, subjects getting larger or smaller in the frame (when moving toward you and then away from you, for example), or scenes in which not much contrast exists between the subject and the background. Oh, and scenes in which there's a great deal of contrast can create problems, too. My take on this feature is that when the conditions are right, it works well, but otherwise, the Wide Area setting gives you a better chance of focusing on a moving subject.

Choosing the right focusing pairs

To recap, the way the camera sets focus during Live View and movie shooting depends on the setting of the Focus-mode selector (AF for autofocus or M for manual focus) and, for autofocusing, your Autofocus mode and AF-area mode. If you use the kit lens (or a similar lens), you also need to set the switch on the lens barrel to either A for autofocusing or M for manual focusing.

Until you get fully acquainted with all the various focusing options and can make your own decisions about which pairings you like best, I recommend keeping things simple (okay, sort of simple) by breaking things down like this:

✓ **For moving subjects:** Set the Autofocus mode to AF-F and the AF-area mode to Wide Area. You also can try the Subject Tracking AF-area mode, but see my comments in the preceding section regarding which subjects may not be well suited to that mode. Either way, remember that in AF-F mode, you don't press the shutter button halfway until you're ready to lock focus and take the picture — focusing begins immediately after you switch the Autofocus mode to AF-F and continues *until* you press the shutter button halfway.

For movie recording, keep your finger off the shutter button if you want the camera to continuously adjust focus during the recording. And again, note that if you use the camera's internal microphone, the sound of the autofocus motor may be audible in the movie. (One solution is to use an external microphone placed away from the camera.)

✓ **For stationary subjects:** Set the Autofocus mode to AF-S and the AF-area mode to Wide Area. Or, if you're shooting a portrait, give the Face Priority AF-area option a try. Note that in a group shot, the camera usually locks on the closest face. Press the shutter button halfway to initiate focusing; after the camera finds the focusing point, focus is locked. For movie recording, you can then release the shutter button. For still photography, keep your finger on the button — otherwise, focus will be reset at the time you press the button to take the picture.

✔ **For difficult-to-focus subjects:** If the camera has trouble finding the right focusing point when you use autofocus, don't spend too much time fiddling with the different autofocus settings. Just set the camera to manual focusing and twist the focusing ring to set focus yourself.

Autofocusing in Live View and movie mode

Having laid out all the whys and wherefores of the Live View autofocusing options, I offer the following summary of the steps involved in choosing the autofocus settings and then actually setting focus:

1. **Choose the Autofocus mode (AF-S or AF-F).**

   Dial in the setting quickly by pressing the AF mode button while rotating the Main command dial. (Refer to Figure 4-9 if you need help locating the button.)

   In AF-F mode, the autofocus system perks up and starts hunting for a focus point immediately.

2. **Choose the AF-area mode by pressing the AF mode button while rotating the Sub-command dial.**

   This setting determines what part of the frame the camera considers when establishing focus.

3. **Locate the focus frame in the Live View display.**

   The appearance of the frame depends on the AF area mode, as follows:

   Figure 4-13: The red box represents the focusing frame in Wide Area and Normal Area AF-area mode.

   - *Wide Area and Normal Area:* You see a red rectangular frame, as shown in Figure 4-13. (The figure shows the frame at the size it appears in Wide Area mode; it's smaller in Normal Area mode.)

   - *Face Priority:* If the camera locates faces, you see a yellow focus frame around each one, as shown on the left in Figure 4-14. Note that one of the frames has double yellow lines — in the figure, it's the center frame.

The double yellow line indicates the face that the camera will use to set focusing distance.

If you don't see any yellow boxes but instead see the red frame, the camera can't detect a face and will set focus as it would if you were using Wide Area mode.

- *Subject Tracking:* A white focusing frame like the one shown on the right in Figure 4-14 appears.

Selected face   Subject Tracking focus frame

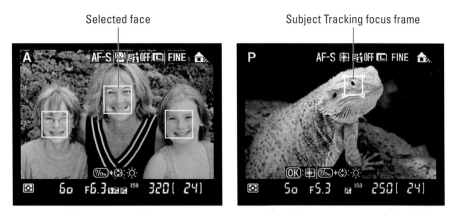

Figure 4-14: The focusing frame appears differently in Face Priority mode (left) and Subject Tracking mode (right).

In AF-F mode, the frame turns green when the object under the frame is in focus.

4. Use the Multi Selector to position the focusing frame over your subject.

For example, I moved the focus frame over the garnish on the soup bowl for my example image, as shown on the left in Figure 4-15.

Figure 4-15: The focus frame turns green if the autofocus system was successful.

In Face Priority mode, you can use the Multi Selector to move the box with the double-yellow border — which indicates the final focusing point — from face to face in a group portrait. In the Wide Area and Normal Area modes, press OK to quickly move the focus point to the center of the frame.

5. **In Subject Tracking AF-area mode, press OK to initiate focus tracking.**

   If your subject moves, the focus frame moves with it. To stop tracking, press OK again. (You may need to take this step if your subject leaves the frame — press OK to stop tracking, reframe, and then press OK to start tracking again.)

6. **In AF-S autofocus mode, press the shutter button halfway down to start autofocusing.**

7. **Wait for the focus frame to turn green, as shown on the right in Figure 4-15.**

   What happens next depends on your Autofocus mode:

   - *AF-S mode:* You also hear a little beep (assuming you didn't disable the beep, which you can do via the Setup menu), and focus is locked.

   - *AF-F mode:* Focus will be adjusted if the subject moves. The focus frame turns back to red (or yellow or white) if focus is lost; green signals that focus has been achieved again. You can lock focus by pressing the shutter button halfway. (In most cases, the camera will reset focus on your subject when you press the button even if the focus frame is already green.)

QUAL

8. **(Optional) Press the Qual button to magnify the display to double-check focus.**

   Each press gives you a closer look at the subject.

   As when you magnify an image when you're viewing photos in playback mode, a small thumbnail in the corner of the monitor appears, with the yellow highlight box indicating the area that's currently being magnified, as shown in Figure 4-16. Press the Multi Selector to scroll the display if needed.

ISO

To zoom out, press the ISO button. If you're not using Subject Tracking mode, you can also press OK to quickly return to normal magnification.

Figure 4-16: Press the Qual button to magnify the display and double-check focus.

Manual focusing in Live View and movie mode

For manual focusing, simply set the Focus-mode selector on the camera to M and, if you're using the kit lens or a similarly featured lens, set its Focus-mode selector to M as well. Then twist the lens focusing ring to bring the scene into focus. But note a few quirks:

- ✔ The focusing frame doesn't turn green when you set focus as it does with autofocusing.

- ✔ Even with manual focusing, you still see the focusing frame; its appearance depends on the current AF-area mode setting. In Face Priority mode, the frame will automatically jump into place over a face, if it detects one. And if you press OK when Subject Tracking mode is enabled, the camera tries to track the subject under the frame until you press OK again. I find these two behaviors irritating, so I always set the AF-area mode to Wide Area or Normal Area for manual focusing.

- ✔ You can press the Qual button to check focus in manual mode just as you can during autofocusing. See Step 8 in the preceding section for details. Press the ISO button to reduce the magnification level.

Shooting Still Pictures in Live View Mode

After sorting out the focusing options, the rest of the steps involved in taking a picture in Live View mode are essentially the same as for viewfinder photography. Here's the drill:

1. **Turn the Mode dial (on top of the camera) to select an exposure mode.**

   Remember, the exposure mode determines what picture settings you can control. Chapter 3 introduces you to the fully automatic modes (Auto, Auto Flash Off, and Scene modes). Chapter 7 provides help with the advanced modes (P, S, A, and M). Chapter 11 explains the two custom user settings, U1 and U2.

2. **Enable Live View by rotating the Live View switch to the right and releasing it.**

3. **Review and adjust picture settings.**

   In Live View mode, the Information screen, which normally displays the critical picture settings, isn't available. But you can view most of the same settings on the Live View display, as shown in Figure 4-17. This display mode is the default; to view other displays, press the Info button. Note that some settings, such as Exposure Compensation and Flash Compensation, appear only when those features are enabled. If you enable automatic bracketing, you also see a BKT symbol near the f-stop setting. (See Chapter 7 for information about these options.)

Note that Exposure Compensation adjustments aren't always reflected by the monitor brightness. When you increase or decrease exposure using this feature, available only in the P, S, A, and M modes, the image on the monitor becomes brighter or darker only up to shifts of EV +/–3.0, even though you can select values as high as +5.0 and as low as –5.0. See Chapter 7 to get a primer on Exposure Compensation.

4. **If focusing manually, twist the focusing ring to set focus.**

5. **If using autofocusing, position the focus frame over the subject.**

   And if you're using Subject Tracking autofocus, press OK to initiate tracking. See the preceding section for details.

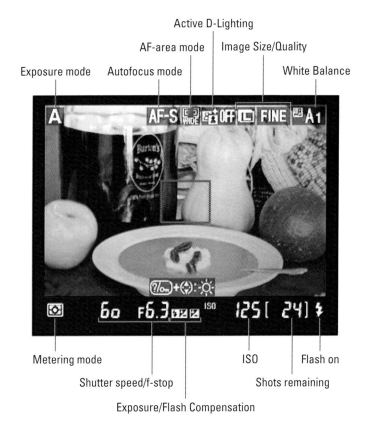

Figure 4-17: You can view these picture settings in the default Live View display mode.

6. **Press the shutter button halfway.**

   If you're autofocusing, focus is locked when the focus frame turns green.

   Regardless of the Autofocus mode, exposure metering begins when you adjust the shutter button halfway and is adjusted up to the time you take the picture.

7. **Press the shutter button the rest of the way to take the picture.**

Shooting Digital Movies

Your D7000 offers the capability to record digital movies — it can even create high-def movies that look stunning on a large TV screen. Although recording live action with a dSLR involves a few limitations and difficulties that you don't experience with a real video camera, it's a fun option to have onboard nonetheless. The next two sections explain how to choose recording options, such as resolution; following that, you can find step-by-step instructions for recording, playing, and editing a movie.

Choosing the video type and quality

The first two recording options to consider are the Video Mode and Movie Quality settings.

Video Mode, found on the Setup menu and shown in Figure 4-18, tells the camera whether you want your movies to adhere to the NTSC or PAL video standard. *NTSC* is used in North America; *PAL* is used in Europe and certain other countries. Your camera should already be set to match the country in which it was purchased, but it never hurts to check. (Don't worry about what NTSC and PAL mean — they're just anagrams for the technical names of the standards.)

Figure 4-18: The Video Mode determines what Movie Quality settings are available.

Okay, that one's straightforward enough. Now onto the really complex technical soup: Open the Shooting menu and choose Movie Settings, as shown on the left in Figure 4-19. Press OK to access the generically named Movie Quality option, as shown on the right in the figure. This setting determines the resolution (frame size), aspect ratio, and frame rate of the movie, as well as the level of file compression — which all affect the final quality of the movie.

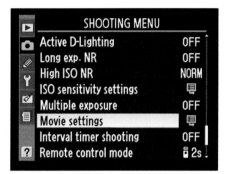

Figure 4-19: Set the Movie Quality option and enable audio recording via the Shooting menu.

To start looking at your options, select Movie Quality and press OK. You also can bring up the Information display, activate the control strip, and choose the option shown in Figure 4-20. Either way, if NTSC is selected as your Video Mode setting, you see the screen shown in Figure 4-21. (More about how it varies when PAL is selected in a moment.)

The first thing to note is that you can choose from various combinations of resolution, or frame size, and frames per second, as follows:

Figure 4-20: You also can access the setting via the Information screen control strip.

  ✔ **Resolution:** You can choose from three resolution settings, or frame sizes, measured in pixels: 1920 x 1080, which produces a so-called Full HD (High Definition) movie that has a 16:9 aspect ratio; 1280 x 720, for Standard HD, also 16:9; and 640 x 424, a much smaller frame size with an aspect ratio of 3:2, the same as still images captured by the D7000. (This smaller resolution can be useful for online videos.)

🖛 **Frame rate (fps):** The *frame rate,* measured in *frames per second (fps),* determines the smoothness of the playback. If NTSC is selected as the Video Mode, frame rate options include 24 fps, which is the same frame rate as film motion pictures, or 30 fps, the NTSC standard for television-quality video. (Well, technically, the NTSC frame rate is 29.97 fps.) If the Video Mode setting is PAL, you can choose from 24 fps and the PAL video standard, 25 fps.

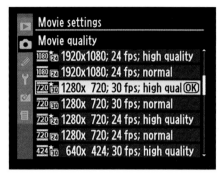

Figure 4-21: The Movie Quality setting determines resolution, aspect ratio, frames per second, and file compression amount.

Again, assuming NTSC as the video standard, you can choose from 24 or 30 fps when the resolution is 1280 x 720. For the 1920 x 1080 frame size, you're limited to 24 fps; this setting is the default. When you select 640 x 424 as the resolution, the only available frame rate is 30 fps.

For each combination, you also can choose a High or Normal setting. Your choice determines how much compression is applied to the video file, which in turn affects the bit rate, or how much data is used to represent one second of video. The High setting results in a higher bit rate, which means better quality and larger files. Choose Normal for a lower bit rate and smaller files.

In addition to the High and Normal settings, the resolution and frame rate also affect file size. Table 4-1 shows you the file size of a 20-minute video — the maximum movie length on the D7000 — at each of the eight Movie Quality settings. (Again, the table assumes NTSC as the Video Mode.)

Table 4-1	Twenty-Minute Movie File Sizes*		
Frame Size	*FPS*	*Quality*	*File Size*
1920 x 1080	24	High	2.9GB
		Normal	1.7GB
1280 x 720	30	High	1.7GB
		Normal	1.1GB
	24	High	1.4GB
		Normal	1.0GB
640 x 424	30	High	0.8GB
		Normal	0.5GB

*Settings available when NTSC is selected as the Video Mode setting.

Reviewing other movie settings

Compared to the mind-numbing intricacies of the video specifications outlined in the preceding section, the rest of the movie settings you can adjust are fairly straightforward. Here's a look at your options:

✔ **Sound recording:** You can record sound using the camera's built-in microphone, labeled in Figure 4-22, or attach an external microphone to the jack labeled on the right. Either way, to enable sound recording and adjust the microphone sensitivity, select the Movie Settings option on the Shooting menu and then select Microphone, as shown on the left in Figure 4-23. Press OK to display the settings shown on the right in the figure.

If you enable sound and choose the Auto Sensitivity option, the camera automatically adjusts the volume according to the level of the ambient noise. Or you can choose one of the other settings to control the microphone sensitivity yourself. Choose Microphone Off to record a silent movie.

When using the built-in microphone, make sure that you don't inadvertently cover it up with your finger. And keep in mind that anything *you* say will be picked up by the mike along with any other audio present in the scene. When an external microphone is attached, the internal microphone goes to sleep.

Internal microphone   External microphone jack

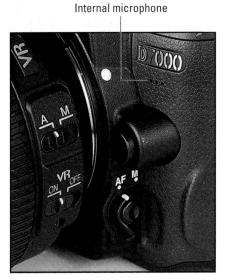 

Figure 4-22: You can capture audio using the internal microphone (left) or attach an external microphone into the microphone jack (right).

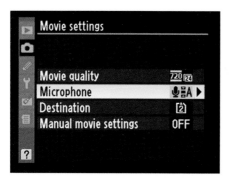 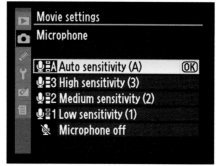

Figure 4-23: Disable audio recording or set the microphone sensitivity level through this menu option.

✔ **Destination:** By default, movie files are always recorded to the memory card in the top card slot (Slot 1). If you have two cards installed, choose the Destination option on the Movie Settings menu, as shown on the left in Figure 4-24, to select Slot 2 as the storage location. The screen tells you the length of the movie that will fit on each card at your current Movie Quality settings.

✔ **Manual Movie Settings:** The final option on the Movie Settings menu (refer to the left screen in Figure 4-24) determines whether you can adjust ISO and shutter speed manually during recording. You also must set the exposure mode to M (on the Mode dial) to take this level of control. Unless you're really an expert in these two options, leave the Manual Movie Settings option set to Off. The camera then automatically controls shutter speed and ISO for you.

Figure 4-24: To change the movie storage location, choose the Destination option.

If you do enable the setting, you can choose shutter speeds from 1/30 second to 1/8000 second and ISO values from ISO 100 to Hi 2. The Auto ISO Sensitivity option doesn't work in this case. Chapter 7 explains shutter speed and ISO. (Shutter speed issues for video are different than they are for still photography, however; again, this level of control is for videophiles only.) And one more caveat: You must select the f-stop setting before switching to Live View; after Live View is enabled, you no longer can adjust that setting.

✔ **Exposure:** Normally, the camera automatically sets exposure for you, assuming that you don't enable the Manual Movie Settings option. But you still have a couple ways to affect exposure:

- *Select an aperture:* If you set the exposure mode to M or A, you can select an f-stop and thereby control depth of field for the movie. Chapter 7 explains f-stops. Be careful, though — at some apertures, the camera may not be able to expose the movie properly. To adjust the aperture, rotate the Sub-command dial. And remember that when the Manual Movie Settings option is set to On, you can adjust f-stop only before switching to Live View mode.

- *Exposure Compensation:* When the Mode dial is set to P, S, or A, you can apply Exposure Compensation, which tells the camera that you prefer a brighter or darker exposure. You can also use Exposure Compensation when the Mode dial is set to M, but only if you turn off the Manual Movie Settings option.

  Either way, you're limited to an adjustment range of EV +3.0 or –3.0 rather than the usual five steps that are possible during normal photography. See Chapter 7 to find out more about this feature. To adjust the setting, press and hold the Exposure Compensation button while rotating the Main command dial.

- *Autoexposure lock:* You can lock exposure at the current settings by pressing and holding the AE-L/AF-L button. Chapter 7 also tells you more about autoexposure lock.

You can adjust these settings during recording if needed.

✔ **Focusing:** You can choose auto or manual focusing and control autofocusing behavior via the Autofocus mode and AF-area mode settings. Earlier parts of this chapter provide a primer in focusing.

✔ **White Balance and Picture Control:** The colors in your movie are rendered according to the current White Balance and Picture Control settings. Chapter 8 explains how to adjust these settings, but you have control over the options only when the Mode dial is set to P, S, A, or M.

Want to record a black-and-white movie? Open the Shooting menu, choose Set Picture Control, and select Monochrome. Instant *film noir*.

One more technical point: Movies are created in the MOV format, which means you can play them on your computer using most movie-playback programs. If you want to view your movies on a TV, you can connect the camera to the TV, as explained in Chapter 5. Or if you have the necessary computer software, you can convert the MOV file to a format that a standard DVD player can recognize and then burn the converted file to a DVD disk. You also can edit your movie in a program that can work with MOV files.

Starting and stopping recording

After you establish all the options explained in the preceding section, there's not much left to do to shoot a movie:

1. **Rotate the Live View switch to the right and release it to switch to Live View mode.**

   Press Info to change the Show Movie Indicators display mode, which displays the data shown in Figure 4-25. You can view the Movie Quality setting, whether sound is enabled, and the length of the movie that will fit in the remaining space on your memory card. You also see the current autofocus settings, the White Balance settings and, at the bottom of the screen, the standard exposure settings (shutter speed, f-stop, and so on).

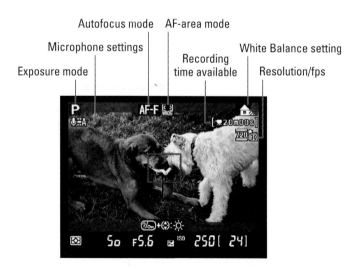

Figure 4-25: These settings are specifically related to movie recording.

2. **Set focus as outlined earlier in this chapter.**

To take advantage of continuous autofocusing, set the Autofocus mode to AF-F. The camera starts focusing on the object under the focus frame automatically and adjusts focus as necessary throughout the recording. You can lock focus at a specific distance by pressing the shutter button halfway.

If the Autofocus mode is set to AF-S, press the shutter button halfway to set and lock focus. You then can lift your finger off the shutter button; focus remains set at the established distance unless you press the button halfway again to reset focus.

3. **To begin recording, press the red movie-record button in the center of the Live View switch.**

Some of the shooting data disappears from the screen, and a red Rec symbol flashes in the top-left corner, as shown in Figure 4-26. As recording progresses, the area labeled time remaining in the figure shows you how many more seconds of video you can record. (The length is dependent on the Movie Quality settings you choose and the amount of space on your memory card.) Also note the number found within the brackets in the lower-right corner of the screen — 24, in Figure 4-26. If you're putting the movie file on the memory card currently being used for still photo storage, the number indicates how many still photos you can fit in the empty card space if you stop recording. As each second of recording ticks by and card space is depleted, the number of still shots remaining drops.

Recording symbol   Time remaining

Figure 4-26: The red Rec symbol flashes while recording is in progress.

4. **To stop recording, press the movie-record button again.**

You can stop your recording and capture a still image in one fell swoop: Just press and hold the shutter button down until you hear the shutter release.

Screening Your Movies

To play your movie, press the Playback button. In single-image playback mode, you can spot a movie file by looking for the little movie-camera icon in the top-left corner of the screen, as shown on the left in Figure 4-27. Press OK to start playback.

In the thumbnail and Calendar playback modes, you see little filmstrip dots along the edges of movie files. This time, press OK twice: once to shift to single-image view and again to start movie playback.

After playback begins, a little playback control icon appears in the lower-right corner of the screen, as shown in Figure 4-28. It represents the Multi Selector and reminds you that you can use these techniques to control the playback:

✔ **Stop playback:** Press the Multi Selector up.

✔ **Pause/resume playback:** Press down to pause playback; press OK to resume playback.

✔ **Fast-forward/rewind:** Press the Multi Selector right or left to fast-forward or rewind the movie. Press again to double the fast-forward or rewind speed; keep pressing to increase the speed to 8 times or 16 times normal. Hold the button down to fast-forward or rewind all the way to the end or beginning of the movie.

✔ **Advance frame by frame:** First, press the Multi Selector down to pause playback. Then press the Multi Selector right to advance one frame; press left to go back one frame.

✔ **Adjust playback volume:** See the little markings labeled volume control symbols in Figure 4-28? They remind you that you can press the Qual button to increase playback volume. For a quieter playback, press the ISO button.

Movie icon   Length of movie

Resolution

Frames per second

Figure 4-27: The little movie-camera symbol tells you you're looking at a movie file.

Volume control symbols

Playback control symbols

Figure 4-28: The icons at the bottom of the screen remind you which buttons to use to control playback.

Chapter 5 explains how to connect your camera to a television so you can play your movies "on the big screen."

Trimming movies

You can do some limited movie editing in camera. I emphasize: *limited* editing. You can trim frames from the start of a movie and clip off frames from the end, and that's it.

To eliminate frames from the beginning of the movie, take these steps:

1. **Display your movie in full-frame view.**

2. **Press OK to begin playback.**

3. **When you reach the first frame you want to keep, press the Multi Selector down to pause the movie.**

   The playback screen looks similar to the one on the left in Figure 4-29.

WB

4. **Press the WB button.**

   Note the symbols centered under the picture frame in the left image in Figure 4-29: They're the same ones on the face of the WB button, cluing you into the fact that you use the button to access the trimming feature. After you press the button, you see the Edit Movie screen, as shown on the right in Figure 4-29.

5. **Highlight Choose Start Point and press OK.**

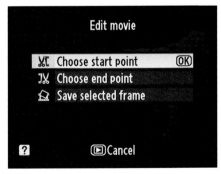

Figure 4-29: After pausing playback, press the WB button to access the movie-editing tools.

The screen appears similar to the one in Figure 4-30. Notice that in the Multi Selector icon, the up arrow now sports a little scissors icon. That's your cue about how to take the next step . . .

6. **Press the Multi Selector up to lop off all frames that came before the current frame.**

   Don't worry that you'll lose your original movie — the trimmed version is saved as a separate file.

   After you press the Multi Selector up, you see a confirmation screen asking for permission to proceed.

7. **Highlight Yes and press OK.**

   A message appears telling you that the trimmed movie is being saved. During playback, edited files are indicated by a little scissors icon that appears in the area noted in Figure 4-31.

To instead trim footage from the end of a film, take the same steps, but this time pause playback on the last frame you want to keep in Step 3. Then, in Step 5, select Choose End Point instead of Choose Start Point.

Figure 4-30: Press the Multi Selector up to proceed with the edit.

Trimmed movie icon

Figure 4-31: The scissors tell you that you're looking at an edited movie file.

Saving a movie frame as a still image

In addition to trimming frames from the beginning and end of a movie, you can do a *screen grab* — that is, save a single frame of the movie as a regular image file. Here's how:

1. **Begin playing your movie.**

2. **When you reach the frame you want to capture, press the Multi Selector down to pause playback.**

WB

3. **Press the WB button to bring up the Edit Movie screen.**

4. **Choose Save Selected Frame, as shown in Figure 4-32, and press OK.**

5. **Press the Multi Selector up to initiate the screen grab.**

6. **On the confirmation screen that appears, select Yes and press OK.**

   Your frame is saved as a JPEG photo.

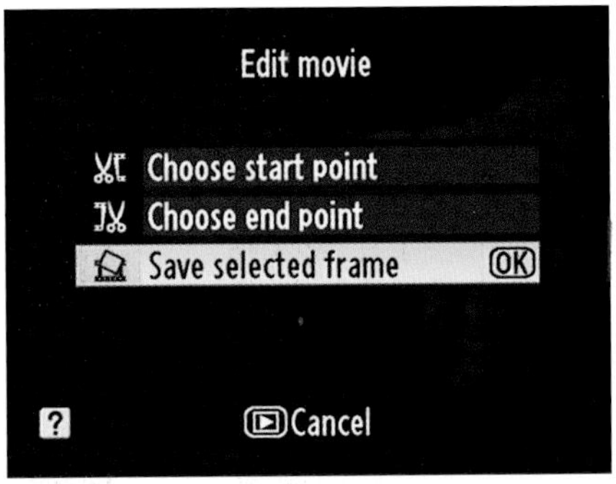

Figure 4-32: Through this option, you can save a single movie frame as a still photo.

Remember a few things about pictures you create this way:

Movie-frame icon

- ✔ When you view the image, it's marked with a little movie-frame icon in the upper-left corner, as shown in Figure 4-33.

- ✔ The resolution of the picture depends on the resolution of the movie. For example, if the movie resolution is 1280 x 720, the picture has that same number of pixels. The resolution appears in blue, in the lower-right corner of the playback screen, as shown in Figure 4-33.

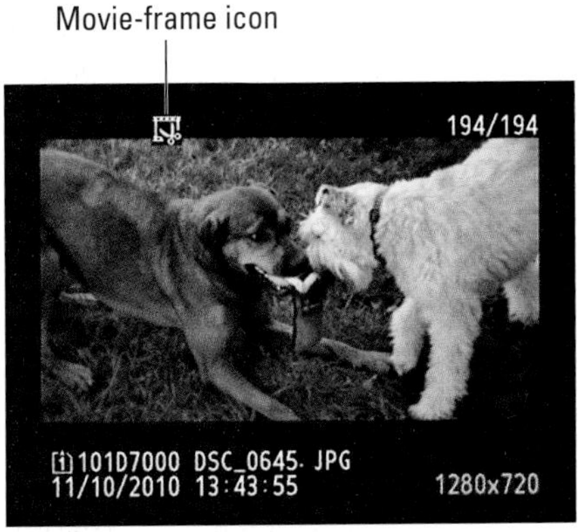

Figure 4-33: This icon marks pictures snipped from a movie.

- ✔ You can't apply editing features from the Retouch menu to the file, and you also can't view all the shooting data that's normally associated with a JPEG picture.

For more about JPEG and picture resolution, visit Chapter 2.

Part II
Working with Picture Files

The 5th Wave — By Rich Tennant

"Remember, when the subject comes into focus, the camera makes a beep. But that's annoying, so I set it on vibrate."

In this part . . .

You have a memory card full of pictures. Now what? Now you turn to the first chapter in this part, Chapter 5, which explains all your camera's picture-playback features, including options that help you evaluate exposure and zoom the display so that you can check small details. The same chapter shows you how to delete lousy pictures and protect great ones from accidental erasure.

When you're ready to move pictures from the camera to your computer, Chapter 6 shows you the best ways to get the job done. In addition, Chapter 6 offers step-by-step guidance on printing your pictures and preparing them for online sharing.

5

Playback Mode: Viewing, Erasing, and Protecting Photos

*W*ithout question, my favorite thing about digital photography is being able to view my pictures on the camera monitor the instant after I shoot them. No more guessing whether I captured the image I wanted or I need to try again; no more wasting money on developing and printing pictures that stink. In fact, this feature alone was reason enough for me to turn my back forever on my closetful of film photography hardware and all the unexposed film remaining from my predigital days.

But seeing your pictures is just the start of the things you can do when you switch your D7000 to playback mode. You also can review all the camera settings you used to take the picture, display graphics that alert you to serious exposure problems, and add file markers that protect the picture from accidental erasure.

This chapter tells you how to use all these playback features and also explains how to connect your camera to a television so that you can view your photos and movies on a bigger screen. (Note that the on-camera playback information in this chapter deals with still pictures, however; see Chapter 4 for help with movie playback.)

Customizing Basic Playback Options

You can control many aspects of picture playback on the D7000. Later sections show you how to choose what type of data appears with your pictures, how to display multiple images at a time, and how to magnify an image for a close-up look. But first, the next few sections explain options that affect overall playback performance, including how long your pictures appear onscreen and how they're oriented on the monitor.

Adjusting playback timing

You can adjust the length of time the camera displays your images on the monitor as follows:

✏ **Adjust the timing of automatic playback shutoff.** After you press the Playback button to begin reviewing your pictures, the monitor turns off automatically if ten seconds go by without any further button presses. I find that playback time maddeningly brief when I'm trying to study a picture. Fortunately, you can adjust the shutoff timing through the Monitor Off Delay option, found in the Timers/AE Lock section of the Custom Setting menu and shown on the left in Figure 5-1. Choose Playback, as shown on the right, to access the timing options, which range from four seconds to ten minutes.

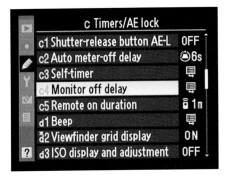
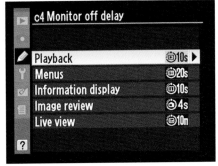

Figure 5-1: You can control how long pictures are displayed before automatic monitor shutdown occurs.

✔ **Enable instant review.** You can tell the camera to display each image for a quick review immediately after you shoot it. Because any monitor use is a strain on battery power, this feature is disabled by default; enable it through the Image Review option on the Playback menu, shown in Figure 5-2.

✔ **Adjust the length of the instant-review period.** By default, the instant-review period lasts four seconds, but you can adjust this

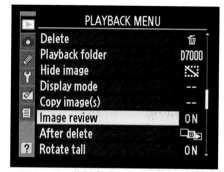

Figure 5-2: Head for the Playback menu to enable instant review.

timing through the Monitor Off Delay option shown in Figure 5-1 as well. Just choose Image Review instead of Playback when you get to the right screen in the figure. Again, settings range from four seconds to ten minutes.

Enabling automatic picture rotation

When you take a picture, the camera can record the image *orientation* — whether you held the camera normally, creating a horizontally oriented image, or turned the camera on its side to shoot a vertically oriented photo. This bit of data is simply added into the picture file.

During playback, the camera can then read the data and automatically rotate the image so that it appears in the upright position, as shown on the left in Figure 5-3. The image is also automatically rotated when you view it in Nikon ViewNX 2, Capture NX 2, and some other photo programs that can interpret the data. Or you can disable rotation, in which case vertically oriented pictures appear sideways, as shown on the right in Figure 5-3.

Official photo lingo uses the term *portrait orientation* to refer to vertically oriented pictures and *landscape orientation* to refer to horizontally oriented pictures. The terms stem from the traditional way that people and places are captured in paintings and photographs — portraits, vertically; landscapes, horizontally.

On the D7000, set up your rotation wishes through the following two menu options, both shown in Figure 5-4:

✔ **Auto Image Rotation:** This option, on the Setup menu, determines whether the orientation data is included in the picture file. The default setting is On; select Off to leave out the data.

✔ **Rotate Tall:** Found on the Playback menu, this option controls whether the camera pays attention to the orientation data. The default setting is Off. Select On, as shown in the figure, if you want the camera to rotate the image during playback.

Figure 5-3: You can display vertically oriented pictures in their upright position (left) or sideways (right).

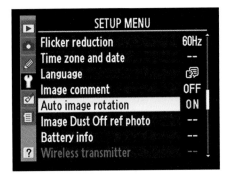 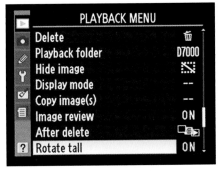

Figure 5-4: Visit the Setup and Playback menus to enable or disable image rotation.

Regardless of these settings, your pictures aren't rotated during the instant-review period. Also, be aware that shooting with the lens pointing directly up or down sometimes confuses the camera, causing it to record the wrong data in the file. Rotating the camera while shooting a burst of images in one of the Continuous Release modes also causes a playback glitch: The camera tags all files with the orientation of the first image, so some may not be rotated properly during playback. Chapter 2 explains the Release mode setting.

Viewing Images in Playback Mode

To review your photos, take these steps:

1. **Press the Playback button.**

   The monitor displays the last picture you took, along with some picture data, such as the frame number of the photo and the memory card that holds the photo, as shown in Figure 5-5. To find out how to interpret the picture information and specify what data you want to see, see the upcoming section "Viewing Picture Data."

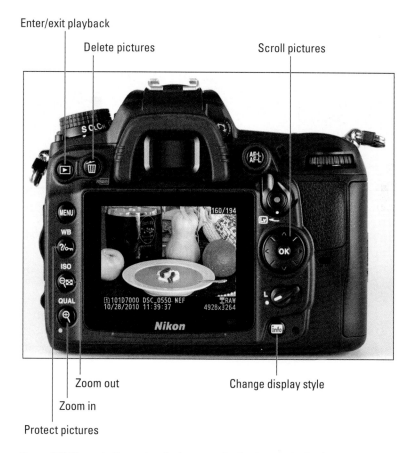

Figure 5-5: These buttons play the largest roles in picture playback.

For details on how to specify which memory card or image storage folder you want to view, skip ahead to the section "Choosing which images to view," in this chapter.

2. **To scroll through your pictures, press the Multi Selector right or left.**

Through the Customize Command Dials option on the Custom Setting menu, you can set the Main command dial to perform this function as well as some other playback operations. You can set the Sub-command dial to serve some playback duties, too. Information in this chapter assumes that you haven't taken that step, but see Chapter 11 if you're interested.

3. **To return to picture-taking mode, press the Playback button again or press the shutter button halfway and then release it.**

These steps assume that the camera is currently set to display a single photo at a time, as shown in Figure 5-5. You can also display multiple images at a time, as explained next.

Viewing multiple images at a time

Along with viewing images one at a time, you can choose to display 4 or 9 thumbnails, as shown in Figure 5-6, or even a whopping 72 thumbnails. Use these techniques to change to thumbnails view and navigate your photos:

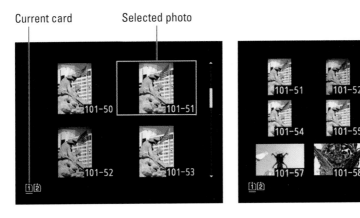

Figure 5-6: You can view multiple image thumbnails at a time.

✔ **Display thumbnails.** Press the ISO button, labeled Zoom out in Figure 5-5, to cycle from single-picture view to 4-thumbnail view, press again to shift to 9-picture view, and press once more to bring up those itty-bitty thumbnails featured in 72-image view. One more press takes you to Calendar view, a nifty feature explained in the next section.

✔ **Display fewer thumbnails.** Pressing the Qual button takes you from Calendar view back to the standard thumbnails display or, if you're already in that display, reduces the number of thumbnails so you can see each one at a larger size — hence the Zoom in label slapped on the button in Figure 5-5. Again, your first press takes you from 72 thumbnails to 9, your second press to 4 thumbnails, and your third press returns you to single-image view.

Notice the icons on these two buttons: The ISO button sports a magnifying glass with a minus sign, the universal symbol for zoom out. And the Qual button's magnifying glass has a plus sign, reminding you that you use this button to zoom in.

✔ **Jump from any thumbnail display to full-frame view.** Press OK. After you return to full-frame view, pressing OK again displays the Retouch menu. Now you can select a retouch option and apply it to the image. See Chapter 10 for a look at the tools found on the Retouch menu.

✔ **Scroll the display.** Press the Multi Selector up and down to scroll to the next or previous screen of thumbnails.

✔ **Select an image.** To perform certain playback functions, such as deleting a photo or protecting it, you first need to select an image. A yellow box surrounds the currently selected image, as shown in Figure 5-6. To select a different image, use the Multi Selector to move the highlight box over the image.

If you're using dual memory cards, you can tell which card contains the selected photo by looking at the card icons, labeled in Figure 5-6. The icon for the current card is yellow. See the upcoming section "Choosing which images to view" for a trick you can use to jump to a specific memory card or folder.

Displaying photos in Calendar view

In Calendar display mode, you see a little calendar on the monitor, as shown in Figure 5-7. By selecting a date on the calendar, you can quickly navigate to all pictures you shot on that day. A thumbnail-free date indicates that neither installed memory card contains any photos from that day.

The key to navigating Calendar view is the ISO button:

1. **Press the ISO button as needed to cycle through the thumbnail display modes until you reach Calendar view.**

   If you're currently viewing images in full-frame view, for example, you need to press the button four times to get to Calendar view.

2. **Using the Multi Selector, move the yellow highlight box over a date that contains an image.**

Figure 5-7: Calendar view makes it easy to view all photos shot on a particular day.

In the left example in Figure 5-7, the 2nd day of October is selected. (The number of the month appears in the top-left corner of the screen.) After you select a date, the right side of the monitor displays a vertical strip of thumbnails of pictures taken on that date.

3. **To view all thumbnails from the selected date, press the ISO button again.**

As a reminder of what button to press, the little icon underneath the calendar displays the symbols that appear on the ISO button.

After you press the button, the vertical thumbnail strip becomes active, as shown on the right in Figure 5-7, and you can scroll through the thumbnails by pressing the Multi Selector up and down. A second highlight box appears in the thumbnail strip to indicate the currently selected image.

QUAL

4. **To temporarily display a larger view of the selected thumbnail, hold down the Qual button.**

Again, note the reminder icon in the bottom-right corner of the screen; it shows the plus-sign magnifying glass that appears on the face of the Qual button.

In the zoomed view, the image filename appears under the larger preview, as shown in Figure 5-8. When you release the Qual button, the large preview disappears, and the calendar comes back into view.

Figure 5-8: Highlight a photo in the thumbnail strip and press the Qual button to temporarily display it at a larger size.

5. **To jump back to the calendar and select a different date, press the ISO button again.**

   You can just keep pressing the button to jump between the calendar and the thumbnail strip as much as you want.

6. **To exit Calendar view and return to single-image view, press OK.**

   If you want to return to Calendar view, press the ISO button four times to cycle from full-frame view through the different thumbnail modes.

Choosing which images to view

Your D7000 organizes pictures automatically into folders that are assigned generic names: 100D7000, 101D7000, and so on. You can see the name of the current folder by looking at the Storage Folder option on the Shooting menu. (The default folder name appears as just 100 on the menu.) You also can create custom-numbered folders through a process outlined in Chapter 11.

During playback, which folder's photos appear depend on the Playback Folder option on the Playback menu, shown in Figure 5-9.

 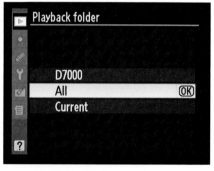

Figure 5-9: Specify which folder you want to view through this option.

You can choose one of three options:

- ✔ **D7000 (default setting):** Displays all pictures shot with your camera, regardless of their folder location. If you're using two memory cards, pictures on both cards are displayed.

- ✔ **All:** Displays all pictures in all folders, even those taken with other cameras (as long as they're in a format the camera can display —

JPEG or NEF). Again, pictures from both memory cards are displayed.

↳ **Current:** Displays images contained in the folder selected as the Storage Folder option on the Shooting menu.

When you're viewing photos in single-image or thumbnails view (but not Calendar view), you can quickly jump from one memory card or folder to another by using this trick:

1. **Press and hold the BKT button (on the left side of the camera, just beneath the Flash button).**

2. **Press the Multi Selector up.**

   You see the screen shown on the left in Figure 5-10.

3. **Highlight a card slot and press right to display a list of folders on that card.**

   The setting of the Playback Folder option on the Playback menu determines which folders appear on the list.

4. **Highlight a folder and press OK.**

   The menu screen disappears, and the first image in your selected folder appears.

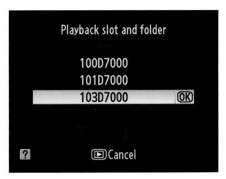

Figure 5-10: During playback, press the BKT button and press the Multi Selector up to display this screen and jump to a specific folder.

Zooming in for a closer view

After displaying a photo in single-frame view, you can magnify it to get a close-up look at important details, such as whether someone's eyes are closed in a portrait. Here's the scoop:

QUAL

✔ **Zoom in.** Press the Qual button. You can magnify the image to a maximum of 15 to 31 times its original display size, depending on the *resolution* (pixel count) of the photo. Just keep pressing the button until you reach the magnification you want. Again: Notice the plus-sign magnifying glass symbol on the button, indicating zoom in.

ISO

✔ **Zoom out.** To zoom out to a reduced magnification, press the ISO button — the one that sports the minus-sign magnifying glass. (That little gridlike thingy next to the magnifying glass reminds you that the button also comes into play when you want to go from full-frame view to one of the thumbnail views.)

✔ **View another part of the magnified picture.** When an image is magnified, a little navigation thumbnail showing the entire image appears briefly in the lower-right corner of the monitor. For example, Figure 5-11 shows a zoomed view of the candle image shown earlier, in Figure 5-8. The yellow outline in this picture-in-picture image indicates the area that's currently consuming the rest of the monitor space. Use the Multi Selector to scroll the yellow box and display a different portion of the image. After a few seconds, the navigation thumbnail disappears; just press the Multi Selector in any direction to redisplay it.

Magnified area

Figure 5-11: Use the Multi Selector to move the yellow outline over the area you want to inspect.

✔ **Inspect faces.** When you magnify portraits, the picture-in-picture thumbnail displays a white border around each face, as shown in Figure 5-12. Rotate the Sub-command dial to examine each face at the magnified view. Unfortunately, the camera sometimes fails to detect faces, especially if the subject isn't looking directly at the camera. But when

Face Detection box

Figure 5-12: Rotate the Sub-command dial to jump between faces in a portrait.

it works correctly, this is a pretty great tool for checking for closed eyes, red-eye, and, of course, spinach in the teeth.

✏ **View more images at the same magnification.** Here's another neat trick: While the display is zoomed, you can rotate the Main command dial to display the same area of the next photo at the same magnification. So if you shot the same subject several times, you can easily check how the same details appear in each one.

✏ **Return to full-frame view.** When you're ready to return to the normal magnification level, you don't need to keep pressing the ISO button until you're all the way zoomed out. Instead, just press OK.

Viewing Picture Data

In single-image picture view, you can choose from several photo information modes, each of which presents different shooting data along with the image.

Upcoming sections provide you with a decoder ring to the details you see in each display mode. First, though, a little setup work is in order, as detailed next.

Enabling hidden data-display options

By default, three of the five display modes are disabled, as is an option that enables you to view the focus point you used when taking the picture. Access these hidden display modes by choosing the Display Mode option on the Playback menu, as shown in Figure 5-13.

Figure 5-13: These display options are disabled by default.

The options work as follows:

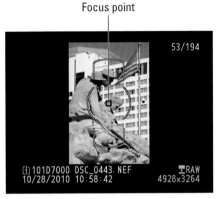

Focus point

Figure 5-14: You can view the focus point you used when taking the photo.

- ✔ **Focus Point:** When this option is turned on, a little red rectangle appears to mark the focus point, as shown in Figure 5-14. You also see the same brackets that represent the autofocus area in the viewfinder. These focus indicators appear only when you use the display mode shown in the figure — File Information mode, covered in the next section. They aren't displayed if you focused manually or used the AF-C AF-area mode setting (or the camera chose that setting for you in AF-A mode). I find the focus marks distracting, but make your own call. Chapter 8 explains the AF-area mode options.

- ✔ **Highlights/RGB Histogram/Data:** These options control the three display modes that are hidden by default, all covered later in this chapter.

A check mark in the box next to the option means that the feature is turned on. In Figure 5-13, for example, all four options are enabled. To toggle the check mark on and off, highlight the option and then press the Multi Selector right.

After turning on the options you want to use, be sure to highlight Done (at the top of the screen) and press OK again. Otherwise, the settings you selected don't stick.

The next sections explain exactly what details you can glean from each display mode. I present them here in the order they appear if you cycle through the modes by pressing the Multi Selector down. You can spin through the modes in the other direction by pressing the Multi Selector up.

File Information mode

In the File Information display mode, the monitor displays the data shown in Figure 5-15. Here's the key to what information appears, starting at the top of the screen and working down:

✔ **Frame Number/Total Pictures:** The first value here indicates the frame number of the currently displayed photo; the second tells you the total number of pictures on the memory card. In Figure 5-15, for example, the image is number 53 out of 194.

✔ **Focus point:** If you enable the Focus Point feature, as outlined in the preceding section, you may see the red focus-point indicator and the autofocus area brackets, as shown in Figure 5-14, depending on the focus settings you used when shooting the picture.

✔ **Card number:** This value tells you which memory-card slot holds the card containing the picture.

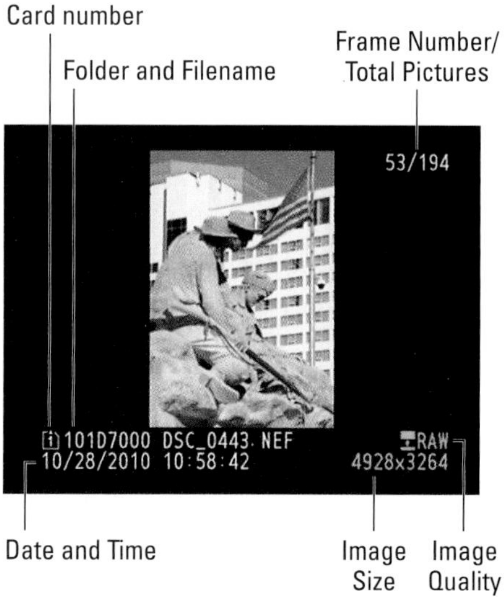

Card number

Folder and Filename

Frame Number/ Total Pictures

53/194

ⓘ 101D7000 DSC_0443. NEF   ☰RAW
10/28/2010 10:58:42   4928x3264

Date and Time

Image Size   Image Quality

Figure 5-15: In File Information mode, you can view these bits of data.

✔ **Folder Name:** Folders are named automatically by the camera unless you create custom folders, an advanced trick you can explore in Chapter 11. The first camera-created folder is named 100D7000. Each folder can contain up to 9999 images; when you exceed that limit, the camera creates a new folder and assigns the next folder number: 101D7000, 102D7000, and so on.

✔ **Filename:** The camera also automatically names your files. Filenames end with a three-letter code that represents the file format, which is either JPG (for JPEG) or NEF (for Camera Raw) for still photos. Chapter 2 discusses these formats. If you record a movie (a project you can explore near the end of this chapter), the file extension is MOV, which represents a digital-movie file format. If you create a dust-off reference image file, an advanced feature designed for use with Nikon Capture NX 2, the camera instead uses the extension NDF. (Because this software must be purchased separately, I don't cover it or the dust-off function in this book.)

The first four characters of filenames also vary. Here's what the two possible codes indicate:

• *DSC_:* This code means you captured the photo at the default Color Space setting, sRGB. You can investigate this option in Chapter 8.

• *_DSC:* If you change the Color Space setting to Adobe RGB, the underscore character comes first.

Each image is also assigned a four-digit file number, starting with 0001. When you reach image 9999, the file numbering restarts at 0001, and the new images go into a new folder to prevent any possibility of overwriting the existing image files. For more information about file numbering, see the Chapter 1 section that discusses the File Number Sequence option, found on the Custom Setting menu.

✔ **Date and Time:** Just below the folder and filename info, you see the date and time that you took the picture. Of course, the accuracy of this data depends on whether you set the camera's date and time values correctly, which you do via the Setup menu. Chapter 1 has details.

✔ **Image Quality:** Here you can see which Image Quality setting you used when taking the picture. Again, Chapter 2 has details, but the short story is this: Fine, Normal, and Basic are the three JPEG recording options, with Fine representing the highest JPEG quality. Raw refers to the Nikon Camera Raw format, NEF.

✔ **Image Size:** This value tells you the image resolution, or pixel count. See Chapter 2 to find out about resolution.

In the top-left corner of the screen, you may see the following two symbols, labeled in Figure 5-16:

Protect status   Retouch Indicator

Figure 5-16: These symbols indicate a protected photo and a retouched photo.

✔ **Protect Status:** A little key icon indicates that you used the file-protection feature to prevent the image from being erased when you use the camera's Delete function. See "Protecting Photos," later in this chapter, to find out more. (*Note:* Formatting your memory card, a topic discussed in Chapter 1, *does* erase even protected pictures.) This area appears empty if you didn't apply protection.

✔ **Retouch Indicator:** This icon appears if you used any of the Retouch menu options to alter the image. For example, I used the Warm filter to create the version of the monument scene shown in Figure 5-16. Chapter 10 explains this filter and other Retouch menu options.

Highlights display mode

One of the most difficult photo problems to correct in a photo-editing program is known as *blown highlights* in some circles and *clipped highlights* in others. In plain English, both terms mean that *highlights* — the brightest areas of the image — are so overexposed that areas that should include a variety of light shades are instead totally white. For example, in a cloud image, pixels that should be light to very light gray become white due to overexposure, resulting in a loss of detail in those clouds.

In Highlights display mode, areas that the camera thinks may be overexposed blink in the camera monitor. To use this mode, follow the instructions in the "Enabling hidden data-display options" section, earlier in this chapter, to enable it.

To fully understand all the features of this mode, though, you need to know a little about digital imaging science. First, digital images are called *RGB images* because they're created out of three primary colors of light: red, green, and blue. In Highlights mode, you can display the exposure warning for all three color components — sometimes called color *channels* — combined or view the data for each individual channel.

When you look at the brightness data for a single channel, though, greatly overexposed areas don't translate to white in photos — rather, they result in a solid blob of some other color. I don't have space in this book to provide a full lesson in RGB color theory, but the short story is that when you mix together red, green, and blue light, and each component is at maximum brightness, you get white. Zero brightness in all three channels gives you black. But if you have maximum red and no blue or green, you have fully saturated red. If you mix together two channels at maximum brightness, you also get full saturation. For example, maximum red and blue produce fully saturated magenta. And wherever colors are fully saturated, you can lose picture detail. For example, a rose petal that should have a range of tones from light to dark red may instead be bright red throughout.

The moral of the story is that when you view your photo in single-channel display, large areas of blinking highlights in one or two channels indicate that you may be losing color details. Blinking highlights that appear in the same spot in all three channels indicate blown highlights — again, because when you have maximum red, green, and blue, you get white. Either way, you may want to adjust your exposure settings and try again.

Okay, with today's science lesson out of the way, Figure 5-17 shows you an image that contains some blown highlights to show you how things look in Highlights display mode. I captured the screen at the moment the highlight blinkies blinked "off" — the black areas in the figure indicate the blown highlights. (I labeled a few of them in the figure.) But as this image proves, just because you see the flashing alerts doesn't mean that you should adjust exposure — the decision depends on where the alerts occur and how the rest of the image is exposed. In my candle photo, for example, it's true that there are small white areas in the flames and the glass vase. Yet exposure in the majority of the photo is fine. If I reduced exposure to darken those spots, some areas of the flowers would be underexposed. In other words, sometimes you simply can't avoid a few clipped highlights when the scene includes a broad range of brightness values.

Blown highlights

Figure 5-17: In Highlights mode, blinking areas indicate blown highlights.

In the lower-left corner of the display, the letters that appear yellow tell you whether you're looking at a single channel (R, G, or B) or the three-channel, composite display (RGB). The latter is selected in the figure. To cycle between the settings, press the ISO button as you press the Multi Selector right or left.

Along with the blinking highlight warning, Highlights display mode presents the Protect Status and Retouch Indicator icons, if you used those features. In the upper-right corner, you see the folder number and the frame number — 101 and 13, in Figure 5-17. The label *Highlights* also appears to let you know the current display mode.

RGB Histogram mode

Press the Multi Selector down to shift from Highlights mode to RGB Histogram mode, which displays your image in the manner shown on the left in Figure 5-18. (**Remember:** You can view your picture in this mode only if you enable it via the Display Mode option on the Playback menu.)

The data just underneath the thumbnail shows the White Balance settings used for the shot. (White balance is a color feature you can explore in Chapter 8.) The first value tells you the setting (Auto 1, in the figure), and the two number values tell you whether you fine-tuned that setting along the amber to blue axis (first value) or green to magenta axis (second value). Zeros, as in the figure, indicate no fine-tuning. You also see the Protect Status and Retouch Indicator symbols if you use those features on the image.

Brightness histogram   RGB histogram

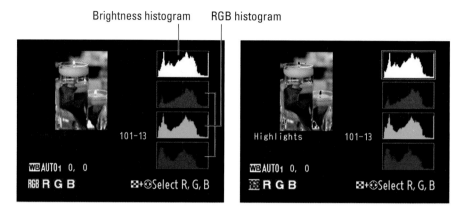

Figure 5-18: In RGB Histogram mode (left), press the ISO button to add the Highlights blinkies to the mix (right).

In addition, you get those chartlike thingies, called *histograms*. You actually get two types of histograms: The top one is a Brightness histogram and reflects the composite, three-channel image data. The three others represent the data for the single red, green, and blue channels. This trio is sometimes called an RGB histogram, thus the display mode name.

The next two sections explain what information you can glean from the two types of histograms. But first, here are two quick tips:

ISO

✔ **Adding Highlights data:** As with Highlights mode, you can display the blinking warning in the image thumbnail and view the warning for either the composite image (RGB) or each individual channel. Press the ISO button as you press the Multi Selector right, and the word Highlights goes from dim to bright, as shown on the right in Figure 5-18, indicating that the highlights are enabled. Keep pressing the button and pressing right to cycle between the single-channel and multichannel views. Again, the yellow highlight appears over the letters in the lower-left corner to tell you which view is active; a yellow box also surrounds the histogram representing the active view. For example, the RGB composite view is active in the figure. To get rid of the blinkies, select the Blue channel and then press the Multi Selector right one more time.

QUAL

✔ **Zooming the view:** Press the Qual button to zoom the thumbnail to a magnified view. The histograms then update to reflect only the magnified area of the photo. To return to the regular view and once again see the whole-image histogram, press OK.

Reading a Brightness histogram

You can get an idea of image exposure by viewing your photo on the camera monitor and by looking at the blinkies in Highlight mode. But the Brightness histogram provides a way to gauge exposure that's a little more detailed.

A Brightness histogram indicates the distribution of shadows, highlights, and *midtones* (areas of medium brightness) in your image. Figure 5-19 shows you the histogram for the candle image, for example.

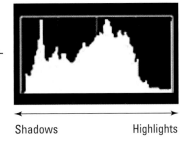

Shadows   Highlights

Figure 5-19: The Brightness histogram indicates tonal range, from shadows on the left to highlights on the right.

The horizontal axis of the histogram represents the possible picture brightness values — the maximum *tonal range,* in photography-speak — from the darkest shadows on the left to the brightest highlights on the right. And the vertical axis shows you how many pixels fall at a particular brightness value. A spike indicates a heavy concentration of pixels at that brightness value.

Keep in mind that there is no one "perfect" histogram that you should try to achieve. Instead, interpret the histogram with respect to the distribution of shadows, highlights, and midtones that comprise your subject. You wouldn't expect to see lots of shadows, for example, in a photo of a polar bear walking on a snowy landscape. Pay attention, however, if you see a very high concentration of pixels at the far right or left end of the histogram, which can indicate a seriously overexposed or underexposed image, respectively. To find out how to resolve exposure problems, visit Chapter 7.

Understanding RGB histograms

When you view your images in RGB Histogram display mode, you see two histograms: the Brightness histogram, covered in the preceding section, and an RGB histogram. Figure 5-20 shows you the RGB histogram for the candle image.

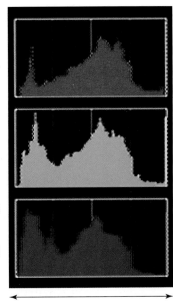

Less   More
saturated   saturated

Figure 5-20: The RGB histogram can indicate problems with color saturation.

As explained in the earlier section about Highlights mode, digital images are made up of red, green, and blue light. With the RGB histograms, you can view the brightness values for each of those color channels. Again, overexposure in one or two channels can produce oversaturated colors and thus a loss of picture detail. So if most of the pixels for one or two channels are clustered toward the right end of the histogram, you may have a problem. Turn on the blinking highlights, take a look at the image thumbnail and note where they occur, and then assess your subject and lighting to determine whether you need to make adjustments and retake the photo.

A savvy RGB histogram reader also can spot color-balance issues by looking at the pixel values. But frankly, color-balance problems are fairly easy to notice just by looking at the image itself on the camera monitor. And understanding how to translate the histogram data for this purpose requires more knowledge about RGB color theory than I have room to present in this book.

For information about manipulating color, see Chapter 8.

Shooting Data display mode

Before you can access this mode, you must enable it via the Display Mode option on the Playback menu. See the earlier section, "Enabling hidden data-display options," for details. After turning on the option, press the Multi Selector down to shift from RGB Histogram mode to Shooting Data mode.

In this mode, you can view up to four screens of information, which you toggle among by pressing the Multi Selector up and down. Figure 5-21 shows you the first two screens. The fourth screen appears only if you include copyright data with your picture, a feature you can explore in Chapter 11.

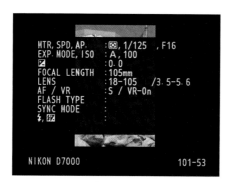 

Figure 5-21: You can view the camera settings used to capture the image in Shooting Data display mode.

Most of the data here won't make any sense to you until you explore Chapters 7 and 8, which explain the exposure, color, and other advanced settings available on your camera. But I want to call your attention to a couple of factoids now:

✔ The top-left corner of the monitor shows the Protect Status and Retouch Indicator icons, if you used these features. Otherwise, the area is empty. (See the earlier section "File Information mode" for details about these particular features.)

✔ The current folder and frame number appear in the lower-right corner of the display.

✔ The Comment item, which is the final item on the third screen, contains a value if you use the Image Comment feature on the Setup menu. I cover this option in Chapter 11.

✔ If the ISO value on Shooting Data Page 1 (the first screen in Figure 5-21) appears in red, the camera is letting you know that it overrode the ISO Sensitivity setting that you selected in order to produce a good exposure. This shift occurs only if you enable automatic ISO adjustment in the P, S, A, and M exposure modes; see Chapter 7 for details.

GPS Data mode

This display mode is available only if the image you're viewing was shot with the optional Nikon GPS (Global Positioning System) unit attached.

If you use the GPS unit, this display mode shows you the latitude, longitude, and other GPS information recorded with the image file. You also see the date and time of the shot along with the folder and frame number, the Protect Status icon, and the Retouch Indicator icon, all explained in the earlier section "File Information mode."

Overview Data mode

Overview Data mode is the second of the two default photo-information modes. (Meaning, you don't have to enable it via the Display Mode option on the Playback menu to use it.) In this mode, the playback screen contains a small image thumbnail along with scads of shooting data — although not quite as much as Shooting Data mode — plus a Brightness histogram. Figure 5-22 offers a look.

The earlier section "Reading a Brightness histogram" tells you what to make of that part of the screen. Just above the histogram, you see the Protect Status and Retouch Indicator, while the Frame Number/Total Pictures data appears at the upper-right corner of the image thumbnail. For details on that data, see the earlier section "File Information mode." (As always, the Protect status and Retouch Indicator icons appear only if you used those two features.)

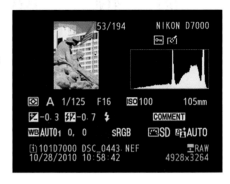

Figure 5-22: In Overview Data mode, you can view your picture along with the major camera settings you used to take the picture.

To sort out the maze of other information, the following list breaks things down into the five rows that appear under the image thumbnail and histogram. In the accompanying figures as well as in Figure 5-22, I include all possible data simply for the purpose of illustration; if any of the items don't appear on your screen, it simply means that the relevant feature wasn't enabled when you captured the shot.

- **Row 1:** This row shows the exposure-related settings labeled in Figure 5-23, along with the focal length of the lens you used to take the shot. As in Shooting Data mode, the ISO value appears red if you had auto ISO override enabled in the P, S, A, or M exposure mode and the camera adjusted the ISO for you. Chapter 7 details the exposure settings; Chapter 8 introduces you to focal length.

- **Row 2:** This row contains a few additional exposure settings, labeled in Figure 5-24. On the right end of the row, the Comment and GPS labels appear if you took advantage of those options when recording the shot. (You must switch to the Shooting Data mode or GPS mode, respectively, to view the actual comment and GPS data.)

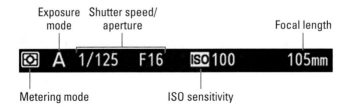

Figure 5-23: Here you can inspect major exposure settings along with the lens focal length.

Exposure Compensation   Flash mode

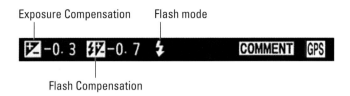

Flash Compensation

Figure 5-24: This row contains additional exposure information.

🖊 **Row 3:** The first three items on this row, labeled in Figure 5-25, relate to color options explored in Chapter 8. Again, the second White Balance value shows the amount of blue-to-amber fine-tuning adjustment, and the third, the amount of green-to-magenta adjustment (both values are 0 in the figure). The last item indicates the Active D-Lighting setting, another exposure option discussed in Chapter 7.

🖊 **Rows 4 and 5:** The final two rows of data (refer to Figure 5-22) show the same information you get in File Information mode, explained earlier in this chapter.

White Balance   Picture Control

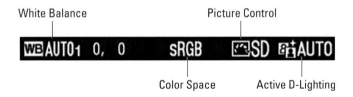

Color Space   Active D-Lighting

Figure 5-25: Look at this row for details about advanced color settings.

Deleting Photos

You can erase pictures from a memory card when it's in your camera in three ways. The next sections give you the lowdown. (Or is it the down low? I can't seem to keep up.)

Regardless of which delete technique you want to use, remember that you can't delete photos that you protected or hid by using the Protect or Hide Image features. Later sections in this chapter explain both features and show you how to unprotect and unhide images so that you can delete them.

Deleting images one at a time

The Delete button is key to erasing single images. But the process varies a little depending on which playback display mode you're using, as follows:

- ✔ In single-image view, you can erase the current image by pressing the Delete button.

- ✔ In thumbnail view (displaying 4, 9, or 72 thumbnails), use the Multi Selector to highlight the picture you want to erase and then press the Delete button.

- ✔ In Calendar view, highlight an image in the thumbnail strip and press Delete.

After you press Delete, you see a message asking whether you really want to erase the picture. If you do, press the Delete button again. Or, to cancel out of the process, press the Playback button.

If you really want to get down into your camera's customization option weeds — and I do believe this is about as weedy as it gets — you can control which picture the camera displays next after you delete the current picture. The option in question lives on the Playback menu and is called After Delete, as shown in Figure 5-26. Select the option and press OK to access your three choices: Show Next displays the picture after the one you just deleted (the default option); Show Previous displays the one that fell before the one you deleted, and Continue as Before tells the camera to keep going in the same direction you were heading before deleting. For example, if you were scrolling forward through your pictures, the camera continues playback in that direction. Wow, now *that's* control. Have you thought about getting some help for that?

Figure 5-26: You can specify which picture appears next after you delete the current one.

Deleting all photos

Erasing all pictures on a memory card is a five-step process:

1. **Open the Playback menu and select Delete, as shown on the left in Figure 5-27.**

2. **Press OK.**

   You see the right screen in Figure 5-27.

3. **Highlight All and press the Multi Selector right.**

4. **On the next screen, highlight the memory card that contains the pictures you want to dump and press the Multi Selector right again.**

   You then see a screen that asks you to verify that you want to delete all your images.

5. **Highlight Yes and press OK.**

Figure 5-27: You can quickly delete all photos from a memory card.

This step deletes only pictures in the folder that's currently selected via the Playback Folder option on the Playback menu. See the section "Choosing which images to view," earlier in this chapter, for information.

Also remember that deleting photos in this way does not erase any pictures that you protected using the Protect feature or hid from display by using the Hide Image option, both described later in this chapter.

Deleting a batch of selected photos

To erase multiple photos — but not all — display the Playback menu, high-light Delete, and press OK. You see the Delete screen shown on the left in Figure 5-28.

Delete marker   Current card

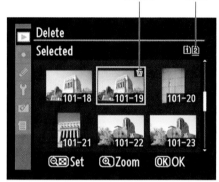

Figure 5-28: Choose this option to tag specific photos for deletion.

You then have two options for specifying which photos to erase:

ISO

✔ **Select photos one by one.** To go this route, highlight Selected, as shown on the left in Figure 5-28, and press the Multi Selector right to display a screen of thumbnails, as shown on the right. Use the Multi Selector to place the yellow highlight box over the first photo you want to delete and then press the ISO button, shown in the margin here. A little trash can icon, the universal symbol for delete, appears in the upper-right corner of the thumbnail, as shown in the figure.

If you change your mind, press the ISO button again to remove the Delete tag from the image. To undo deletion for all selected photos, press the Playback button.

A couple tricks to try:

QUAL

BKT

• For a closer look at the selected image, press and hold the Qual button. When you release the button, the display returns to normal thumbnail view.

• If you have two memory cards installed, the card icon that appears yellow in the upper-right corner of the screen is the currently selected card. You can use the same technique available during playback to jump between cards and folders: Press the BKT button and press the Multi Selector up to get the screen where you can select a card. Highlight the card, press OK to display the list of folders on the card, and select the one you want to view. Press OK to return to the screen where you tag pictures for deletion. The first photo in your chosen folder is automatically selected. Remember that the folders that appear when you use this option depend on the setting you choose for the Playback Folder option, as covered in the earlier section "Choosing which images to view."

✔ **Erase all photos taken on a specific date.** To dump all pictures you shot on a particular day, choose Select Date from the main Delete screen, as shown on the left in Figure 5-29. Press the Multi Selector right to display a list of dates on which you took the pictures on the memory card, as shown on the right in the figure.

Next, highlight a date and press the Multi Selector right. A little check mark appears in the box next to the date, as shown in Figure 5-29, tagging all images taken on that day for deletion. To remove the check mark and save the photos from the digital dumpster, press the Multi Selector right again.

Can't remember what photos are associated with the selected date? Try this:

- To display thumbnails of all images taken on the selected date, press the ISO button.

- To temporarily view the selected thumbnail at full-size view press the Qual button.

- To return to the date list, press the ISO button again.

Figure 5-29: With the Select Date option, you can quickly erase all photos taken on a specific date.

After tagging individual photos for deletion or specifying a shooting date to delete, press OK to start the Delete process. You see a confirmation screen asking permission to destroy the images; select Yes and press OK. The camera trashes the photos and returns you to the Playback menu.

You have one alternative way to quickly erase all images taken on a specific date: In the Calendar display mode, you can highlight the date in question and then press the Delete button instead of going through the Playback menu. You get the standard confirmation screen asking you whether you want to go forward. Press the Delete button again to dump the files. Visit the section "Displaying photos in Calendar view," earlier in this chapter, for the scoop on that display option.

As with the Delete All option, you can't delete protected or hidden photos using any of these techniques. For more about protecting and hiding photos, see the next two sections.

Hiding Photos during Playback

Suppose that you took 100 pictures — 50 at a business meeting and 50 at the wild after-meeting party. You want to show your boss the photos where you and your co-workers look like responsible adults, but you'd rather not share the ones showing you and your assistant dancing on the conference table. You can always delete the party photos; the preceding section shows you how. But if you want to keep them — you never know when a good blackmail picture will come in handy — you can simply hide the incriminating images during playback.

The key to this trick is the Hide Image option on the Playback menu. After highlighting the option, as shown on the left in Figure 5-30, press OK to display the right screen in the figure.

From here, things work pretty much the same as they do for marking a picture for deletion, covered in the preceding section:

✔ **Select and hide photos one by one:** Choose Select/Set, as shown on the right in Figure 5-30, to display thumbnails of your images. Highlight the picture you want to hide and then press the ISO button to tag the photo with the little hide marker, as shown on the left in Figure 5-31.

You can use the same techniques as outlined in the preceding section to jump between memory cards and folders and get a larger view of the selected photo.

 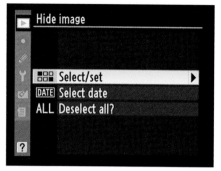

Figure 5-30: The Hide Image function lets you prevent photos from appearing during normal picture playback.

After you tag all the images you want to hide, press OK to return to the Playback menu. Your pictures are now hidden.

🖝 **Select and hide all photos taken on a specific date:** On the screen shown on the right in Figure 5-30, choose Select Date and press the Multi Selector right. Now you see a list of dates, as shown on the right in Figure 5-31. Highlight the date that contains the photos you want to hide. Then press right to put a check in the box to the left of the date. Again, the tricks that work for deleting photos by date work here, too; see the preceding section for details. Press OK to finalize the process.

Hide   Current
marker   card

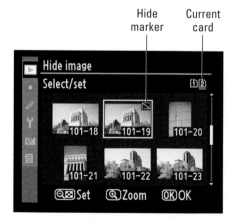 

Figure 5-31: You can select photos one by one (left) or by date (right).

A couple of fine points about this feature:

✓ Hidden images remain viewable from within the Hide Image screens. In other words, if you travel back to the Hide Image menu and choose the Select/Set or Select Date option, you see thumbnails for your hidden images along with those that aren't hidden. So make sure your boss doesn't know how to implement this feature.

✓ To redisplay hidden pictures, just reverse the process, removing the hide marker from photos you want to view again. Or, to redisplay all hidden pictures quickly, choose Deselect All from the first Hide Image screen (the right screen in Figure 5-30). Then press the Multi Selector right to display a screen that asks you to confirm your decision. Highlight Yes and press OK to make it so.

✓ If you protected a photo before hiding it, redisplaying the picture removes its protected status.

✓ Before you can delete hidden photos, you first need to remove the Hide Image tags. Or you can format your memory card, which wipes out all photos, hidden or not. See Chapter 1 for details on card formatting.

Protecting Photos

You can safeguard pictures from accidental erasure by giving them *protected status.* After you take this step, the camera doesn't allow you to erase a picture by using either the Delete button or the Delete option on the Playback menu.

Formatting your memory card, however, *does* erase even protected pictures. In addition, when you protect a picture, it shows up as a read-only file when you transfer it to your computer. Files that have that read-only status can't be altered until you unlock them in your photo software. In Nikon ViewNX 2, you can do this by clicking the image thumbnail and then choosing File↪ Protect Files↪Unprotect.

Protecting a picture is easy:

1. **Display or select the picture you want to protect.**

   • *In single-image view,* just display the photo.

   • *In 4/9/72 thumbnail mode,* use the Multi Selector as needed to place the yellow highlight box over the photo.

• *In Calendar view,* highlight the image in the strip of thumbnails that appears on the right side of the screen. (Press the ISO button to jump between the calendar dates and the thumbnails.)

WB

2. **Press the WB button.**

   See the key symbol on the button? That's your reminder that you use the button to lock a picture. The same symbol appears on protected photos during playback, as shown in Figure 5-32.

3. **To remove protection, display or select the image and then press the WB button again.**

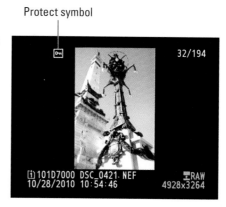

Protect symbol

Figure 5-32: Press the Protect button to prevent accidental deletion of the selected image.

Creating a Digital Slide Show

Many photo-editing and cataloging programs offer a tool for creating digital slide shows that can be viewed on a computer or, if copied to a DVD, on a DVD player. You can even add music, captions, graphics, special effects, and the like to jazz up your presentations.

But if you want to create a simple slide show — that is, one that simply displays the photos on the camera memory card one by one — you can create and run the show right on your camera by using the Slide Show function on the Playback menu. And by connecting your camera to a television, as outlined in the last section of this chapter, you can present your show to a whole roomful of people.

A couple of things to note about the Slide Show feature:

⮮ The pictures displayed in the show depend on the current setting of the Playback Folder option on the Playback menu. For more about choosing which folder (and which memory card, if you're using two at a time) you want to view, see "Choosing which images to view," earlier in this chapter.

⮮ Any pictures that you hid through the Hide Image function, also explained earlier in this chapter, do not appear in the show.

With those details out of the way, follow these steps to present a slide show:

1. **Display the Playback menu and highlight Slide Show, as shown on the left in Figure 5-33.**

2. **Press OK to display the Slide Show screen shown on the right in Figure 5-33.**

3. **Highlight Frame Interval and press the Multi Selector right.**

   On the next screen, you can specify how long you want each image to be displayed. You can set the interval to two, three, five, or ten seconds.

4. **Highlight the frame interval you want to use and press OK.**

   You return to the Slide Show screen.

5. **To start the show, highlight Start and press OK.**

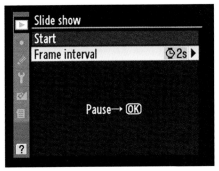

Figure 5-33: Choose Slide Show to set up automatic playback of all pictures on your memory card.

When the show ends, you see a screen offering three options: You can choose to restart the show, adjust the frame interval, or exit to the Playback menu. Highlight your choice and press OK.

During the show, you can control playback as follows:

⮞ **Pause the show.** Press OK. Again, you see three options onscreen. To restart playback, select Restart and press OK. You also can adjust the frame interval or exit to the Playback menu.

▱ **Exit the show.** You have three options:

- *To return to full-frame, regular playback,* press the Playback button.

- *To return to the Playback menu,* press the Menu button.

- *To return to picture-taking mode,* press the shutter button halfway.

▱ **Skip to the next/previous image manually.** Press the Multi Selector right or left.

▱ **Change the information displayed with the image.** Press the Multi Selector up or down to cycle through the display modes. See the section "Viewing Picture Data" for help understanding the various modes.

Viewing Your Photos on a Television

Your camera is equipped with a feature that allows you to play your pictures and movies on a television screen. In fact, you have three playback options:

▱ **Regular (standard definition) video playback:** Haven't made the leap yet to HDTV? No worries: You can set the camera to send a regular standard-definition audio and video signal to the TV. The cable you need is even provided in the D7000 camera box. (Look for the cable that has a yellow plug and a white plug at one end.)

▱ **HDMI playback:** If you have a high-definition television, you can set the camera to high-def playback. However, you need to purchase an HDMI cable to connect the camera and television. You need a Type C mini-pin HD cable; prices start at about $20. Nikon doesn't make its own cable, so just look for a quality third-party version.

By default, the camera decides the proper video resolution to send to the TV after you connect the two devices. But you have the option of setting a specific resolution as well. To do so, select HDMI from the Setup menu, press OK, and then choose Output Resolution, as shown in Figure 5-34.

▱ **For HDMI CEC TV sets:** If your television is compatible with HDMI CEC, your D7000 enables you to use the buttons on the TV's remote control to perform the functions of the OK button and Multi Selector during full-frame picture playback and slide shows. To make this feature work, you must enable it via the Setup menu. Again, start with the HDMI option, but this time, select Device Control and set the option to On.

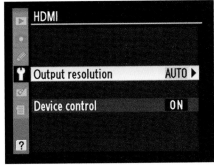

Figure 5-34: Select options for HD playback here.

You need to make one final preflight check before connecting the camera and television: Verify the status of the Video Mode setting, located just above the HDMI option on the Setup menu. (Refer to the left screen in Figure 5-34.) You have just two options: NTSC and PAL. Select the video mode used by your part of the world. (In the United States, Canada, and Mexico, NTSC is the standard.) The mode should've been set at the factory to the right option for the country in which you bought your camera, but it never hurts to check.

After you select the necessary Setup menu options, grab your video cable, turn off the camera, and open the little rubber door on the left side of the camera. There you find two *ports* (connection slots): one for a standard audio/ video (A/V) signal and one for the HDMI signal. Figure 5-35 labels the two ports.

Audio/Video out   HDMI mini-pin connector

Figure 5-35: The video-out ports are under the little rubber door on the side of the camera.

Deleting versus formatting: What's the diff?

In Chapter 1, I introduce you to the Format Memory Card command, which lives on the Setup menu and erases everything on your memory card. What's the difference between erasing photos by formatting and by choosing Delete from the Playback menu and then selecting the All option?

Well, if you happen to have stored other data on the card, such as, say, a music file or a picture taken on another type of camera, you need to format the card to erase those files. You can't use Delete to get rid of them.

Also keep in mind that the Delete function affects only the currently selected folder of camera images. As long as you use the default folder system that the camera creates for you, however, "currently selected folder" is the same as "all images." The section "Choosing which images to view," earlier in this chapter, talks more about this issue; Chapter 11 explains how to create custom folders.

One final — and important — note: Although using the Protect feature (explained elsewhere in this chapter) prevents the Delete function from erasing a picture, formatting erases all pictures, protected or not.

The smaller plug on the A/V cable attaches to the camera. The yellow plug goes into your TV's video jack, and the white one goes into your TV's stereo audio jack. For HDMI playback, a single plug goes to the TV.

At this point, I need to point you to your specific TV manual to find out exactly which jacks to use to connect your camera. You also need to consult your manual to find out which channel to select for playback of signals from auxiliary input devices. Then just turn on your camera to send the signal to the TV set. If you don't have the latest and greatest HDMI CEC capability (or lost your remote), control playback using the same techniques as you normally do to view pictures on your camera monitor. You can also run a slide show by following the steps outlined in the preceding section.

6

Downloading, Printing, and Sharing Your Photos

*F*or many novice digital photographers, the task of moving pictures to the computer is one of the more confusing aspects of the art form. Unfortunately, providing you with detailed downloading instructions is impossible because the steps vary widely depending on which computer software you use to do the job.

To give you as much help as I can, however, this chapter starts with a quick review of photo software, in case you aren't happy with your current solution. Following that, you can find information about downloading images, converting pictures that you shoot in the Raw format to a standard format, and preparing your pictures for print and online sharing.

Choosing the Right Photo Software

Programs for downloading, archiving, and editing digital photos abound, ranging from entry-level software designed for beginners to high-end options geared to professionals. The good news is that if you don't need serious photo-editing capabilities, you may find a free program that serves your needs — in fact, your camera ships with one free program, Nikon ViewNX 2.

The next section offers a look at Nikon ViewNX 2 along with two other free-bies; following that, I offer some advice on a few popular programs to consider when the free options don't meet your needs.

Three free photo programs

If you don't plan on doing a lot of retouching or other manipulation of your photos but simply want a tool for downloading and organizing your pictures, one of the following free programs may be a good solution:

- **Nikon ViewNX 2:** This program is on the CD that shipped in your camera box. As the name implies, the program provides a simple photo organizer and viewer, plus a few basic photo-editing features, including red-eye removal and exposure and color adjustment filters. You also can use the program to download pictures and to convert Raw files to a standard format. (See Chapter 2 for a primer on file formats.) I show you how to accomplish both tasks later in this chapter.

  Figure 6-1 offers a look at the ViewNX 2 window as it appears when you use the Thumbnail Grid view mode, one of three display options available from the View menu.

Figure 6-1: Nikon ViewNX 2 offers a basic photo viewer and some limited editing functions.

After you download your photos, you can view camera *metadata* — the data that records the camera settings you used to take the picture — in ViewNX 2. Just display the Metadata panel, located on the right side of the program window, as shown in Figure 6-1. (If the panel is hidden, click the little triangle on the far right side of the window and then click the triangle at the top of the panel. I labeled both controls in the figure.) Many other photo programs also display metadata, but sometimes can't reveal data that's very camera specific, such as the Picture Control setting on the D7000. Every camera manufacturer records metadata differently, and the Raw data structure may vary even among cameras from the same manufacturer, so it's a little difficult for software companies to keep up with each new model.

ViewNX 2 offers another cool feature that most other browsers don't: By clicking the Focus Point button, labeled in Figure 6-1, you can display a little red rectangle that indicates which focus point the camera used to establish focus for the shot, which can be helpful when you're trying to troubleshoot focus problems. You don't see the point if you used manual focusing or continuous autofocusing when taking the shot, however.

 ✔ **Apple iPhoto:** Most Mac users are very familiar with this photo browser, built into the Mac operating system. Apple provides some great tutorials on using iPhoto at its Web site (www.apple.com) to help you get started if you're new to the program.

 ✔ **Windows Photo Gallery:** Some versions of Microsoft Windows also offer a free photo downloader and browser, Windows Photo Gallery (the name varies slightly depending on your version of the Windows operating system).

Advanced photo programs

Programs mentioned in the preceding section can handle simple photo downloading and organizing tasks. But if you're interested in serious photo retouching or digital-imaging artistry, you need to step up to a full-fledged photo-editing program.

As with software in the free category, you have many choices; the following list describes just the most widely known programs.

 ✔ **Adobe Photoshop Elements:** Elements has been the best-selling consumer-level photo-editing program for some time, and for good reason. With a full complement of retouching tools, onscreen guidance for beginners, and an assortment of templates for creating photo projects like scrapbooks, Elements offers all the features that most consumers need. Figure 6-2 shows the Elements editing window with some of the photo-creativity tools displayed to the right of the photo. The program includes a photo organizer as well, along with built-in tools to help you print your photos and upload them to photo-sharing sites. (www.adobe.com, about $100)

Figure 6-2: Adobe Photoshop Elements offers good retouching tools plus templates for creating scrapbooks, greeting cards, and other photo gifts.

✔ **Nikon Capture NX 2:** Shown in Figure 6-3, this Nikon program offers an image browser/organizer plus a wealth of photo-editing tools, including a sophisticated tool for processing Raw images. But as you can see from the figure, it's not exactly geared to casual photographers or novice photo editors, so expect a bit of a learning curve. Nor does this program offer the sort of photo-creativity tools you find in a program like Photoshop Elements (the same is true for the other advanced tools described in this list). (www.nikon.com, about $180)

✔ **Apple Aperture:** Aperture is geared more to shooters who need to organize and process lots of images but typically do only light retouching work — wedding photographers and school-portrait photographers, for example. (www.apple.com, about $200)

✔ **Adobe Photoshop Lightroom:** Lightroom is the Adobe counterpart to Aperture, although in its latest version, it offers some fairly powerful retouching tools as well. Many pro photographers rely on this program or Aperture for all their work, in fact. (www.adobe.com, about $300)

Figure 6-3: Nikon Capture 2 may appeal to photographers who need more robust image-editing tools than are found in ViewNX 2.

✓ **Adobe Photoshop:** The granddaddy of photo editors, Photoshop offers the industry's most powerful, sophisticated retouching tools, including tools for producing HDR (high dynamic range) and 3D images. In fact, you probably won't use even a quarter of the tools in the Photoshop shed unless you're a digital imaging professional who uses the program on a daily basis — even then, some tools may never see the light of day. (www.adobe.com, about $700)

Not sure which tool you need, if any? Good news: You can download 30-day free trials of all these programs from the manufacturers' Web sites.

Sending Pictures to the Computer

Whatever photo software you choose, you can take the following approaches to downloading images to your computer:

✔ **Connect the camera to the computer via a USB cable.** The USB cable you need is supplied in the camera box.

✔ **Use a memory card reader.** With a card reader, you simply pop the memory card out of your camera and into the card reader instead of hooking the camera to the computer. Many computers and printers now have card readers, and you also can buy standalone readers for less than $30. *Note:* If you use the new SDHC (Secure Digital High Capacity) or SDXC (Secure Digital eXtended Capacity) cards, the reader must specifically support that type.

✔ **Invest in Eye-Fi memory cards and transfer images via a wireless network.** You can find out more about these special memory cards at the manufacturer's Web site, www.eye.fi. Your computer must be connected to a wireless network for the transfer technology to work.

For most people, I recommend a card reader. Sending pictures directly from the camera, whether via cable or wirelessly, requires that the camera be turned on during the entire download process, wasting battery power. Additionally, not all devices can use Eye-Fi memory cards, meaning that you're spending money on cards that may have limited use beyond serving as storage on your D7000. Card readers, on the other hand, can accept cards from any device that uses SD cards, which are fast becoming the standard storage medium for portable devices.

That said, I include information about cable transfer in the next section in case you don't have a card reader. To use a card reader, skip ahead to "Starting the transfer process."

Because Eye-Fi cards aren't yet in widespread use, I don't cover that transfer technology. If you're an Eye-Fi user, check the instructions that ship with the cards and visit the company's Web site for information on how to set up your card and transfer images from it to your computer. Also check the Eye-Fi compatibility and use details provided in the D7000 manual; look for the section related to the Eye-Fi Upload option on the Setup menu. (The menu item appears only when an Eye-Fi card is installed in the camera.)

Connecting the camera and computer for picture download

With the USB cable that shipped with your camera, you can connect the camera to your computer and then transfer images directly to the computer's hard drive.

The next section explains the actual transfer process; the steps here just walk you through the process of connecting the two devices. You need to follow a specific set of steps when connecting the camera to your computer. Otherwise, you can damage the camera or the memory card.

Also note that for your camera to communicate with the computer, Nikon suggests that your computer runs one of the following operating systems:

✔ Windows 7, Vista with Service Pack 2, or XP with Service Pack 3 (Home or Professional edition).

✔ Mac OS X 10.4.11, 10.5.8, or 10.6.4

If you use another OS (operating system, for the nongeeks in the crowd), check the support pages on the Nikon Web site (www.nikon.com) for the latest news about any updates to system compatibility. You can always simply transfer images with a card reader, too.

With that preamble out of the way, here are the steps to link your computer and camera:

1. Check the level of the camera battery.

If the battery is low, charge it before continuing. Running out of battery power during the transfer process can cause problems, including lost picture data. Alternatively, if you purchased the optional AC adapter, use that to power the camera during picture transfers.

2. Turn on the computer and give it time to finish its normal startup routine.

3. Turn off the camera.

USB port

4. Insert the smaller of the two plugs on the USB cable into the USB port on the side of the camera.

Look under the top rubber door on the left side of the camera for this port, labeled in Figure 6-4.

5. Plug the other end of the cable into the computer's USB port.

If possible, plug the cable into a port that's built in to the computer, as opposed to one that's on your keyboard or part of an external USB hub. Those accessory-type connections can sometimes foul up the transfer process.

6. Turn on the camera.

Figure 6-4: The USB slot is hidden under the top rubber door on the left side of the camera.

What happens now depends on your computer operating system and what photo software you have installed on that system. The next section explains the possibilities and how to proceed with the image transfer process.

7. **When the download is complete, turn off the camera and then disconnect it from the computer.**

I repeat: Turn off the camera before severing its ties with the computer. Otherwise, you can damage the camera.

Starting the transfer process

After you connect the camera to the computer or insert a memory card into your card reader, your next step depends, again, on the software installed on your computer and the computer operating system.

Here are the most common possibilities and how to move forward:

Figure 6-5: Windows may display this initial boxful of transfer options.

✔ **On a Windows-based computer, a Windows message box similar to the one in Figure 6-5 appears.** Again, the figure shows the dialog box as it appears on a computer running Windows 7. Whatever its design, the dialog box suggests different programs that you can use to download your picture files. Which programs appear depend on what you have installed on your system. If you installed Nikon ViewNX 2, for example, the list should contain a Nikon Transfer 2 entry, as shown in the figure. Nikon Transfer 2 is the downloading utility built into ViewNX 2.

In Windows 7 and Vista, just click the transfer program that you want to use. In other versions of Windows, the dialog box may sport an OK button; if so, click that button to proceed.

If you want to use the same program for all your transfers, select the Always Do This for Pictures check box, as shown in the figure. (In other versions of Windows, the check box may have a slightly different name.) The next time you connect your camera or insert a memory card, Windows will automatically launch your program of choice instead of displaying the message box.

✔ **An installed photo program automatically displays a photo-download wizard.** For example, the Nikon Transfer 2 downloader or a downloader associated with Adobe Photoshop Elements, iPhoto, or some other photo software may leap to the forefront. Usually, the downloader that appears is associated with the software that you most recently installed. Each new program that you add to your system tries to wrestle control over your image downloads away from the previous program.

If you don't want a program's auto downloader to launch whenever you insert a memory card or connect your camera, you can turn off that feature. Check the software manual to find out how to disable the auto launch.

✔ **Nothing happens.** Don't panic; assuming that your card reader or camera is properly connected, all is probably well. Someone simply may have disabled all the automatic downloaders on your system. Just launch your photo software and then transfer your pictures using whatever command starts that process.

As another option, you can use Windows Explorer or the Mac Finder to drag and drop files from your memory card to your computer's hard drive. Whether you connect the card through a card reader or attach the camera directly, the computer sees the card or camera as just another drive on the system. So the process of transferring files is exactly the same as when you move any other file from a CD, DVD, or other storage device onto your hard drive.

In the next section, I provide details on using Nikon Transfer 2 to download your files. If you use some other software, the concepts are the same, but check your program manual to get the small details. In most programs, you also can find lots of information by simply clicking open the Help menu.

Downloading photos with Nikon ViewNX 2

If you want to use the free Nikon software, Nikon ViewNX 2, to download, view, and organize your photos, dig out the program CD from your camera box and install the software on your system.

Also note that this book features Nikon ViewNX 2 version 2.0.3. If you own an earlier version of the program, visit the Nikon Web site to install the updates. (To find out what version you have installed, open the program. Then, in Windows, choose Help⇨About. On a Mac, choose the About command from the Nikon Transfer or Nikon ViewNX menu.) You also may be able to use the built-in software updater, depending on the age of your software. Open the program and choose Help⇨Check for Updates to give it a go.

One final software-related point: You can use Nikon ViewNX 2 to download your photos and still use any photo-editing or image-management software you prefer. And to do your editing, you don't need to redownload photos — after you transfer photos to your computer, you can access them from any program, just as you can any file that you put on your system. With some programs, you must first take the step of *importing* the photo files, which enables the program to build thumbnails and, in some cases, working copies of your pictures, however.

With that lengthy preamble out of the way, the following steps walk you through the process of downloading via Nikon ViewNX 2:

1. **Attach your camera to the computer or insert a memory card into your card reader, as outlined in the first part of this chapter.**

   Depending on what software you have installed on your system, you may see a dialog box asking you how to download your photos. If the window that appears is the Nikon Transfer 2 window, shown in Figure 6-6, skip to Step 3. *Nikon Transfer 2* is the picture-downloading utility built into ViewNX 2.

   Similarly, if you see a Windows dialog box that contains the Nikon Transfer 2 option, as shown in Figure 6-5, click that option and skip to Step 3.

   If nothing happens, don't worry — just travel to Step 2, which shows you how to launch the Nikon Transfer 2 software if it didn't appear automatically.

2. **Launch Nikon Transfer 2, if it isn't already open.**

   To access the transfer tool, open Nikon ViewNX 2 and then choose File⇨Launch Transfer or click the Transfer button at the top of the window. The window shown in Figure 6-6 appears.

3. **Display the Source tab to view thumbnails of your pictures, as shown in the figure.**

   Don't see any tabs? Click the little Options triangle, located near the top-left corner of the window and labeled in Figure 6-6, to display them. Then click the Source tab. The icon representing your camera or memory card should be selected, as shown in the figure. If not, click the icon.

   If you have two memory cards in the camera, click the little triangle at the bottom-right corner of the camera icon, as shown in Figure 6-6. Then choose which card you want the downloader to access.

   Thumbnails of your images appear in the bottom half of the dialog box. If you don't see the thumbnails, click the arrow labeled in Figure 6-6 to open the thumbnails area.

4. **Select the images that you want to download.**

   A check mark in the little box under a thumbnail tells the program that you want to download the image. Click the box to toggle the check mark on and off.

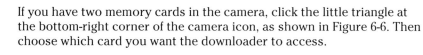

Click to display/hide thumbnails

Click to display/hide options

Select All   Select Protected

Choose memory card

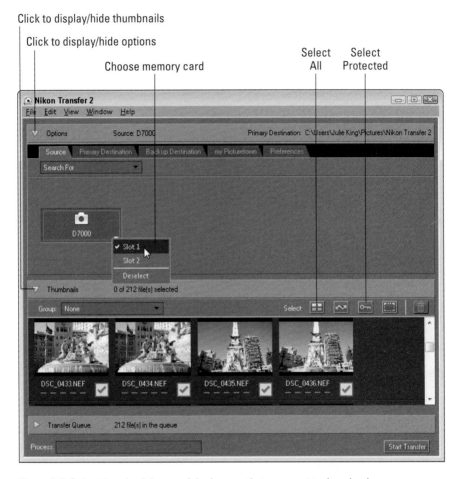

Figure 6-6: Select the check boxes of the images that you want to download.

If you used the in-camera function to protect pictures (see Chapter 5), you can select just those images by clicking the Select Protected icon, labeled in Figure 6-6. To select all images on the card, click the Select All icon instead.

5. **Click the Primary Destination tab at the top of the window.**

When you click the tab, the top of the transfer window offers options that enable you to specify where and how you want the images to be stored on your computer. Figure 6-7 offers a look.

6. **Choose the folder where you want to store the images from the Primary Destination Folder drop-down list.**

The list is labeled in Figure 6-7. If the folder you want to use isn't in the list, open the drop-down list, choose Browse from the bottom of the list, and then track down the folder and select it.

Choose storage folder

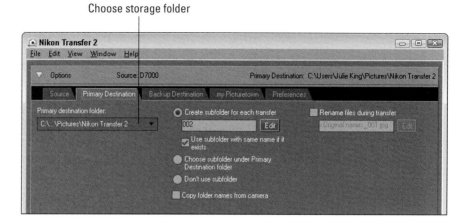

Figure 6-7: Specify the folder where you want to put the downloaded images.

By default, the program puts images in a Nikon Transfer folder, which is housed inside the My Pictures folder in Windows XP and Pictures in Windows 7, Windows Vista, and on a Mac. That My Pictures or Pictures folder is housed inside a folder that your system creates automatically for each registered user of the computer.

You don't have to stick with this default location — you can put your pictures anywhere you please. But because most photo programs automatically look for pictures in these standard folders, putting your pictures there simplifies things a little down the road. *Note:* You can always move your pictures into other folders after you download them if needed, too.

7. **Specify whether you want the pictures to be placed inside a new subfolder.**

   If you select the Create Subfolder for Each Transfer option, the program creates a new folder inside the storage folder you selected in Step 6. Then it puts all the pictures from the current download session into that new subfolder. You can either use the numerical subfolder name the program suggests or click the Edit button to set up your own naming system. You might find it helpful to go with a folder name that includes the date that the batch of photos was taken, for example. (You can reorganize your pictures into this type of setup after download, however.) If you created custom folders on the camera memory card, an option you can explore in Chapter 11, select the Copy Folder Names from Camera check box to use those folder names instead.

8. **Tell the program whether you want to rename the picture files during the download process.**

   If you do, select the Rename Files during Transfer check box. Then click the Edit button to display a dialog box where you can set up your new filenaming scheme. Click OK after you do so to close the dialog box.

9. **Click the Preferences tab to set the rest of the transfer options.**

The tab shown in Figure 6-8 takes over the top of the program window. Here you find a number of options that enable you to control how the program operates, as follows:

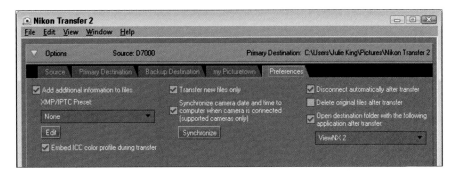

Figure 6-8: Control other aspects of the program's behavior via the Preferences tab.

- *Add Additional Information to Files:* Through this option, you can embed *XMP/IPTC* data in the file. *IPTC* refers to text data that press photographers are often required to tag onto their picture files, such as captions and copyright information. *XMP* refers to a data format developed by Adobe to enable that kind of data to be added to the file. IPTC stands for International Press Telecommunications Council; XMP stands for Extensible Metadata Platform.

Click the Edit button beneath the option to create and store a preset that contains the data you want to add. On your next visit to the dialog box, you can choose the preset from the drop-down list above the Edit button.

You also can tag a file with text comments in the camera, using the Image Comment feature that I cover in Chapter 11.

- *Embed ICC Color Profile during Transfer:* This option relates to the Color Space option on the Shooting menu. Nikon recommends that you enable this option if you capture images using the Adobe RGB color space instead of the default, sRGB space. Otherwise, some photo programs may simply assume that the files are in the sRGB space. Chapter 8 explains the Color Space setting.

- *Transfer New Files Only:* This option, when selected, ensures that you don't waste time downloading images that you've already transferred but are still on the memory card.

- *Synchronize Camera Date and Time . . . :* If you connect your camera to the computer via USB cable, selecting this option tells the camera to reset its internal clock to match the date and time of the computer.

• *Disconnect Automatically after Transfer:* Choose this option to tell the transfer tool to shut itself down automatically when the download is complete.

• *Delete Original Files after Transfer:* Turn off this option, as shown in Figure 6-8. Otherwise, your pictures are automatically erased from your memory card when the transfer is complete. Always make sure the pictures really made it to the computer before you delete them from your memory card. (See Chapter 5 to find out how to use the Delete function on your camera.)

• *Open Destination Folder with the Following Application after Transfer:* By default, Nikon ViewNX 2 starts automatically at the end of the download process if it isn't already open. If you want to use a program other than ViewNX 2 to view and edit your photos, open the drop-down list, choose Browse, and select the program from the dialog box that appears. Click OK after doing so.

Your choices remain in force for any subsequent download sessions, so you don't have to revisit this tab unless you want the program to behave differently.

10. **When you're ready to start the download, click the Start Transfer button.**

It's located in the lower-right corner of the program window. (Refer to Figure 6-6.) After you click the button, the Process bar in the lower-left corner indicates how the transfer is progressing. Again, what happens when the transfer completes depends on the choices you made in Step 9; by default, Nikon Transfer closes, and ViewNX 2 opens, automatically displaying the folder that contains your just-downloaded images.

Processing Raw (NEF) Files

Chapter 2 introduces you to the Raw file format. The advantage of capturing Raw files, or NEF files on Nikon cameras, is that you make the decisions about how to translate the original picture data into an actual photograph. You can specify attributes such as color intensity, image sharpening, contrast, and so on — which are all handled automatically by the camera if you use its other file format, JPEG. You take these steps by using a software tool known as a *Raw converter.*

The bad news: Until you convert your NEF files into a standard file format, you can't share them online or print them from most programs other than Nikon ViewNX 2. You also can't get prints from most retail outlets or open them in many photo-editing programs.

To process your D7000 NEF files, you have the following options:

- **Use the in-camera processing feature.** Through the Retouch menu, you can process your Raw images right in the camera. You can specify only limited image attributes, and you can save the processed files only in the JPEG format, but still, having this option is a nice feature.

- **Process and convert in ViewNX 2.** ViewNX 2 also offers a Raw processing feature. Again, the controls for setting picture characteristics are a little limited, but you can save the adjusted files in either the JPEG or TIFF format. See the next section for an explanation of TIFF.

- **Use Nikon Capture NX 2 or a third-party Raw conversion tool.** For the most control over your Raw images, you need to open your wallet and invest in a program that offers a truly capable converter. See the first part of this chapter for a review of Capture NX 2 as well as some other programs with good Raw converters.

The next two sections show you how to convert Raw files using your camera and ViewNX 2. If you opt for a third-party conversion tool, check the program's Help system for details on how to use the various controls, which vary from program to program.

Processing Raw images in the camera

Through the NEF (RAW) Processing option on the Retouch menu, you can convert Raw files right in the camera — no computer or other software required. I want to share two reservations about this option, however:

- First, you can save your processed files only in the JPEG format. As discussed in Chapter 2, that format results in some quality loss because of the file compression that JPEG applies. You can choose the level of JPEG compression you want to apply during Raw processing; you can create a JPEG Fine, Normal, or Basic file. Each of those settings produces the same quality that you get when you shoot new photos in the JPEG format and select Fine, Normal, or Basic from the Image Quality menu.

  Chapter 2 details the JPEG options, but, long story short, choose Fine for the best JPEG quality. And if you want to produce the absolute best quality from your Raw images, use a software solution and save your processed file in the TIFF format instead. TIFF is a *lossless* format, which means that all original image quality is retained. TIFF is the publishing industry standard format, so almost every photo program can open TIFF files.

- You can make adjustments to exposure, color, and a few other options as part of the in-camera Raw conversion process. Evaluating the effects of your adjustments on the camera monitor can be difficult because of the size of the display compared to your computer monitor. So for really tricky images, you may want to forgo in-camera conversion and do the job on your computer, where you can get a better — and bigger — view of things. If you do go the in-camera route, make sure that the monitor brightness is set to its default position so that you aren't misled by the display. (Chapter 1 shows you how to adjust monitor brightness.)

That said, in-camera Raw processing offers a quick and convenient solution when you need JPEG copies of your Raw images for immediate online sharing — JPEG is the standard format for online use — or to share with someone who doesn't have photo software that can handle Raw images. Follow these steps to get the job done:

1. **Press the Playback button to switch to playback mode.**

2. **Display the picture you want to process in the single-image (full-frame) view.**

   If necessary, you can shift from thumbnails view to single-image view by just pressing OK. Chapter 5 has more playback details.

3. **Press OK.**

   The Retouch menu then appears atop your photo, as shown in Figure 6-9.

4. **Use the Multi Selector to scroll to the NEF (RAW) Processing option, as shown in Figure 6-9.**

5. **Press OK to display your processing options, as shown in Figure 6-10.**

   This screen is command central for specifying what settings you want the camera to use when creating the JPEG version of your Raw image.

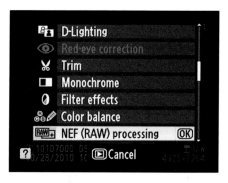

Figure 6-9: In single-image playback mode, press OK to display the Retouch menu over your photo.

6. **Set the conversion options.**

   Along the right side of the screen, you see a vertical column offering the conversion options labeled in Figure 6-10. To establish the setting for an option, highlight it and then press the Multi Selector right. You then see the available settings for the option. For example, if you choose the Image Quality option, you see the screen shown in Figure 6-11. Highlight the setting you want to use and press OK to return to the main Raw conversion screen.

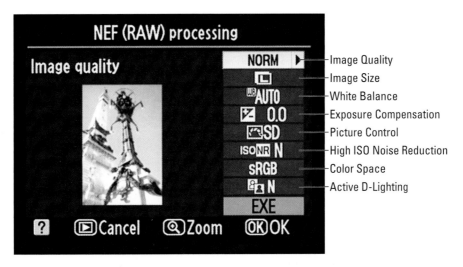

Figure 6-10: Specify Raw conversion settings here.

Rather than detailing all the options here, the following list points you to the chapter where you can explore the settings available for each:

- *Image Quality:* See the Chapter 2 section related to the JPEG quality settings for details on this option. Choose Fine to retain maximum picture quality.

- *Image Size:* Chapter 2 explains this one, too. Choose Large to retain all the original image pixels.

- *White Balance:* Check out Chapter 8 for details about White Balance options, which affect picture colors.

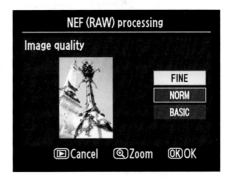

Figure 6-11: This option determines the JPEG quality level of the processed image.

- *Exposure Compensation:* With this option, you can adjust image brightness by applying Exposure Compensation, a feature that I cover in Chapter 7.

- *Picture Control:* This option enables you to adjust color, contrast, and image sharpness. For a review of the available settings, see the last part of Chapter 8.

- *High ISO Noise Reduction:* See Chapter 7 for an explanation of this feature, which is designed to reduce the amount of noise in pictures shot using a high ISO Sensitivity setting.

• *Color Space:* You can choose from two settings, sRGB and Adobe RGB; Chapter 8 explains the difference. (The default color space is sRGB.)

• *Active D-Lighting:* This feature helps brighten too-dark areas of a picture without blowing out highlights at the same time. You can specify the level of correction to apply (High, Normal, Low, or none). Chapter 7 offers more advice regarding Active D-Lighting.

7. **When you finish setting all the conversion options, highlight EXE on the main conversion screen (refer to Figure 6-10) and then press OK.**

The camera records a JPEG copy of your Raw file and displays the copy in the monitor. To remind you that the image was created with the help of the Retouch menu, the top-left corner of the display sports the little Retouch icon, as shown in Figure 6-12.

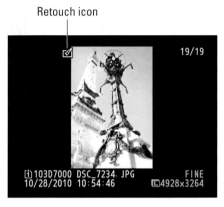

Retouch icon

Figure 6-12: The Retouch icon indicates that you created the picture file by using an option on the Retouch menu.

Processing Raw files in ViewNX 2

In ViewNX 2, you can convert your Raw files to the JPEG format or, for top picture quality, to the TIFF format. Although the ViewNX 2 converter isn't as full-featured as the ones in Nikon Capture NX 2 and some other photo-editing programs, it does enable you to make some adjustments to your Raw images. Follow these steps to try it out.

1. **Open ViewNX 2 and click the thumbnail of the image that you want to process.**

You may want to set the program to Image Viewer mode, as shown in Figure 6-13, so that you can see a larger preview of your image. Just choose View⊏>Image Viewer to switch to this display mode. To give the photo even more room, also choose Window⊏>Filmstrip to turn off the row of thumbnails that normally appears at the bottom of the window.

2. **Display the Adjustments panel on the right side of the program window.**

I labeled the panel in Figure 6-13. You show and hide this panel and the Metadata panel by clicking the triangle on the far right side of the window. You can then display and collapse the individual panels by clicking the triangles to the left of their names. (I labeled the triangles in the figure.) To allow the maximum space for the Raw conversion adjustments, collapse the Metadata panel, as shown in the figure. If necessary, drag the vertical bar between the image window and the Adjustments panel to adjust the width of the panel.

3. **To display all available image settings, choose All from the Adjustments drop-down list at the top of the panel, as shown in the figure.**

   Unless you use a large monitor, you may need to use the scroll bar on the right side of the panel to scroll the display to see all the options.

4. **Use the panel controls to adjust your image.**

   The preview you see in the image window reflects the default conversion settings chosen by Nikon. But you can play with any of the settings as you see fit. If you need help understanding any of the options, open the built-in help system (via the Help menu), where you can find descriptions of how each adjustment affects your image.

Click to hide/display Adjustments panel

Reset button   Save button

Figure 6-13: Display the Adjustments panel to tweak Raw images before conversion.

To return to the original image settings, click the Reset button at the bottom of the panel, labeled in Figure 6-13.

5. Click the Save button at the bottom of the panel (refer to Figure 6-13).

This step stores your conversion settings as part of the image file but doesn't actually create your JPEG or TIFF copy of the photo.

6. To save the processed file, choose File⇨Convert Files.

Or just click the Convert Files button on the toolbar at the top of the program window. Either way, you see the Convert Files dialog box, as shown in Figure 6-14.

Figure 6-14: To retain the best image quality, save processed Raw files in the TIFF format.

7. Select TIFF(8 Bit) from the File Format drop-down list.

A *bit* is a unit of computer data; the more bits you have, the more colors your image can contain. Although you can create 16-bit TIFF files in the converter, many photo-editing programs either can't open them or limit you to a few editing tools, so I suggest you stick with the standard, 8-bit image option. Your image will contain more than enough colors, and you'll avoid potential conflicts caused by so-called *high-bit* images.

Don't select JPEG; the JPEG format applies *lossy compression,* thereby sacrificing some image quality. If you need a JPEG copy of your processed Raw image for online sharing, you can easily create one from your TIFF version by following the steps laid out near the end of this chapter.

8. **Deselect the Use LZW Compression option, as shown in the figure.**

   Although LZW compression reduces the file size somewhat and does not cause any quality loss, some programs can't open files that were saved with this option enabled. So turn it off.

9. **Deselect the Change the Image Size check box.**

   This step ensures that you retain all the original pixels in your image, which gives you the most flexibility in terms of generating quality prints at large sizes. For details on this issue, check out Chapter 2.

10. **Deselect each of the three Remove check boxes.**

    If you select the check boxes, you strip image *metadata* — the extra text data that's stored by the camera — from the file. Unless you have some specific reason to do so, clear all three check boxes so that you can continue to access the metadata when you view your processed image in programs that know how to display metadata.

    The first check box relates to data that you can view on the Metadata tab in ViewNX; the first section of the chapter gives you the lowdown. The second box refers to the XMP/IPTC data that you can embed during file transfer; see the section "Downloading photos with Nikon ViewNX 2" for a discussion of that issue. The ICC profile item refers to the image *color space,* which is either sRGB or Adobe RGB on your D7000. Chapter 8 explains the difference.

11. **Select a storage location for the processed TIFF file.**

    You do this in the Save In area of the dialog box. Select the top option to save your processed file in the same folder as the original Raw file. Or, to put the file in a different folder, click the Specified Folder button. The name of the currently selected alternative folder appears below the button, as shown in Figure 6-14. You can change the storage destination by clicking the Browse button and then selecting the drive and folder where you want to put the file.

     By selecting the Create a New Subfolder for Each File Conversion check box, you can put your TIFF file into a separate folder within the destination folder. If you select the box, click the Naming Options button and then specify how you want to name the subfolder.

12. **Specify whether you want to give the processed TIFF a different file-name from the original Raw image.**

    To do so, select the Change File Names check box, click the Naming Options button, and enter the name you want to use.

If you don't change the filename, the program gives the file the same name as the original Raw file. But you don't overwrite that Raw file because you're storing the copy in a different file format (TIFF). In Windows, the filename of the processed TIFF image has the three-letter extension TIF.

13. **Click the Convert button.**

A window appears to show you the progress of the conversion process. When the window disappears, your TIFF image appears in the storage location you selected in Step 11.

One neat thing about working with Raw images is that you can easily create as many variations of your photo as you want. For example, you might choose one set of options when processing your Raw file the first time and then use an entirely different set to create another version of the photo.

Planning for Perfect Prints

Images from your D7000 can produce dynamic prints, and getting those prints made is easy and economical, thanks to an abundance of digital printing services in stores and online. For home printing, today's printers are better and less expensive than ever, too. That said, getting the best prints from your picture files requires a little bit of knowledge and prep work on your part, whether you decide to do the job yourself or use a retail lab. To that end, the next three sections offer tips to help you avoid the most common causes of printing problems.

Check the pixel count before you print

Resolution — the number of pixels in your digital image — plays a huge role in how large you can print your photos and still maintain good picture quality. You can get the complete story on resolution in Chapter 2, but here's a quick recap as it relates to printing:

- **Choose the right resolution before you shoot:** Set resolution via the Image Size option, found on the Shooting menu, or by pressing the Qual button while rotating the Sub-command dial.

    You must select the size *before* you capture an image, which means that you need some idea of the ultimate print size before you shoot. When you do the resolution math, remember to take any cropping you plan to do into account.

- **Aim for a minimum of 200 pixels per inch (ppi):** You'll get a wide range of recommendations on this issue, even among professionals. But in general, if you aim for a resolution in the neighborhood of 200 ppi, you should be pleased with your results. If you want a 4-x-6-inch print, for example, you need at least 800 x 1200 pixels.

Depending on your printer, you may get even better results at a slightly lower resolution. On the other hand, some printers do their best work when fed 300 ppi, and a few request 360 ppi as the optimum resolution. However, using a resolution higher than that typically doesn't produce any better prints.

Unfortunately, because most printer manuals don't bother to tell you what image resolution produces the best results, finding the right pixel level is a matter of experimentation. (Don't confuse *ppi* with the manual's statements related to the printer's dpi. *Dots per inch (dpi)* refers to the number of dots of color the printer can lay down per inch; many printers use multiple dots to reproduce one image pixel.)

If you're printing photos at a retail kiosk or at an online site, the software you use to order prints should determine the resolution of your files and then suggest appropriate print sizes. If you're printing on a home printer, though, you need to be the resolution cop.

What do you do if you don't have enough pixels for the print size you have in mind? You have the following two choices, neither of which provides a good outcome:

- ✒ **Keep the existing pixel count and accept lowered photo quality.** In this case, the pixels simply get bigger to fill the requested print size. When pixels grow too large, they produce a defect known as *pixelation:* The picture starts to appear jagged, or stairstepped, along curved or oblique lines. Or, at worst, your eye can make out the individual pixels, and your photo begins to look more like a mosaic than, well, like a photograph.

- ✒ **Add more pixels and accept lowered photo quality.** In some photo programs, you can add pixels to an image (the technical term for this process is *upsampling*). Some other photo programs even upsample the photo automatically for you, depending on the print settings you choose.

Although adding pixels might sound like a good option, it actually doesn't help in the long run. You're asking the software to make up photo information out of thin air, and the resulting image usually looks worse than the original. You don't see pixelation, but details turn muddy, giving the image a blurry, poorly rendered appearance.

Just to hammer home the point and remind you again of the impact of resolution picture quality, Figures 6-15 through 6-17 show you the same image as it appears at 300 ppi (the resolution required by the publisher of this book), at 50 ppi, and then resampled from 50 ppi to 300 ppi. As you can see, there's just no way around the rule: If you want the best-quality prints, you need the right pixel count from the get-go.

300 ppi

Figure 6-15: A high-quality print depends on a high-resolution original.

50 ppi

Figure 6-16: At 50 ppi, the image has a jagged, pixelated look.

50 ppi resampled to 300 ppi

Figure 6-17: Adding pixels in a photo editor doesn't rescue a low-resolution original.

Allow for different print proportions

The D7000 produces images that have a 3:2 aspect ratio, which matches the proportions of a 4-x-6-inch print. To print your photo at other traditional sizes — 5 x 7, 8 x 10, and so on — you need to crop the photo to match those proportions. Alternatively, you can reduce the photo size slightly and leave an empty margin along the edges of the print as needed.

As a point of reference, both images in Figure 6-18 are original, 3:2 images. The red outlines indicate how much of the original can fit within a 5-x-7-inch frame and an 8-x-10-inch frame, respectively.

Chapter 10 shows you how to crop your image using the Trim option on the Retouch menu. You also can usually crop your photo using the software provided at online printing sites and at retail print kiosks. If you plan to simply drop off your memory card for printing at a lab, be sure to find out whether the printer automatically crops the image without your input. If so, use your photo software to crop the photo, save the cropped image to your memory card, and deliver that version of the file to the printer.

5 x 7   8 x 10

Figure 6-18: Composing your shots with a little head room enables you to crop to different frame sizes.

To allow yourself some printing flexibility, leave at least a little margin of background around your subject when you shoot (refer to Figure 6-18). That way, you don't clip off the edges of the subject, no matter what print size you choose. (Some people refer to this margin padding as *head room,* especially when describing portrait composition.)

Get print and monitor colors in sync

Ah, your photo colors look perfect on your computer monitor. But when you print the picture, the image is too red or too green or has another nasty color tint. This problem, which is probably the most prevalent printing issue, can occur because of any or all the following factors:

- **Your monitor needs to be calibrated.** When print colors don't match the ones you see on your monitor, the most likely culprit is the monitor, not the printer. If the monitor isn't accurately calibrated, the colors it displays aren't a true reflection of your image colors. The same caveat applies to monitor brightness: You can't accurately gauge the exposure of a photo if the brightness of the monitor is cranked way up or down.

It's worth noting that many of today's new monitors are very bright, providing ideal conditions for Web browsing and watching movies but not necessarily for photo editing. So you may need to turn the brightness way, way down to get to a true indication of image exposure.

To ensure that your monitor displays photos on a neutral canvas, you can start with a software-based *calibration utility,* which is just a small program that guides you through the process of adjusting your monitor. The program displays various color swatches and other graphics, and then asks you to provide feedback about the colors you see onscreen.

If you use a Mac, its operating system (OS) offers a built-in calibration utility, the Display Calibrator Assistant; Windows 7 offers a similar tool: Display Color Calibration. You also can find free calibration software for both Mac and Windows systems online; just enter the term *free monitor calibration software* into your favorite search engine.

Software-based tools, though, depend on your eyes to make decisions during the calibration process. For a more reliable calibration, you may want to invest in a hardware solution, such as the Huey Pro (about $100, www.pantone.com) or the Spyder3Express (about $90, www.datacolor.com). These products use a device known as a *colorimeter* to accurately measure display colors.

Whichever route you take, the calibration process produces a monitor *profile,* which is simply a data file that tells your computer how to adjust the display to compensate for any monitor color casts or brightness and contrast issues. Your Windows or Mac operating system loads this file automatically when you start your computer. Your only responsibility is to perform the calibration every month or so because monitor colors drift over time.

- **One of your printer cartridges is empty or clogged.** If your prints look great one day but are way off the next, the number-one suspect is an empty ink cartridge or a clogged print nozzle or head. Check your manual to find out how to perform the necessary maintenance to keep the nozzles or print heads in good shape.

  If black-and-white prints have a color tint, a logical assumption is that your black ink cartridge is to blame, if your printer has one. But the truth is that images from a printer that doesn't use multiple black or gray cartridges always have a slight color tint. Why? Because to create gray, the printer instead has to mix yellow, magenta, and cyan in perfectly equal amounts, and that's a difficult feat for the typical inkjet printer to pull off. If your black-and-white prints have a strong color tint, however, a color cartridge might be empty, and replacing it may help somewhat. Long story short: Unless your printer is marketed for producing good black-and-white prints, you'll probably save yourself some grief by simply having your black-and-whites printed at a retail lab.

When you buy replacement ink, by the way, keep in mind that third-party brands (though perhaps cheaper) may not deliver the same performance as cartridges from your printer manufacturer. A lot of science goes into getting ink formulas to mesh with the printer's ink-delivery system, and the printer manufacturer obviously knows most about that delivery system.

✓ **You chose the wrong paper setting in your printer software.** When you set up a print job, be sure to select the right setting from the paper type option — glossy or matte, for example. This setting affects the way the printer lays down ink on the paper.

✓ **Your photo paper is low quality.** Sad but true: Cheap, store-brand photo papers usually don't render colors as well as the higher-priced, name-brand papers. For best results, try papers from your printer manufacturer; again, those papers are engineered to provide top performance with the printer's specific inks and ink-delivery system.

Some paper manufacturers, especially those that sell fine-art papers, offer downloadable *printer profiles,* which are simply little bits of software that tell your printer how to manage color for the paper. Refer to the manufacturer's Web site for information on how to install and use the profiles. And note that a profile mismatch can also cause incorrect colors in your prints, including the color tint in black-and-white prints alluded to earlier.

✓ **Your printer and photo software fight over color management duties.** Some photo programs offer *color management* tools, which enable you to control how colors are handled as an image passes from camera to monitor to printer. Most printer software also offers color management features. The problem is, if you enable color management controls in both your photo software and printer software, you can create conflicts that lead to wacky colors. Check your photo software and printer manuals for color management options and ways to turn them on and off.

Even if all the aforementioned issues are resolved, however, don't expect perfect color matching between printer and monitor. Printers simply can't reproduce the entire spectrum of colors that a monitor can display. In addition, monitor colors always appear brighter because they are, after all, generated with light.

Finally, be sure to evaluate print colors and monitor colors in the same ambient light — daylight, office light, whatever — because that light source has its own influence on the colors you see. Also allow your prints to dry for 15 minutes or so before you make any final judgments.

DPOF, PictBridge, and computerless printing

The D7000 offers two features that enable you to print directly from your camera or a memory card assuming that your printer offers the required options.

One of the direct-printing features is *Digital Print Order Format,* or *DPOF.* With this option, accessed via the Print Set (DPOF) option on the Playback menu, you select pictures from your memory card to print and then specify how many copies you want of each image. Then, if your photo printer has a Secure Digital (SD) memory card slot (or SDHC/SDXC slots, if you use these new, high-capacity cards) and supports DPOF, you just pop the memory card into that slot. The printer reads your "print order" and outputs just the requested copies of your selected images. (You use the printer's own controls to set paper size, print orientation, and other print settings.)

A second direct-printing feature, *PictBridge,* works a little differently. If you have a PictBridge-enabled photo printer, you can connect the camera to the printer by using a USB cable. (You use the same cable as for picture downloads.) A PictBridge interface appears on the camera monitor, and you use the camera controls to select the pictures you want to print. With PictBridge, you specify additional print options from the camera, such as page size and whether to print a border around the photo.

Both DPOF and PictBridge are especially useful when you need fast printing. For example, if you shoot pictures at a party and want to deliver prints to guests before they go home, DPOF offers a quicker option than firing up your computer, downloading pictures, and so on. And, if you invest in one of the tiny portable photo printers on the market today, you can easily make prints away from your home or office. You can take both your portable printer and camera along to your regional sales meeting, for example.

If you're interested in exploring either printing feature, your camera manual provides complete details.

Preparing Pictures for E-Mail and Online Sharing

How many times have you received an e-mail message that looks like the one in Figure 6-19? Some well-meaning friend or relative sent you a digital photo that's so large you can't view the whole thing on your monitor.

The problem is that computer monitors can display only a limited number of pixels. The exact number depends on the monitor's resolution setting and the capabilities of the computer's video card, but suffice it to say that the average photo from one of today's digital cameras has a pixel count in excess of what the monitor can handle.

In general, a good rule is to limit a photo to no more than 640 pixels at its longest dimension. That ensures that people can view your entire picture without scrolling, as in Figure 6-20. This image measures 640 x 428 pixels.

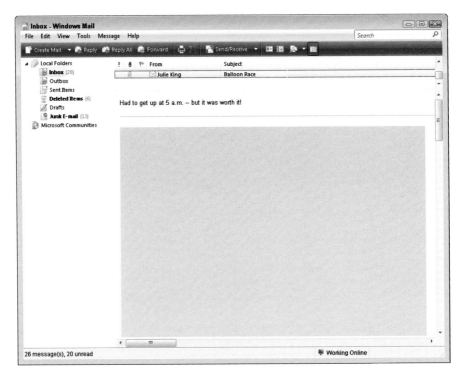

Figure 6-19: The attached image has too many pixels to be viewed without scrolling.

This size recommendation means that even if you shoot at your D7000's lowest Image Size setting (2464 x 1632), you wind up with lots more pixels than you need for onscreen viewing. Some new e-mail programs have a photo-upload feature that creates a temporary low-res version for you, but if not, creating your own copy is easy. (Details later.) If you're posting to an online photo-sharing site, you may be able to upload all your original pixels, but many sites have resolution limits.

In addition to resizing high-resolution images, check their file types; if the photos are in the Raw (NEF) or TIFF format, you need to create a JPEG copy for online use. Web browsers and e-mail programs can't display Raw or TIFF files.

You can tackle both bits of photo prep in the following ways:

✓ **Use ViewNX 2:** Just choose the Convert Files command, found on the File menu. When the Convert Files dialog box appears, set up things as follows:

• *Select JPEG as the file format.* Make your choice from the File Format drop-down list, as shown in Figure 6-21.

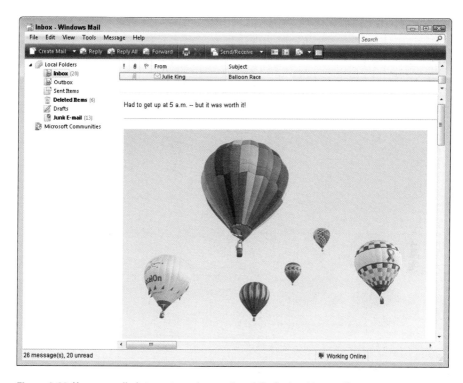

Figure 6-20: Keep e-mail pictures to no larger than 640 pixels wide or tall.

- *Set the picture quality level.* Use the Quality slider, labeled in the figure, to set the picture quality, which is controlled by how much JPEG compression is applied when the file is saved. For best quality, drag the slider all the way to the right, but remember the tradeoff: As you raise the quality, less compression occurs, which results in a larger file size. (See Chapter 2 for more information about JPEG compression.)

- *Set the image size (number of pixels):* To resize the photo, select the Change the Image Size check box and then enter a value (in pixels) for the longest dimension of the photo. The program automatically fills in the other value.

For pictures that you want to share online, also select all three of the Remove check boxes, as shown in the figure, to eliminate adding to file sizes unnecessarily.

The rest of the options work just as they do during Raw conversion; see the "Processing Raw files in ViewNX 2," earlier in this chapter, for details.

✓ **Use the in-camera tools:** Use the Resize option on the Retouch menu to create a small JPEG copy of either a JPEG or Raw original, as outlined in the next two sections.

Quality slider

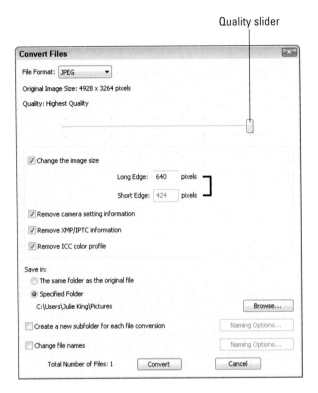

Figure 6-21: In ViewNX 2, select the Convert Files option to create a JPEG version of a Raw or TIFF photo.

One last point about onscreen images: Remember that pixel count has *absolutely no effect* on the quality of pictures displayed onscreen. Pixel count determines only the size at which your images are displayed.

Resizing a single photo

The in-camera resizing tool works on both JPEG and Raw images. If you apply it directly to a Raw image, though, you lose the chance to adjust the resized image through the camera's Raw conversion tool. So you may prefer to do the conversion first, which creates a JPEG copy at the original size, and then create a small copy of that JPEG image.

Either way, to create a small copy of just one image, take these steps:

1. **Press the Playback button to set your camera to playback mode.**

2. **Display the picture in single-image view.**

   If the monitor currently displays multiple thumbnails, just press OK to switch to single-image view.

3. **Press OK to display the Retouch menu over your image, as shown on the left in Figure 6-22.**

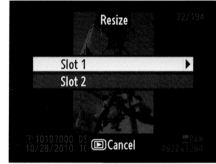

Figure 6-22: The Resize feature creates a low-resolution, e-mail–friendly copy of a photo.

4. **Highlight Resize and press OK or press the Multi Selector right.**

   You see the screen shown on the right in the figure.

5. **If two memory cards are installed, highlight the card where you want to store the small copy.**

6. **Press the Multi Selector right.**

   The screen shown in Figure 6-23 appears, offering the list of size options (stated in pixels) available for your small copy.

7. **Highlight the size you want to use for your copy.**

8. **Press OK or press the Multi Selector right.**

   A screen appears, asking you to confirm that you want to create a small copy.

Figure 6-23: The size values are stated in pixels.

9. **Highlight Yes and press OK.**

   The camera duplicates the selected image and *downsamples* (eliminates pixels from) the copy to achieve the size you specified in Step 7. Your original picture file remains untouched.

When you view your small-size copies on the camera monitor, they appear with a Retouch icon at the top of the screen and a Resize icon at the bottom, as shown in Figure 6-24. You can't zoom in to magnify the view of copies creating using the two smallest sizes. (See Chapter 5 for details on magnifying images during playback.)

Retouch icon   Resize icon

Resizing a batch of images

If you want to create small copies of several photos on your memory card, you can save time by using the following alternative in-camera resizing process. (As with the steps outlined in the preceding section, these steps work with both JPEG and Raw files.)

Figure 6-24: The Resize icon indicates a small-size copy.

1. **Press the Menu button and then display the Retouch menu.**

2. **Select the Resize option, as shown on the left in Figure 6-25, and press OK.**

Figure 6-25: Start directly from the Retouch menu to resize a bunch of pictures at the same time.

You see the screen shown on the right in Figure 6-25.

3. **If two memory cards are installed, select Choose Destination and then select which card you want to use to store the resized images.**

4. **Select Choose Size to choose the size for the small copies.**

5. **Choose Select Image and press OK to display thumbnails of all your pictures, as shown in Figure 6-26.**

6. **Move the yellow highlight box over a thumbnail and press the ISO button to "tag" the photo for copying.**

   You see a little icon in the top-right corner of the thumbnail, as shown in Figure 6-26. Press the button again to remove the tag if you change your mind.

7. **After selecting all your pictures, press OK to display the copy-confirmation screen.**

8. **Highlight Yes and press OK once more to wrap things up.**

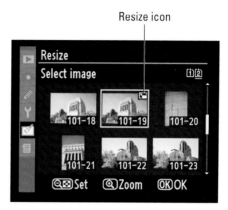

Figure 6-26: Press the ISO button to tag a picture for resizing.

Copying Pictures between Cards

When you have two memory cards installed in the camera, you can use the Copy Image(s) option on the Playback menu to copy one or more pictures from the card in one slot to the card in the other slot. You might use this feature to create safety backups of your best photos, for example, instead of using the Backup setting for the card in Slot 2, which creates duplicates of every image you take. (Chapter 1 explains the Backup option and other choices for configuring your cards.)

To copy images from card to card, follow these steps:

1. **On the Playback menu, choose Copy Image(s), as shown on the left in Figure 6-27, and press OK.**

Figure 6-27: You can copy cards from one installed memory card to another.

You see the right screen in the figure.

2. **Highlight Select Source and press OK.**

   You see a screen listing both memory cards (Slot 1 and Slot 2).

3. **Highlight the memory card that contains the pictures you want to copy and press OK.**

   You return to the main Copy Image(s) screen.

4. **Highlight Select Image(s), as shown on the right in Figure 6-28, and press OK.**

   You then see a screen listing all folders on the selected card, as shown on the right in Figure 6-28. If you haven't created any custom folders, a topic covered in Chapter 11, you see just one folder.

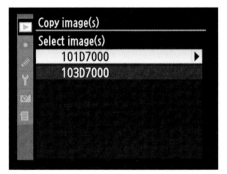

Figure 6-28: Select the folder that contains the pictures you want to copy.

5. **Highlight the folder that contains your pictures and press OK.**

   The camera displays the screen shown on the left in Figure 6-29.

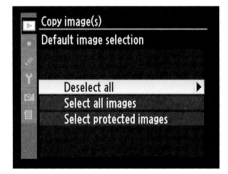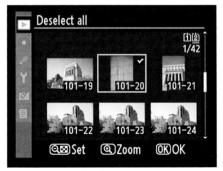

Figure 6-29: Press the ISO button to add or remove the check mark that tags a picture for copying.

6. **Choose an initial picture-selection option.**

   Two of the options are pretty clear-cut: Choose Select All Images if you want to copy every picture on the card; choose Select Protected Images to copy just photos that you tagged with the Protect feature, covered in Chapter 5.

   The third option, Deselect All, is a little counterintuitive. Here's the deal: The camera initially assumes that you want to copy every picture on the card, so it tries to help by automatically preselecting all them. You can later deselect the ones you don't want to copy, but if you're copying just a few pictures out of a large group, it's faster to choose Deselect All so that you start out with no pictures selected. Then you don't have to waste time "untagging" all the ones you don't want to copy.

7. **Press OK to display thumbnails of your photos, as shown on the right in Figure 6-29.**

   Checkmarks appear with any photos currently selected for copying. In the figure, the top center photo is selected.

8. **Press the ISO button to add or remove a photo from the selection.**

   Pressing the button toggles the checkmark on and off.

9. **After selecting the photos you want to copy, press OK.**

   You're returned to the main Copy Image(s) screen once more.

10. **Choose Select Destination Folder and press OK.**

    You see a screen offering two options: The first, Select Folder by Number, enables you to specify a three-digit folder number. (Press the Multi Selector left or right to highlight a value, and press up or down to change the number.) The second option, Select Folder from List, displays all available folders. After choosing a folder number or folder, press OK.

11. **Choose Copy Image(s)? and press OK.**

12. **Highlight Yes and press OK to copy the photos.**

A couple fine points:

- ✔ If the destination card doesn't have enough space for all the selected images, the camera alerts you that all images may not be copied. You can choose to go forward or cancel the operation and install a card that has more free space.

- ✔ If the destination card contains an image that has the same filename as one you select for copying, the camera gives you the option to overwrite the existing file, skip copying that file, or cancel out of the copy operation altogether.

- ✔ When you copy a protected picture, both the copy and the original remain protected. See Chapter 5 for details about protecting images.

Safeguarding your digital photo files

To make sure that your digital photos enjoy a long, healthy life, follow these storage guidelines:

- Don't rely on your computer's hard drive for long-term, archival storage. Hard drives occasionally fail, wiping out all files in the process. This warning applies to both internal and external hard drives. At the very least, having a dual-drive backup is in order — you might keep one copy of your photos on your computer's internal drive and another on an external drive. If one breaks, you still have all your goodies on the other one.

- Camera memory cards, flash memory keys, and other portable storage devices, such as one of those wallet-sized media players, are similarly risky. All are easily damaged if dropped or otherwise mishandled. And being of diminutive stature, these portable storage options also are easily lost.

- The best way to store important files is to copy them to nonrewritable CDs. (The label should say CD-R, not CD-RW.) Look for quality, brand-name CDs that have a gold coating, which offer a higher level of security than other coatings and boast a longer life than your garden-variety CDs.

- Recordable DVDs offer the advantage of holding lots more data than a CD. However, be aware that the DVDs you create on one computer may not be playable on another because multiple recording formats and disc types exist: DVD minus, DVD plus, dual-layer DVD, and so on. If you do opt for DVD, look for the archival, gold-coated variety, just as for CDs.

- For a double backup, you may want to check into online storage services, such as Mozy (www.mozy.com) and IDrive (www.idrive.com). You pay a monthly subscription fee to back up your important files to the site's servers.

Note, though, the critical phrase here: *double backup*. Online storage sites have a troubling history of closing down suddenly, taking all their customers' data with them. (One extremely alarming case was the closure of a photography-oriented storage site called Digital Railroad, which gave clients a mere 24-hours' notice before destroying their files.) So anything you store online should be also stored on DVD or CD and kept in your home or office. Also note that photo-sharing sites such as Shutterfly, Kodak Gallery, and the like *aren't* designed to be long-term storage tanks for your images. Usually, you get access to only a small amount of file storage space, and the site may require you to purchase prints or other photo products periodically to maintain your account.

Part III
Taking Creative Control

In this part . . .

As nice as it is to be able to set your D7000 to automatic mode and let the camera handle most of the photographic decisions, I encourage you to take creative control and explore the advanced exposure modes (P, S, A, and M). In these modes, you can make your own decisions about the exposure, focus, and color characteristics of your photo, which are key to capturing a compelling image as you see it in your mind's eye. And don't think that you have to be a genius or spend years to be successful — adding just a few simple techniques to your photographic repertoire can make a huge difference in the quality of the pictures you take.

The first two chapters in this part explain everything you need to know to do just that, providing both some necessary photography fundamentals as well as details about using the advanced exposure modes. Following that, Chapter 9 helps you draw together all the information presented earlier in the book, summarizing the best camera settings and other tactics to use when capturing portraits, action shots, landscapes, and close-up shots. In short, this part helps you get the most out of your camera, which results in you becoming a better photographer.

7

Getting Creative with Exposure and Lighting

Mastering the art of exposure is one of the most challenging aspects of photography. First, you have to grapple with a seemingly endless list of technical terms — *aperture, metering, shutter speed, ISO, stop,* and so on. Add to that the equally large number of exposure-related options on your D7000, and, well . . . suffice it to say that if you're feeling a little intimidated, you're in good company. I know, I've been there.

From years of working with beginning photographers, though, I can promise that when you take things nice and slow, digesting a piece of the exposure pie at a time, the topic is not nearly as complicated as it seems. And I guarantee that the payoff will be well worth your time and brain energy. You'll not only learn how to solve just about any exposure problem, but you'll also discover ways to use exposure to put your creative stamp on a scene.

To that end, this chapter provides everything you need to know to exploit all your camera's exposure options, including a primer in exposure science. (It's not as bad as it sounds.) Explore a paragraph or two one day, a few more the next, and before long, you'll have it all down pat.

Introducing the Exposure Trio: Aperture, Shutter Speed, and ISO

Any photograph, whether taken with a film or digital camera, is created by focusing light through a lens onto a light-sensitive recording medium. In a film camera, the film negative serves as that medium; in a digital camera, it's the image sensor, which is an array of light-responsive computer chips.

Between the lens and the sensor are two barriers, known as the *aperture* and *shutter,* which together control how much light makes its way to the sensor. The actual design and arrangement of the aperture, shutter, and sensor vary depending on the camera, but Figure 7-1 offers an illustration of the basic concept.

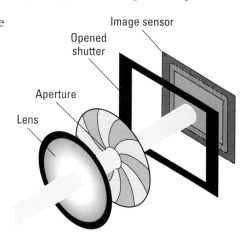

The aperture and shutter, along with a third feature known as *ISO,* determine *exposure* — what most would describe as the picture's overall brightness and contrast. This three-part exposure formula works as follows:

Figure 7-1: The aperture size and shutter speed determine how much light strikes the image sensor.

✏ **Aperture (controls amount of light):** The *aperture* is an adjustable hole in a diaphragm set just behind the lens. By changing the size of the aperture, you control the size of the light beam that can enter the camera. Aperture settings are stated as *f-stop numbers,* or simply *f-stops,* and are expressed with the letter *f* followed by a number: f/2, f/5.6, f/16, and so on. The lower the f-stop number, the larger the aperture, and the more light is permitted into the camera, as illustrated by Figure 7-2. (If it seems backward to use a higher number for a smaller aperture, think of it this way: A higher value creates a bigger light barrier than a lower value.)

The range of possible f-stops varies from lens to lens, so check your lens manual to see what aperture choices are available to you. With many zoom lenses, the range of f-stops depends on the current focal length of the lens. You typically can open the aperture to a wider setting when you zoom out to a short focal length than when you zoom to the maximum focal length. (See Chapter 8 for a discussion of focal lengths.)

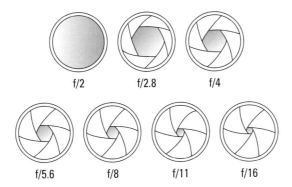

f/2   f/2.8   f/4

f/5.6   f/8   f/11   f/16

Figure 7-2: A lower f-stop number means a larger aperture, allowing more light into the camera.

- **Shutter speed (controls duration of light):** Set behind the aperture, the shutter works something like, er, the shutters on a window. When you aren't taking pictures, the camera's shutter stays closed, preventing light from striking the image sensor, just as closed window shutters prevent sunlight from entering a room. When you press the shutter button, the shutter opens briefly to allow light that passes through the aperture to hit the image sensor.

  The length of time that the shutter is open is the *shutter speed* and is measured in seconds: 1/60 second, 1/250 second, 2 seconds, and so on. Shutter speeds on the D7000 range from 30 seconds to 1/8000 second when you shoot without flash. For flash photography with the built-in flash, the range is more limited; for some external flash units, you can still access the entire range of shutter speeds, although there are trade-offs to be made for the privilege. See the section "Enabling high-speed flash (Auto FP)," later in this chapter, for information.

  Should you want a shutter speed longer than 30 seconds, manual (M) exposure mode also provides a *bulb* exposure feature. At this setting, the shutter stays open indefinitely as long as you press the shutter button.

- **ISO (controls light sensitivity):** *ISO,* which is a digital function rather than a mechanical structure on the camera, enables you to adjust how responsive the image sensor is to light. The term ISO is a holdover from film days, when an international standards organization rated each film stock according to light sensitivity: ISO 200, ISO 400, ISO 800, and so on.

  On a digital camera, the sensor itself doesn't actually get more or less sensitive when you change the ISO — rather, the light "signal" that hits the sensor is either amplified or dampened through electronics wizardry, sort of like how raising the volume on a radio boosts the audio signal.

  But the upshot is the same as changing to a more light-reactive film stock: A higher ISO means that less light is needed to produce the image, enabling you to use a smaller aperture, faster shutter speed, or both. (In other words, from now on, don't worry about the technicalities and just remember that ISO equals light sensitivity.)

The normal ISO settings on the D7000 range from ISO 100 to 6400. But if you really need to push things, you can extend that range all the way to ISO 25600. (This uber-high setting goes by the name Hi 2.) High ISO settings have a downside that you can explore in the upcoming section "ISO affects image noise."

Distilled down to its essence, the image-exposure formula is just this simple:

✔ Aperture and shutter speed together determine how much light strikes the image sensor.

✔ ISO determines how much the sensor reacts to that light and thus how much light is needed to expose the picture.

The tricky part of the equation is that aperture, shutter speed, and ISO settings affect your pictures in ways that go *beyond* exposure. You need to be aware of these side effects, explained in the next section, to determine which combination of the three exposure settings will work best for your picture.

Understanding exposure-setting side effects

You can create the same exposure with many combinations of aperture, shutter speed, and ISO. You're limited only by the available light, the aperture range of the lens, and the shutter speeds and ISO settings offered by the camera. But the settings you select impact your image beyond mere exposure, as follows:

✔ Aperture affects *depth of field,* or the zone of sharp focus.

✔ Shutter speed determines whether moving objects appear blurry or sharply focused.

✔ ISO affects the amount of image *noise,* which is a defect that looks like tiny specks of sand.

As you can imagine, understanding how aperture, shutter speed, and ISO affect your image enables you to have much more creative control over your photographs — and, in the case of ISO, to also ensure the quality of your images. The next three sections explore these exposure side effects in detail.

Aperture affects depth of field

The aperture setting, or f-stop, affects *depth of field,* which is the range of sharp focus in your image. I introduce this concept in Chapter 3, but here's a quick recap: With a shallow depth of field, your subject appears more sharply focused than faraway objects; with a large depth of field, the sharp-focus zone spreads over a greater distance.

As you reduce the aperture size — or *stop down the aperture,* in photo lingo — by choosing a higher f-stop number, you increase depth of field. As an example, take a look at the two images in Figure 7-3. For both shots, I established focus on the female statue atop the fountain. Notice that the background in the first image, taken at an aperture setting of f/14, is softer than in the right example, taken at f/29. Aperture is just one contributor to depth of field, however; the focal length of your lens and the distance between that lens and your subject also affect how much of the scene stays in focus. See Chapter 8 for the complete story.

f/14, 1/80 second, ISO 100   f/29, 1/20 second, ISO 100

Figure 7-3: Stopping down the aperture (by choosing a higher f-stop number) increases depth of field.

One way to remember the relationship between f-stop and depth of field is to think of the *f* as standing for *focus.* A higher f-stop number produces a larger depth of field, so if you want to extend the zone of sharp focus to cover a greater distance from your subject, you set the aperture to a higher f-stop. The higher the *f*-stop number, the greater the zone of sharp *f*ocus. (Please *don't* share this tip with photography elites, who will roll their eyes and inform you that the *f* in *f-stop* most certainly does *not* stand for focus but for the ratio between the aperture size and lens focal length — as if *that's* helpful to know if you're not an optical engineer. Again, Chapter 8 explains focal length, which *is* helpful to know.)

Shutter speed affects motion blur

At a slow shutter speed, moving objects appear blurry, whereas a fast shutter speed captures motion cleanly. This phenomenon has nothing to do with the actual focus point of the camera but rather on the movement occurring — and being recorded by the camera — during the time that the shutter is open.

Compare the photos in Figure 7-3, for example. The static elements are perfectly focused in both images, although the background in the right photo appears slightly sharper because I shot that image using a higher f-stop, increasing the zone of sharp focus. But the way the camera rendered the moving portion of the scene — the fountain water — was determined by the shutter speed. At a shutter speed of 1/20 second (right photo), the water blurs, giving it a misty look. At 1/80 second (left photo), the droplets appear more sharply focused. How high a shutter speed you need to freeze action depends on the speed of your subject.

If your picture suffers from overall blur, where even stationary objects appear out of focus, the camera itself moved during the exposure, which is always a danger when you handhold the camera. The slower the shutter speed, the longer the exposure time and the longer you have to hold the camera still to avoid the blur that's caused by camera shake. For example, I was able to successfully handhold the 1/80 second exposure you see on the left in Figure 7-3, but at 1/20 second, there was enough camera movement to result in the blurry shot shown in Figure 7-4. I mounted the camera on the tripod to get the shake-free version shown on the right in Figure 7-3.

Figure 7-4: If both stationary and moving objects are blurry, camera shake is the usual cause.

Keep in mind that freezing action isn't the only way to use shutter speed to creative effect. When shooting waterfalls, for example, most photographers use a very slow shutter speed to give the water even more of a flowing, romantic look than you see in my fountain example. With colorful moving subjects, a slow shutter can produce some cool abstract effects and create a heightened sense of motion. Chapter 9 offers examples of both effects.

Handholding the camera: How low can you go?

My students often ask how slow they can set the shutter speed and still handhold the camera instead of using a tripod. Unfortunately, there's no one-size-fits-all answer to this question.

The slow-shutter safety limit varies depending on a couple factors, including your physical abilities and your lens — the heavier the lens, the harder it is to hold steady. For reasons that are too technical to get into, camera shake also affects your picture more when you shoot with a lens that has a long focal length. So you may be able to use a much slower shutter speed when you shoot with a lens that has a focal length of 55mm, for example, than if you switch to a 200mm telephoto lens. (Chapter 8 explains focal length, if the term is new to you.)

A standard photography rule is to use the inverse of the lens focal length as the minimum handheld shutter speed. For example, with a 50mm lens, use a shutter speed no slower than 1/50 second. But that rule was developed before the advent of today's modern lenses, which tend to be significantly lighter and smaller than older lenses, as do cameras themselves. I have a very light, super-zoom lens that I can handhold at speeds as low as 1/80 second even when I zoom to focal lengths way beyond 80mm, for example.

The best idea is to do your own tests to see where your handholding limit lies. Start with a slow shutter speed — say, in the 1/40 second neighborhood, and then click multiple shots, increasing the shutter speed for each picture. If you have a zoom lens, run the test first at the minimum focal length (widest angle) and then zoom to the maximum focal length for another series of shots. Then it's simply a matter of comparing the images in your photo-editing program. (You may not be able to accurately judge the amount of blur on the camera monitor.) See Chapter 6 to find out how to see the shutter speed you used for each picture when you view your images. That information, along with other camera settings, appears in the file *metadata*, which you can display in Nikon ViewNX 2 and many other programs.

Remember, too, that if your lens offers Vibration Reduction (as does the D7000 kit lens), turning on that feature can compensate for small amounts of camera shake, enabling you to capture sharp images at slightly slower shutter speeds than normal when handholding the camera. Again, your mileage may vary, but most people can expect to go at least two or three notches down the shutter-speed ramp. See Chapter 1 for more information about this feature.

ISO affects image noise

As ISO increases, making the image sensor more reactive to light, you increase the risk of producing noise. *Noise* is a defect that looks like sprinkles of sand and is similar in appearance to film *grain,* a defect that often mars pictures taken with high ISO film. Figure 7-5 offers an example.

Ideally, then, you should always use the lowest ISO setting on your camera to ensure top image quality. But sometimes, the lighting conditions simply don't permit you to do so and still use the aperture and shutter speeds you need. Take my rose image as an example. When I shot these pictures, I didn't have a tripod, so I needed a shutter speed fast enough to allow a sharp handheld image. I opened the aperture to f/6.3, which was the maximum on the lens I was using, to allow as much light as possible into the camera. At ISO 100, I needed a shutter speed of 1/40 second to expose the picture, and that shutter speed wasn't fast enough for a successful handheld shot. By raising the ISO to 200, I was able to use a shutter speed of 1/80 second, which enabled me to capture the flower cleanly, as shown in Figure 7-6.

Fortunately, you don't encounter serious noise on the D7000 until you really crank up the ISO. In fact, you may even be able to get away with a fairly high ISO if you keep your print or display size small. Some people probably wouldn't even notice the noise in the left image in Figure 7-5 unless they were looking for it, for example. But as with other image defects, noise becomes more apparent as you enlarge the photo, as shown on the right in that same figure. Noise is also easier to spot in shadow areas of your picture and in large areas of solid color.

How much noise is acceptable, and, therefore, how high an ISO is safe, is a personal choice. Even a little noise isn't acceptable for pictures that require the highest quality, such as images for a product catalog or a travel shot that you want to blow up to poster size.

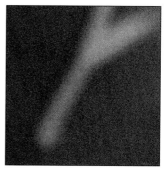

Figure 7-5: Caused by a very high ISO or long exposure time, noise becomes more visible as you enlarge the image.

ISO 100, f/6.3, 1/40 second   ISO 200, f/6.3, 1/80 second

Figure 7-6: Raising the ISO enabled me to bump up the shutter speed enough to permit a blur-free handheld shot.

It's also important to know that a high ISO isn't the only cause of noise: A long exposure time (slow shutter speed) can also produce the defect. So how high you can raise the ISO before the image gets ugly varies depending on shutter speed. I can pretty much guarantee, though, that your pictures will exhibit visible noise at the camera's four highest ISO settings, which produce ISO sensitivity ranging from ISO 8000 to 25600. In fact, that's why Nikon gave these settings their special labels, Hi 0.3, Hi 0.7, Hi 1, and Hi 2 — it's a way to let you know that you should use these settings only if the light is so bad that you have no other way to get the shot.

Doing the exposure balancing act

As you change any of the three exposure settings — aperture, shutter speed, and ISO — one or both of the others must also shift to maintain the same image brightness. Say that you're shooting a soccer game, for example, and you notice that although the overall exposure looks great, the players appear slightly blurry at your current shutter speed. If you raise the shutter speed, you have to compensate with a larger aperture, to allow in more light during the shorter exposure, or a higher ISO setting, to make the camera more sensitive to the light — or both.

As the previous sections explain, changing these settings impacts your image in ways beyond exposure. As a quick reminder:

- ✔ Aperture affects depth of field, with a higher f-stop number producing a greater zone of sharp focus.

- ✔ Shutter speed affects whether motion of the subject or camera results in a blurry photo. A faster shutter "freezes" action and also helps safeguard against all-over blur that can result from camera shake when you're handholding the camera.

- ✔ ISO affects the camera's sensitivity to light. A higher ISO makes the camera more responsive to light but also increases the chance of image noise.

So when you boost that shutter speed to capture your soccer subjects, you have to decide whether you prefer the shorter depth of field that comes with a larger aperture or the increased risk of noise that accompanies a higher ISO.

Everyone has their own approach to finding the right combination of aperture, shutter speed, and ISO, and you'll no doubt develop your own system as you become more practiced at using the advanced exposure modes. In the meantime, here's how I handle things:

- ✔ I use the lowest ISO setting (ISO 100) unless the lighting conditions are so poor that I can't use the aperture and shutter speed I want without raising the ISO.

- ✔ If my subject is moving (or might move, as with a squiggly toddler or antsy pet), I give shutter speed the next highest priority in my exposure decision. I might choose a fast shutter speed to ensure a blur-free photo or, on the flip side, select a slow shutter to intentionally blur that moving object, an effect that can create a heightened sense of motion.

- ✔ For images of nonmoving subjects, I make aperture a priority over shutter speed, setting the aperture according to the depth of field I have in mind. For portraits, for example, I use the largest aperture (the lowest f-stop number, known as shooting *wide open,* in photographer-speak) so that I get a short depth of field, creating a nice, soft background for my subject. For landscapes, I usually go the opposite direction, stopping down the aperture as much as possible to capture the subject at the greatest depth of field.

Keeping all this straight is a little overwhelming at first, but the more you work with your camera, the more the whole exposure equation will make sense to you. You can find tips for choosing exposure settings for specific types of pictures in Chapter 9; keep moving through this chapter for details on how to actually adjust aperture, shutter speed, and ISO settings.

Exploring the Advanced Exposure Modes

In the automatic modes described in Chapter 3, you have very little control over exposure. You may be able to choose from one or two Flash modes, and you can adjust ISO. But to gain full control over exposure, set the Mode dial to one of the advanced modes highlighted in Figure 7-7: P, S, A, or M. You also need to shoot in these modes to use certain other features, such as manual white balancing, a color control that you can explore in Chapter 8.

The major difference among the four advanced modes is the level of control over aperture and shutter speed, as follows:

Figure 7-7: You can control exposure and certain other picture properties fully only in P, S, A, or M mode.

- ✔ **P (programmed autoexposure):** In this mode, the camera selects both aperture and shutter speed. But you can choose from different combinations of the two for creative flexibility.

- ✔ **S (shutter-priority autoexposure):** In this mode, you select a shutter speed, and the camera chooses the aperture setting that produces a good exposure at your selected ISO setting.

- ✔ **A (aperture-priority autoexposure):** The opposite of shutter-priority autoexposure, this mode asks you to select the aperture setting. The camera then selects the appropriate shutter speed to properly expose the picture.

- ✔ **M (manual exposure):** In this mode, you specify both shutter speed and aperture.

To sum up, the first three modes are semi-automatic exposure modes that are designed to help you get a good exposure while still providing you with some photographic flexibility. Note one important point about the semi-auto modes, however: In extreme lighting conditions, the camera may not be able to select settings that will produce a good exposure, and it doesn't stop you from taking a poorly exposed photo. You may be able to solve the problem by using features designed to modify the autoexposure results, such as Exposure Compensation (explained later in this chapter), but there are no guarantees.

Manual mode puts all exposure control in your hands. If you're a longtime photographer who comes from the days when manual exposure was the only game in town, you may prefer to stick with this mode. If it ain't broke, don't fix it, as they say. And in some ways, manual mode is simpler than the semi-auto modes because if you're not happy with the exposure, you just change the aperture, shutter speed, or ISO setting and shoot again. You don't have to fiddle with features that enable you to modify your autoexposure results.

My own personal choice is to use aperture-priority autoexposure when I'm shooting still subjects and want to control depth of field — aperture is my *priority* — and to switch to shutter-priority autoexposure when I'm shooting a moving subject and so I'm most concerned with controlling shutter speed. Frankly, my brain is taxed enough by all the other issues involved in taking pictures — what my White Balance setting is, what resolution I need, where I'm going for lunch as soon as I make this shot work — that I just appreciate having the camera do some of the exposure lifting.

However, when I know exactly what aperture and shutter speed I want to use, or I'm after an out-of-the-ordinary exposure, I use manual exposure. For example, sometimes when I'm doing a still life in my studio, I want to create a certain mood by underexposing a subject or even shooting it in silhouette. The camera is always going to fight you on that result in the P, S, and A modes because it so dearly wants to provide a good exposure. Rather than dialing in all the autoexposure tweaks that could eventually force the result I want, I simply set the mode to M, adjust the shutter speed and aperture directly, and give the autoexposure system the afternoon off.

But even in manual mode, you're never really flying without a net — the camera assists you by displaying the exposure meter, explained next.

Reading (And Adjusting) the Meter

To help you determine whether your exposure settings are on cue in M (manual) exposure mode, the camera displays an *exposure meter* in the viewfinder and Information display. The meter is the little linear graphic highlighted in Figure 7-8. You can see a close-up look at how the meter looks in the viewfinder in Figure 7-9. To activate the meter displays, just press the shutter button halfway and then release it.

The minus-sign end of the meter represents underexposure; the plus sign, overexposure. So if the little notches on the meter fall to the right of 0, as shown in the first example in Figure 7-9, the image will be underexposed. If the

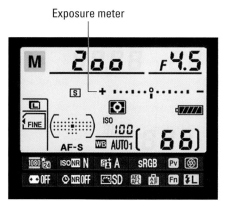

Figure 7-8: In M exposure mode, the exposure meter appears in the Information display and viewfinder.

indicator moves to the left of 0, as shown in the second example, the image will be overexposed. The farther the indicator moves toward the plus or minus sign, the greater the potential problem. When the meter shows a balanced exposure, as in the third example, you're good to go.

| Underexposure | Overexposure | Good exposure |

Figure 7-9: The meter indicates whether your exposure settings are on target.

In the other exposure modes, the meter appears if the camera anticipates an exposure problem. The word Lo at the end of the meter tells you that the photo may be seriously underexposed; the word Hi indicates severe overexposure. In dim lighting, you may also see a blinking flash symbol. It's a not-so-subtle suggestion to add some light to the scene. (You can disable the flash alert through the Flash Warning option on the Custom Setting menu if you like.)

Keep in mind, too, that the meter's suggestion on exposure may not always be the one you want to follow. For example, you may want to shoot a backlit subject in silhouette, in which case you *want* that subject to be underexposed. In other words, the meter is a guide, not a dictator. In addition, remember that the exposure information the meter reports is based on the *exposure metering mode,* which determines which part of the frame the camera considers when calculating exposure. At the default setting, exposure is based on the entire frame, but you can select two other metering modes. See the upcoming section "Choosing an Exposure Metering Mode" for details.

If you're so inclined, you can customize the meter in the following ways:

✔ **Adjust the meter shutoff timing.** The meter turns on anytime you press the shutter button halfway. But then it turns off automatically if you don't press the button again for a period of time — six seconds, by default. You can adjust the shut-off timing through the Auto Meter-Off Delay option, found on the Timers/AE Lock submenu of the Custom Setting menu, as shown on the left in Figure 7-10. Choices range from 4 seconds to 30 minutes. You can also disable the auto meter shutdown by choosing the No Limit option, but remember that the metering system uses battery power, so keeping it active for long periods of time on a regular basis isn't a good move.

✔ **Reverse the meter orientation.** For photographers used to a camera that orients the meter with the positive (overexposure) side appearing on the right and the negative (underexposure) side on the left, the D7000 offers the option to flip the meter to that design. This option also lies on the Custom Setting menu, but on the Controls submenu. Look for the Reverse Indicators option, as shown on the right in the figure. The setting shown in the figure is the default.

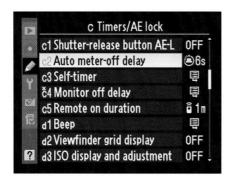

Figure 7-10: You can customize the behavior of the exposure meter.

Setting Aperture, Shutter Speed, and ISO

The next sections detail how to view and adjust these three critical exposure settings. For a review of how each setting affects your pictures, check out the first part of this chapter.

Adjusting aperture and shutter speed

You can view the current aperture (f-stop) and shutter speed in the Control panel, viewfinder, and Information display, as shown in Figure 7-11. If you don't see the values, the exposure meter isn't awake; press the shutter button halfway to bring it out of its slumber.

Shutter speed   Aperture

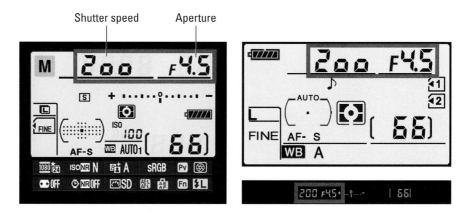

Figure 7-11: You can view the f-stop and shutter speed setting in all three displays.

Exposure stops: How many do you want to see?

In photography, the term *stop* refers to an increment of exposure. To increase exposure by one stop means to adjust the aperture or shutter speed to allow twice as much light into the camera as the current settings permit. To reduce exposure a stop, you use settings that allow half as much light. Doubling or halving the ISO value also adjusts exposure by one stop.

By default, all the major exposure-related settings on the D7000 are based on one-third stop adjustments. For example, when you adjust the Exposure Compensation value, a feature that enables you to request a brighter or darker picture than the camera's autoexposure system thinks is correct, you can choose settings of EV 0.0 (no adjustment), +0.3, +0.7, and +1.0 (a full stop of adjustment).

If you prefer, you can tell the camera to present exposure adjustments in half-stop increments so that you don't have to cycle through as many

settings each time you want to make a change. Make your preferences known through these two options, found in the Metering/Exposure section of the Custom Setting menu. (The menu uses the term *step* instead of *stop,* but the results are the same.) The two settings affect specific exposure components:

- **ISO Sensitivity Step Value:** Affects ISO settings only.
- **EV Steps for Exposure Cntrl (Control):** Affects shutter speed, aperture, Exposure Compensation, Flash Compensation, and exposure bracketing settings. Also determines the increment used to indicate the amount of under- or overexposure in the meter.

Obviously, the default setting, 1/3 stop, provides the greatest degree of exposure fine-tuning, so I stick with that option. In this book, all instructions also assume that you're using the defaults.

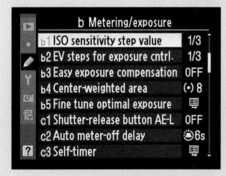 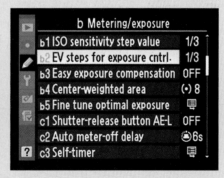

Before I explain how to select the f-stop and shutter speed, I need to share a few notes about the latter setting:

- Shutter speeds are presented as whole numbers, even if the shutter speed is set to a fraction of a second. For example, the number 125 indicates a shutter speed of 1/125 second. When the shutter speed slows to one second or more, quote marks appear after the number — 1" indicates a shutter speed of one second, 4" means four seconds, and so on.

✔ When you set the exposure mode to M (manual) or S (shutter-priority auto), you have access to shutter speeds not displayed in the other modes:

- *Bulb:* At this setting, the shutter remains open as long as you hold down the shutter button. You can shoot bulb exposures only in the M (manual) exposure mode. If you select the bulb setting in M mode and then change to the S (shutter-priority auto) mode, the word Bulb flashes in the display to remind you to change to manual exposure. Well, to remind you that something's amiss, anyway.

- *x250:* In addition, you also see a setting that has an *x* before the value — x250, by default. The *x,* when used with shutter speeds, indicates the *flash sync speed,* which is the fastest shutter speed that works with flash. On the D7000, the default sync speed is 1/250 second, but you can set another speed through a Custom Setting option. See the later section "Enabling high-speed flash (Auto FP)" for details. If you want to use 1/250 second as your shutter speed, you can select either the x250 setting or the plain ol' 1/250 setting.

- *Time:* This setting, represented by two dashes (- -) in the displays, is available in M mode when you set the Release mode to Remote Control and use the optional ML-L3 wireless remote control. The shutter opens when you press the remote's shutter-release button and stays open for 30 minutes or until you press the button a second time.

The following list tells you how to select the aperture and shutter speed in each exposure mode:

✔ **P (programmed auto):** In this mode, the camera shows you its recommended f-stop and shutter speed when you press the shutter button halfway. But you can rotate the Main command dial to select a different combination of settings. The number of possible combinations depends upon the aperture settings and shutter speeds the camera can select, which in turn depend on the lighting conditions, your lens, and the ISO setting.

An asterisk (*) appears next to the P exposure mode symbol in the Information display after you rotate the Main command dial. The same symbol appears in the upper-right corner of the Control panel. The asterisk indicates that you adjusted the aperture/shutter speed settings from those the camera initially suggested. To get back to the initial combo of shutter speed and aperture, rotate the Main command dial until the asterisk disappears.

✔ **S (shutter-priority autoexposure):** In this mode, you select the shutter speed. Just rotate the Main command dial to get the job done.

As you change the shutter speed, the camera adjusts the aperture as needed to maintain what it considers the proper exposure. Remember that as the aperture shifts, so does depth of field — so even though you're working in shutter-priority mode, keep an eye on the f-stop, too, if depth of field is important to your photo. Also note that in extreme lighting conditions, the camera may not be able to adjust the aperture enough to produce a good exposure at your current shutter speed — again, possible aperture settings depend on your lens. So you may need to compromise on shutter speed or ISO.

✔ **A (aperture-priority autoexposure):** In this mode, you control aperture, and the camera adjusts shutter speed automatically. To set the aperture (f-stop), rotate the Sub-command dial.

When you stop down the aperture (raise the f-stop value), be careful that the shutter speed doesn't drop so low that you run the risk of camera shake if you handhold the camera — unless you have a tripod handy, of course. And if your scene contains moving objects, make sure that when you dial in your preferred f-stop, the shutter speed that the camera selects is fast enough to stop action (or slow enough to blur it, if that's your creative goal). These same warnings apply when you use P mode, by the way.

✔ **M (manual exposure):** In this mode, you select both aperture and shutter speed, like so:

   • *To adjust shutter speed:* Rotate the Main command dial.

   • *To adjust aperture:* Rotate the Sub-command dial.

Understand that when you use P, S, or A modes, the settings that the camera handles are selected based on what the exposure meter thinks is the proper exposure. If you don't agree with the camera, you have two options: You can switch to manual exposure mode and simply dial in the aperture and shutter speed that deliver the exposure you want; or if you want to stay in P, S, or A mode, you can tweak exposure by applying Exposure Compensation, enabling Active D-Lighting, or changing the metering mode. See the next section for ISO details; later sections in this chapter address the other issues.

Controlling ISO

The ISO setting, introduced at the start of this chapter, adjusts the camera's sensitivity to light. At a higher ISO, you can use a faster shutter speed or a smaller aperture (higher f-stop number) because less light is needed to expose the image. But remember that a higher ISO also increases the possibility of noise, as illustrated in Figure 7-5. (Be sure to check out the upcoming sidebar "Dampening noise" for features that may help calm noise somewhat.)

On the D7000, you can choose ISO values ranging from 100 to 6400, plus four Hi settings, 0.3, 0.7, 1, and 2, which stretch the ISO range from 8000 (Hi 0.3) to 25600 (Hi 1). You also have the option of choosing Auto ISO; at this setting, the camera selects the ISO needed to expose the picture at the current shutter speed and aperture.

The number of settings available between the top and bottom of the ISO range depend on the ISO Sensitivity Step Value option, covered in the sidebar "Exposure stops: How many do you want to see?" earlier in this chapter. By default, ISO settings are presented in one-third stop increments.

 You can view the current ISO setting in the Information display, as shown on the left in Figure 7-12. But the viewfinder and Control panel show the ISO setting *only* when Auto ISO is enabled. At other settings, press the ISO button to hide all other data but the ISO value in the Control panel, as shown on the right in the figure. In the viewfinder, the ISO value replaces the shots remaining value while the button is pressed.

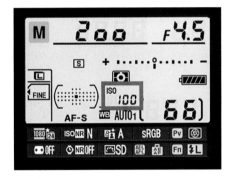
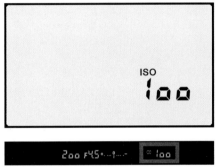

Figure 7-12: Press the ISO button while rotating the Main command dial to adjust ISO.

You can adjust the setting in two ways:

✔ **Press the ISO button while rotating the Main command dial.** In the P, S, A, and M modes, the Auto setting doesn't appear as an option when you rotate the dial, but you can request auto ISO control by another means. (More on that bit of business momentarily.)

✔ **Shooting menu:** Select ISO Sensitivity Settings, as shown on the left in Figure 7-13, and then choose ISO Sensitivity, as shown on the right. Again, things work differently depending on your exposure mode; the settings shown on the second screen of the figure are available in the P, S, A, and M modes only. In other modes, the ISO Sensitivity option is available but the others are off limits.

If you don't like this setup, you can modify things a little through the ISO Display and Adjustment option found on the Custom Setting menu. At the default setting, Off (Show Frame Count), things work as just described. Choose Show ISO Sensitivity to replace the Shots Remaining value in the viewfinder and Control panel with the ISO value at all times. You can still see the Shots Remaining value in the Information display. A third option, Show ISO/Easy ISO, is a little complicated: If you select this setting, the ISO value appears in the Shots Remaining area, just as with the Show ISO Sensitivity option. But at this setting, you can adjust the setting by simply rotating the Main command dial in the A exposure mode and the Sub-command dial in the P and S modes. For all other modes, you stick with the original plan: Press the ISO button and rotate the Main command dial. I think all that's a little complicated, so I stick with the default setting.

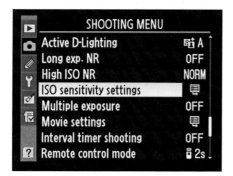 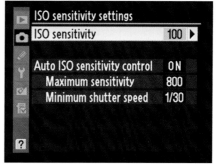

Figure 7-13: You can access additional ISO options through the Shooting menu.

A more important ISO topic to consider is the way that the camera handles ISO adjustment when you enable Auto ISO:

- **Auto ISO in the fully automatic exposure modes:** In Auto, Auto Flash Off, and Scene modes, the camera selects the ISO for you, but doesn't go up any higher than ISO 1600.

- **Auto ISO in P, S, A, and M modes:** Auto ISO doesn't appear on the ISO settings list, but you can enable Auto ISO as sort of a safety net. Here's how it works: You dial in a specific ISO setting — say, ISO 100. If the camera decides that it can't properly expose the image at that ISO given your current aperture and shutter speed, it automatically adjusts ISO as necessary.

  To use this feature, set the Auto ISO Sensitivity Control option to On, as shown in Figure 7-14. Then use these two options to tell the camera exactly when and how it should step in and offer ISO assistance:

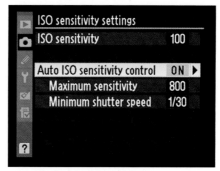

Figure 7-14: In P, S, A, and M modes, you can set limits for Auto ISO override.

- *Maximum Sensitivity:* Specify the highest ISO setting the camera may select when it overrides your ISO decision. Note that this setting also limits the top ISO speed you can select manually. For example, if you set the Maximum Sensitivity option to ISO 640 and then set the ISO Sensitivity setting to ISO 800, the camera overrides your choice and uses ISO 640 when you take the picture.

- *Minimum Shutter Speed:* Set the minimum shutter speed at which the ISO override engages. For example, you can specify that you want the camera to amp up ISO when the shutter speed drops to 1/30 second or below, as shown in the figure.

If the camera is about to override your ISO setting, it alerts you by blinking an ISO-Auto label in the displays. And in playback mode, the ISO value appears in red if you view your photos in a display mode that includes the ISO value. (Chapter 5 has details.)

To disable Auto ISO override for the P, S, A, and M modes, just reset the Auto ISO Sensitivity Control option to Off.

Choosing an Exposure Metering Mode

To fully interpret what your exposure meter tells you, you need to know which metering mode is active. The metering mode determines which part of the frame the camera analyzes to calculate the proper exposure. The metering mode affects more than the meter, however: It also determines the exposure settings that the camera selects for you when you shoot in the P, S, and A exposure modes as well as in the fully automatic exposure modes.

In the P, S, A, and M modes, you can adjust the metering mode by pressing the Metering button while rotating the Main command dial. An icon representing the current metering mode appears in the Information display and Control panel, as shown in Figure 7-15.

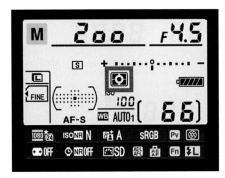
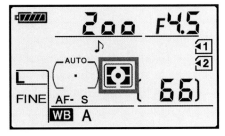

Figure 7-15: This symbol represents the matrix metering mode.

TIP

Dampening noise

Both high ISO settings and long exposure times can result in *noise*, the digital defect that gives your pictures a speckled look. (Refer to Figure 7-5.) To help solve the problem, the D7000 offers two noise-removal filters: *High ISO Noise Reduction,* designed to reduce the appearance of ISO-related noise; and *Long Exposure Noise Reduction,* which dampens the type of noise that occurs during long exposures.

You can enable both filters through the Shooting menu, as shown in the left figure below, or through the control strip along the bottom of the Information display. To activate the strip, press the Info button twice. Then use the Multi Selector to highlight a filter. In the figure here, the High ISO Noise Reduction filter is active; the Long Exposure Noise Reduction filter is directly below. Press OK to access the available settings.

If you turn on Long Exposure Noise Reduction, the camera applies the filter to pictures taken at shutter speeds of longer than eight seconds. For High ISO Noise Reduction, you can choose from four settings. The High, Normal, and Low settings apply the filter at ISO 800 or higher; the setting you choose determines the strength of the filter. At the fourth setting, Off, the camera

actually still applies a tiny amount of noise removal, but only at ISO 1600 or higher.

Before you enable noise reduction, be aware that doing so has a few disadvantages. First, the filters are applied after you take the picture, as the camera processes the image data. While the Long Exposure Noise Reduction filter is being applied, the message "Job Nr" appears in the viewfinder and Control panel, in the area normally reserved for the shutter speed and aperture. The time needed to apply this filter can significantly slow down your shooting speed — in fact, it can double the time the camera needs to record the file to the memory card.

Second, although filters that go after long-exposure noise work fairly well, those that attack high ISO noise work primarily by applying a slight blur to the image. Don't expect this process to totally eliminate noise, and do expect some resulting image softness. You may be able to get better results by using the blur tools or noise-removal filters found in many photo editors because you can blur just the parts of the image where noise is most noticeable — usually in areas of flat color or little detail, such as skies.

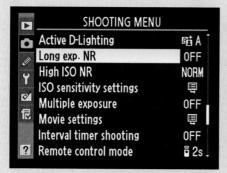

Part III: Taking Creative Control

Your camera offers three metering modes, represented by the icons you see in the margins here:

✔ **Matrix:** The camera bases exposure on the entire frame. This setting is always used when you shoot in Auto, Auto Flash Off, or any of the Scene exposure modes.

✔ **Spot:** In this mode, the camera bases exposure on a single, circular area about 3.5mm in diameter. Exactly which part of the frame that circle covers depends on focus settings that I detail in Chapter 8:

- If you use autofocusing and set the AF-area mode to Auto Area, in which the camera chooses the focus point for you, exposure is based on the center focus point, as illustrated on the left in Figure 7-16.

- When you use the other AF-area mode settings or manual focusing, you use the Multi Selector to select a focus point, and the camera bases metering on that point.

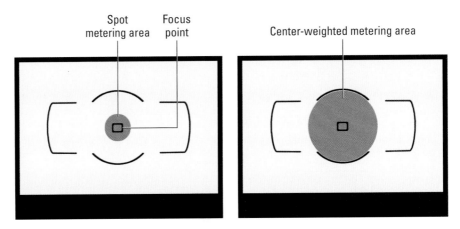

Figure 7-16: Spot metering is linked to the current focus point; center-weighted metering references a larger area at the center of the frame.

✔ **Center-weighted:** A blend of matrix and spot metering, this mode bases exposure on the entire frame but puts extra emphasis — or *weight* — on the center of the frame.

Normally, the area that's given priority in this mode is about 8mm in diameter, as illustrated on the right in Figure 7-16. But you can alter the critical metering area through the Center-Weighted Area option, found in the Metering/Exposure section of the Custom Setting menu and shown in Figure 7-17. You can change the size of the metering circle to 6mm, 10mm, or 13mm. (The menu option is available only when the Mode dial is set to P, S, A, or M.)

The Center-Weighted Area option also offers an Avg setting, which tells the camera to take a reading of the entire frame and then base exposure on the average brightness values it sees. The difference between this option and the Matrix setting is that Matrix is based on a newer, more capable technology, whereas Avg is based on a system used in earlier Nikon cameras. Longtime Nikon shooters who are familiar with this metering option may appreciate its inclusion on the D7000, but the matrix system typically delivers a better exposure if you're concerned about objects throughout the frame, so I suggest that you stick with that when you want to expose the photo with the entire frame in mind.

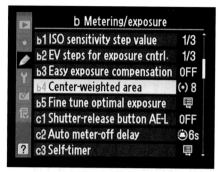

Figure 7-17: You can customize the center-weighted metering area.

As an example of how metering mode affects exposure, Figure 7-18 shows the same image captured at each mode. In the matrix example, the bright background caused the camera to select an exposure that left the statue quite dark. Switching to center-weighted metering helped somewhat, but didn't quite bring the statue out of the shadows. Spot metering produced the best result as far as the statue goes, although the resulting increase in exposure left the sky and background monument a little washed out.

Matrix metering   Center-weighted metering   Spot metering

Figure 7-18: Spot and center-weighted metering can produce a better exposure of backlit subjects.

In theory, the best practice is to check the metering mode before you shoot and choose the one that best matches your exposure goals. But in practice, that's a bit of a pain, not just in terms of having to adjust yet one more capture setting but in terms of having to *remember* to adjust one more capture setting. So here's my advice: Until you're really comfortable with all the other controls on your camera, just stick with the default setting, which is matrix metering. That mode produces good results in most situations, and, after all, you can see in the monitor whether you disagree with how the camera metered or exposed the image and simply reshoot after adjusting the exposure settings to your liking. This option, in my mind, makes the whole metering mode issue a lot less critical than it is when you shoot with film. Just remember that if you're shooting a series of photos like the one in the figure, where your subject is significantly darker or lighter than the background, switching to spot or center-weighted metering is one way to make sure that the subject is properly exposed.

One final point about metering: The Fine Tune Optimal Exposure option, found on the Metering/Exposure submenu of the Custom Setting menu, enables you to fiddle with the metering system beyond just specifying the size of the center-weighted metering area. For each metering mode, you can specify that you always want a brighter or darker exposure than what Nikon's engineers determined to be optimal when developing the camera. In essence, you're recalibrating the meter. Although it's nice to have this level of control, I advise against making this adjustment unless you really know what you're doing, both in terms of using the camera and calculating exposure. It's sort of like reengineering your oven so that it heats to 300 degrees when the dial is set to 325 degrees — it's easy to forget that you made the shift and not be able to figure out why your exposure settings aren't delivering the results you expected.

If your camera consistently under- or overexposes your pictures when you use the semi-automatic exposure modes (P, S, or A) or fully auto modes, it may be time for a service check at your local camera-repair shop, assuming that the problems occur even in normal lighting situations. For intermittent exposure issues, tweak picture brightness by using Exposure Compensation, explained next, when you use the semi-autoexposure modes (P, S, and A), or just adjust the aperture, shutter speed, or ISO in manual exposure mode (M). Also investigate the upcoming section about Active D-Lighting, which gives you yet another way to manipulate exposure.

Applying Exposure Compensation

When you set your camera to the P, S, or A modes, you can enjoy autoexposure support but still retain some control over the final exposure. If you think that the image the camera produced is too dark or too light, you can use the *Exposure Compensation* feature.

This feature enables you to tell the camera to produce a darker or lighter exposure than what its autoexposure mechanism thinks is appropriate. Best of all, this feature is probably one of the easiest on the whole camera to understand. Here's all there is to it:

- Exposure Compensation settings are stated in terms of EV values, as in EV +2.0. Possible values range from EV +5.0 to EV –5.0. (The *EV* stands for *exposure value.*)

  Each full number on the EV scale represents an exposure shift of one *stop.* If you're new to this terminology, see the sidebar "Exposure stops: How many do you want to see?" earlier in this chapter. That sidebar also explains how you can tweak the increments of EV adjustment the camera offers.

- A setting of EV 0.0 results in no exposure adjustment.

- For a brighter image, raise the EV value. The higher you go, the brighter the image becomes.

- For a darker image, lower the EV value.

As an example, take a look at the first image in Figure 7-19. The initial exposure selected by the camera left the balloon a tad too dark for my taste. So I just amped the Exposure Compensation setting to EV +1.0, which produced the brighter exposure on the right.

To apply Exposure Compensation, hold down the Exposure Compensation button, found near the shutter button. All data except the Exposure Compensation value then disappears from the Control panel and is dimmed in the Information display. In the viewfinder, the Shots Remaining value is replaced by the Exposure Compensation value. While holding the button, rotate the Main command dial to adjust the EV value. The exposure meter reflects your change as you adjust the value.

After you release the button, the 0 on the meter in the viewfinder blinks to remind you that Exposure Compensation is active. You also see a little plus/minus symbol (the same one that decorates the Exposure Compensation button) in the Control panel and Information display, and in the Information display, the meter readout indicates the amount of compensation you applied. For example, in the left screen in Figure 7-20, the meter indicates an adjustment of EV +1.0. (If you have difficulty making out the meter reading, just press the Exposure Compensation button again to view the numerical value in the displays.)

Your Exposure Compensation setting remains in force until you change it, even if you power off the camera. So you may want to make a habit of checking the setting before each shoot or always setting the value back to EV 0.0 after taking the last shot for which you want to apply compensation.

EV 0.0   EV +1.0

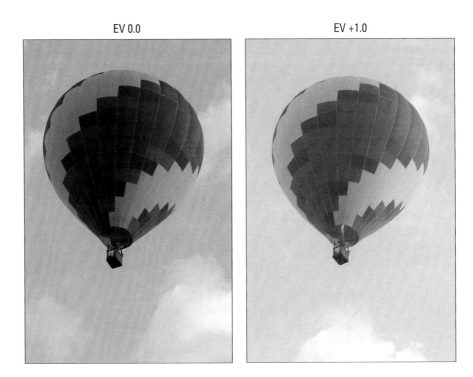

Figure 7-19: For a brighter exposure, raise the EV value.

Exposure Compensation amount   Exposure Compensation symbol

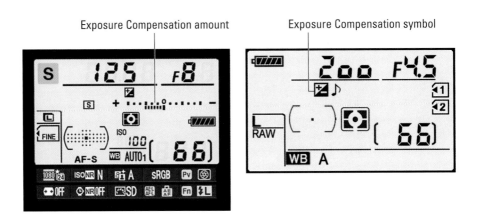

Figure 7-20: The plus/minus symbol tells you that Exposure Compensation is being applied.

Here are a few other tips about Exposure Compensation:

✔ How the camera arrives at the brighter or darker image you request through your Exposure Compensation setting depends on the exposure mode:

- *In A (aperture-priority autoexposure) mode,* the camera adjusts the shutter speed but leaves your selected f-stop in force. Be sure to check the resulting shutter speed to make sure that it isn't so slow that camera shake or blur from moving objects is problematic.

- *In S (shutter-priority autoexposure) mode,* the opposite occurs: The camera opens or stops down the aperture, leaving your selected shutter speed alone.

- *In P (programmed autoexposure) mode,* the camera decides whether to adjust aperture, shutter speed, or both.

- *In all three modes,* the camera may also adjust ISO if you have Auto ISO Sensitivity Control enabled.

Don't forget that the camera can adjust f-stop only so much, according to the aperture range of your lens. And the range of shutter speeds, too, is limited by the camera itself, although you're not likely to reach those limits on the D7000, which offers speeds from 30 seconds to 1/8000 second. If you hit the aperture or shutter speed wall, you either have to compromise on shutter speed or aperture or adjust ISO. Remember that the exposure meter blinks if the camera can't adjust the settings enough to produce a good exposure.

✔ When you use flash, the Exposure Compensation setting affects both background brightness and flash power. But you can further modify the flash power through a related option, Flash Compensation. You can find out more about that feature later in this chapter.

✔ The Metering/Exposure section of the Custom Setting menu contains an Easy Exposure Compensation option. If you enable this feature, you can adjust the Exposure Compensation setting in the P and S exposure modes simply by rotating the Sub-command dial. In A exposure mode, you use the Main command dial instead of the Sub-command dial (because you use the Sub-command dial in A mode to adjust the f-stop). I don't recommend enabling this feature: You can easily rotate the dials by mistake and not realize that you adjusted the setting.

✔ Finally, if you don't want to fiddle with Exposure Compensation, just switch to manual exposure mode and select whatever aperture and shutter speed settings produce the exposure you're after. Start with the settings selected by the camera in the autoexposure mode you were using and then just go from there. Exposure Compensation has no effect on manual exposures; again, that adjustment is made only in the P, S, and A modes.

Although the camera doesn't change your selected exposure settings in manual mode even if Exposure Compensation is enabled, the exposure *meter is* affected by the current setting, which can lead to some confusion. The meter indicates whether your shot will be properly exposed based on the Exposure Compensation setting. So if you don't realize that Exposure Compensation is enabled, you may mistakenly adjust your exposure settings when they're actually on target for your subject. This is yet another reason why it's best to always reset the Exposure Compensation setting back to EV 0.0 after you're done using that feature.

Using Autoexposure Lock

To help ensure a proper exposure, your camera continually meters the light in a scene until the moment you depress the shutter button fully and capture the image. In autoexposure modes — that is, any mode but M — it also keeps adjusting exposure settings as needed to maintain a good exposure.

For most situations, this approach works great, resulting in the right settings for the light that's striking your subject at the moment you capture the image. But on occasion, you may want to lock in a certain combination of exposure settings. For example, perhaps you want your subject to appear at the far edge of the frame. If you were to use the normal shooting technique, you'd place the subject under a focus point, press the shutter button halfway to lock focus and set the initial exposure, and then reframe to your desired composition to take the shot. The problem is that exposure is then recalculated based on the new framing, which can leave your subject under- or overexposed.

The easiest way to lock in exposure settings is to switch to M (manual) exposure mode and use the f-stop, shutter speed, and ISO settings that work best for your subject. But if you prefer to stay in P, S, or A mode, you can press the AE-L/AF-L button to lock exposure and focus before you reframe. By keeping the button pressed between shots, you can even keep using the same exposure and focus for a series of photographs. Here's the technique I recommend:

1. **Set the metering mode to spot metering.**

    Press the Metering button while rotating the Main command dial to change the setting.

2. **If autofocusing, set the Autofocus mode to AF-S and the AF-area mode to Single Point.**

   Press the AF-mode button and rotate the Main command dial to change the Autofocus mode; press the button while spinning the Sub-command dial to change the AF-area mode. (The AF-mode button is the unmarked button at the center of the Focus-mode selector on the left front side of the camera.)

When using these autofocus settings or manual focusing, you see a single focus point in the viewfinder.

3. **Use the Multi Selector to move the focus point over your subject.**

   You sometimes need to press the shutter button halfway and release it to activate the exposure meters before you can do so. Also, be sure that the Focus Selector Lock switch (on back of the camera, just below the Multi Selector) is set to the little white dot and not the L (locked) position. Otherwise, you can't adjust the focus point.

   In spot metering mode, the focus point determines the area used to calculate exposure, so this step is critical whether you use autofocusing or manual focusing.

4. **Press the shutter button halfway.**

   The camera sets the initial exposure settings. If you're using autofocusing, focus is also set at this point. For manual focusing, twist the focusing ring on the lens to bring the subject into focus. The green focus indicator dot in the viewfinder lights when focus is achieved.

5. **Press and hold the AE-L/AF-L button.**

   This button's just to the right of the viewfinder.

   While the button is pressed, the letters AE-L appear at the left end of the viewfinder to remind you that exposure lock is applied.

   By default, focus is locked at the same time if you're using autofocusing. You can change this behavior by customizing the AE-L/AF-L button function, as outlined in Chapter 11.

6. **Reframe the shot if desired and take the photo.**

   Be sure to keep holding the AE-L/AF-L button until you release the shutter button! And if you want to use the same focus and exposure settings for your next shot, just keep the AE-L/AF-L button pressed.

Expanding Tonal Range with Active D-Lighting

A scene like the one in Figure 7-21 presents the classic photographer's challenge: Choosing exposure settings that capture the darkest parts of the subject appropriately causes the brightest areas to be overexposed. And if you instead *expose for the highlights* — that is, set the exposure settings to capture the brightest regions properly — the darker areas are underexposed.

In the past, you had to choose between favoring the highlights or the shadows. But thanks to the Nikon feature Active D-Lighting, you have a better chance of keeping your highlights intact while better exposing the darkest areas. In my seal scene, turning on Active D-Lighting produced a brighter rendition of the darkest parts of the rocks and the seals, for example, and yet the color in the sky didn't get blown out as it did when I captured the image with Active D-Lighting turned off. The highlights in the seal and in the rocks on the lower-right corner of the image also are toned down a tad in the Active D-Lighting version.

 Active D-Lighting actually does its thing in two stages. First, it selects exposure settings that result in a slightly darker exposure than normal. This half of the equation guarantees that you retain details in your highlights. After you snap the photo, the camera brightens the darkest areas of the image. This adjustment rescues shadow detail.

Active D-Lighting Off   Active D-Lighting On

Figure 7-21: Active D-Lighting captured the shadows without blowing out the highlights.

In Auto, Auto Flash Off, and Scene modes, the camera decides how much Active D-Lighting adjustment is needed. In the P, S, A, and M modes, you can specify the amount of adjustment in two ways:

   ✐ **Shooting menu:** Select Active D-Lighting from the Shooting menu, as shown on the left in Figure 7-22. Press OK to display the second screen in the figure. You can disable the feature, choose from four levels of adjustment, or select Auto to let the camera control the adjustment.

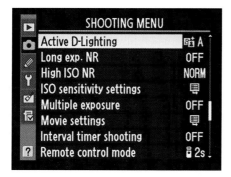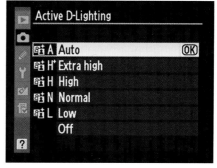

Figure 7-22: At the Auto setting, the camera automatically applies the amount of Active D-Lighting adjustment as it sees fit.

✔ **Information display:** Press the Info button twice to activate the control strip at the bottom of the Information display. Then use the Multi Selector to highlight the Active D-Lighting icon, as shown in Figure 7-23, and press OK. You're then taken to the menu screen where you can choose the level of adjustment.

A couple of pointers:

✔ You'll get the best Active D-Lighting results in matrix metering mode.

✔ In the M exposure mode, the camera doesn't change your shutter speed or f-stop to achieve the darker exposure it needs for Active D-Lighting to work; instead, the meter readout guides you to select the right settings unless you have automatic ISO override enabled. In that case, the camera may instead adjust ISO to manipulate the exposure.

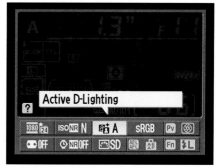

Figure 7-23: You can also access the D-Lighting options from the Information display control strip.

✔ You can't use Active D-Lighting at ISO Hi 0.3 or above.

✔ If you're not sure how much adjustment to apply, try Active D-Lighting *bracketing,* which automatically records the scene using different adjustment levels. See the last section in this chapter for details.

✔ The Retouch menu offers a D-Lighting filter that applies a similar adjustment to existing pictures. (See Chapter 10 for help.) Some photo-editing programs, such as Adobe Photoshop Elements and Photoshop, also have good shadow and highlight recovery filters. In either case, when you shoot with Active D-Lighting disabled, you're better off setting the initial exposure settings to record the highlights as you want them. It's very difficult to bring back lost highlight detail after the fact, but you typically can unearth at least a little bit of detail from the darkest areas of the image.

Exploring Flash Photography

Sometimes, no amount of fiddling with aperture, shutter speed, and ISO produces a bright-enough exposure — in which case, you simply have to add more light. The built-in flash on your D7000 offers the most convenient solution, but you can also attach an external flash to the camera's *hot shoe*, labeled in Figure 7-24. When you first take the camera out of the box, the contacts on the shoe are protected by a little cover, as shown in the figure; remove the cover to attach a flash.

Figure 7-24: Press the Flash button to pop up the built-in flash in the P, S, A, and M exposure modes.

How much flash control you have depends on your exposure mode:

↳ **Auto and Scene modes:** With one exception, the Food Scene mode, these modes all feature automatic flash, meaning that in dim lighting, the camera automatically raises and fires the built-in flash (assuming that an external flash isn't attached, in which case popping up the built-in flash would deliver a nasty punch in the nose). You may be able to choose from a couple Flash modes, including Flash Off, which disables the flash. But other flash controls are roped off.

↳ **P, S, A, and M modes and the Food Scene mode:** In these modes, you take total control over flash. If you want to use the built-in flash, press the Flash button, also labeled in Figure 7-24. To go flash free, just press the top of the flash unit gently down to close it.

Even in these modes, however, the camera displays a blinking flash (lightning bolt) symbol in the viewfinder if it thinks you're off your rocker not to use flash. Find that feature annoying? You can disable it via the Flash Warning option on the Custom Setting menu. Look for the option in the Shooting/Display section of the menu. (You have to set the Mode dial to P, S, A, or M to access the setting.)

Chapter 3 offers assistance with using the flash in the Auto and Scene modes; the rest of this chapter digs into features available in the advanced exposure modes.

Like everything else on the D7000, those features range from fairly simple to fairly not. Unfortunately, to keep this book from being exorbitantly large (and expensive), I can cover only the basics here. So I point you toward a couple of my favorite resources for delving more deeply into flash photography:

- Nikon's United States Web site (www.nikonusa.com) offers some great tutorials on flash photography (as well as other subjects). Start in the Learn and Explore section of the site.

- A Web site completely dedicated to flash photography, www.strobist.com, enables you to learn from and share with other photographers.

- You can find several good books detailing the entire Nikon flash system, which it calls the *Creative Lighting System* (*CLS,* for short).

- Chapter 9 of this book offers additional flash and lighting tips related to portraits and other specific types of photographs.

Before moving on, though, here's one preliminary tip: Pay careful attention to your results when you use the built-in flash with a telephoto lens that's very long. You may find that the flash casts an unwanted shadow when it strikes the lens. For best results, try switching to an external flash head.

Setting the Flash mode

Whether you're using the built-in flash or an external flash, you can choose from several *Flash modes.* This setting determines the timing of the flash and also affects how much of the picture is exposed by ambient light and how much is lit by the flash.

To set the mode, press the Flash button while rotating the Main command dial. As soon as you press the button, the Information display and Control panel change to show an icon representing the Flash mode and, in P, S, A, and M exposure modes, the Flash Compensation value, as shown in Figure 7-25. (Flash Compensation enables you to adjust flash power; look for details later in this chapter.) In the viewfinder, you see only the Flash Compensation value plus a little lightning bolt icon indicating that flash is enabled, charged, and ready to fire.

Flash mode   Flash Compensation setting

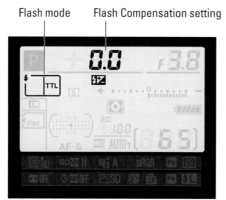
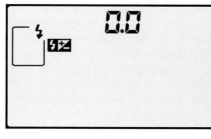

Figure 7-25: Press the Flash Mode button while rotating the Main command dial to change the Flash mode.

The Flash mode icon shown in the Information display in Figure 7-25 reflects the current setting of the Flash Cntrl for Built-in Flash menu option, shown in Figure 7-26. The option lives in the Bracketing/Flash suburb of the Custom Setting menu. For normal flash, stick with the default setting, TTL, as shown in the figures. TTL stands for *through-the-lens* and refers to the fact that the camera bases the necessary flash power on the amount of light actually coming through the lens. For a look at what the other

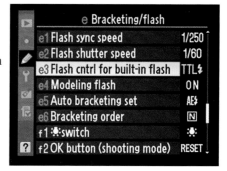

Figure 7-26: For normal flash operation, set this menu item to TTL.

options do, see the section "Enabling manual, repeating, or commander-mode flash," later in this chapter.

In the P, S, A, and M exposure modes, your flash mode choices break down into three basic categories, described in the next sections: normal flash; red-eye reduction flash; and the special-purpose sync modes, slow-sync and rear-sync. In the Auto exposure mode, you have access to the first two flash options, although they go by different names (Auto and Auto with Red-Eye Reduction), and the camera fires the flash only if the ambient light is sufficiently dim. In the Scene modes, flash choices depend on the scene you choose, so see Chapter 3 for details.

Normal flash (front-curtain sync)

For normal flash, select the setting represented in the Control panel by the symbol you see in the margin here. The symbol looks nearly the same in the Information display, but includes the letters TTL, as shown in Figure 7-25.

This mode is officially named *front-curtain sync,* which refers to how the flash is synchronized with the opening of the shutter. Here's the deal: The D7000 uses a type of shutter that involves two curtains moving across the frame each time you press and release the shutter button. When you press the shutter button, the first curtain opens, allowing light through to the sensor. At the end of the exposure, the second curtain draws across the frame to once again shield the sensor from light. With front-curtain sync, the flash fires at the moment the front curtain opens. This arrangement produces normal flash exposures. *Rear-curtain sync,* in which the flash fires at the end of the exposure, is a special-effects Flash mode, as illustrated a little later in this chapter.

Although most people think of flash as a tool to use only in dim lighting, it can really improve outdoor photos taken in strong daylight, too. As an example, Figure 7-27 shows a floral image taken with and without the built-in flash. Flash can also be extremely beneficial when shooting subjects that happen to be slightly shaded, such as the carousel horses featured later in this chapter. For outdoor portraits, a flash is even more important; the section on shooting still portraits in Chapter 9 discusses that subject and offers a look at the difference a flash can make.

Figure 7-27: Adding flash resulted in better illumination and a slight warming effect.

You do need to beware of a couple complications with using flash in bright light, however:

✔ **Colors may need tweaking when you mix light sources.** When you combine multiple light sources, such as flash with daylight, colors may appear warmer or cooler than neutral. In Figure 7-27, colors became warmer with the addition of flash. For outdoor portraits, the warming effect is usually flattering, and I usually like the result with nature shots as well. But if you prefer a neutral color rendition, see the Chapter 8 section related to the white balance control to find out how to address this issue. You can adjust white balance only in P, S, A, and M exposure modes.

✔ **You may need to stop down the aperture or lower ISO to avoid over-exposing the photo.** Because of the way the camera needs to synchro-nize the firing of the flash with the opening of the shutter, the fastest shutter speed you can use with the built-in flash by default is 1/250 second. The upcoming section "Enabling high-speed flash (Auto FP)" explains how you can raise the top shutter speed to 1/320 for the built-in flash, but even so, you may need to stop down the aperture significantly or lower the ISO setting to avoid overexposing the image when shooting in bright sun. When you use some external flash units, you can set the flash to sync at any shutter speed, however.

As another option, you can place a neutral density filter over your lens; this accessory reduces the light that comes through the lens without affecting colors. Of course, if possible, you can simply move your sub-ject into the shade.

✔ **In P and A modes, shutter speeds may drop low enough to require a tripod to steady the camera.** Remember, in these two modes, the camera controls shutter speed. And by default, the camera can drop the shut-ter speed as low as 1/60 second to ensure a good exposure when you use flash. A slower shutter speed raises the risk of blurring caused by camera shake or any movement of the subject, as explained in the introduction to shutter speed at the beginning of this chapter. Use a tripod if you're unsure whether you can handhold the camera at 1/60 second, and warn your sub-ject to stay still as well.

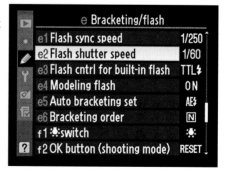

Figure 7-28: You can set the minimum shutter speed the camera can select when you use flash in the P and A exposure modes.

✔ **You can lower the slow limit of the shutter speed used for the P and A modes.** Again, the camera restricts itself to using a shutter speed no slower than 1/60 second when you use flash in the P and A modes. But if you need a longer exposure, you can waive that limit. Through the Flash Shutter Speed option, shown in Figure 7-28, you can set the mini-mum shutter speed as slow as 30 seconds. The option appears in the Bracketing/Flash section of the Custom Setting menu.

This setting applies only to the normal, front-curtain sync Flash mode as well as to the red-eye reduction mode and rear-sync mode, both discussed in upcoming sections. The camera completely ignores your limit if you choose slow-sync flash, slow-sync with red eye, or slow rear-curtain sync, also discussed later.

Red-eye reduction flash

Red-eye is caused when flash light bounces off a subject's retinas and is reflected back to the camera lens. Red-eye is a human phenomenon, though; with animals, the reflected light usually glows yellow, white, or green.

Man or beast, this issue isn't nearly the problem with the type of pop-up flash found on your D7000 as it is on non-SLR cameras. Your camera's flash is positioned in such a way that the flash light usually doesn't hit a subject's eyes straight on, which lessens the chances of red-eye. However, red-eye may still be an issue when you use a lens with a long focal length (a telephoto lens) or you shoot subjects from a distance.

 If you do notice red-eye, you can try the red-eye reduction mode, represented by the icon shown in the margin here. In this mode, the AF-assist lamp on the front of the camera lights up briefly before the flash fires. The subject's pupils constrict in response to the light, allowing less flash light to enter the eye and cause that glowing red reflection. Be sure to warn your subjects to wait for the flash, or they may step out of the frame or stop posing after they see the light from the AF-assist lamp.

For an even better solution, try the flash-free portrait tips covered in Chapter 9. If you do a lot of portrait work that requires flash, you may also want to consider an external flash unit that offers a rotating head. You then can aim the flash toward the ceiling and "bounce" the light off the ceiling instead of aiming it directly at your subject. That technique produces softer lighting and also virtually eliminates the possibility of red-eye.

If all else fails, check out Chapter 10, which shows you how to use the built-in red-eye removal tool on your camera's Retouch menu. Sadly, though, this feature removes only red-eye, not the yellow/green/white eye that you get with animal portraits.

Slow-sync and rear-curtain sync flash

In front-curtain sync (normal flash) and red-eye reduction Flash modes, the flash and shutter are synchronized so that the flash fires at the exact moment the shutter opens. As mentioned earlier, technical types refer to this flash arrangement as *front-curtain sync*.

Your D7000 also offers some special-sync modes, which work as follows:

✔ **Slow-sync flash:** This mode, available in the P and A exposure modes and used by default in some Scene modes, also uses front-curtain sync but allows a shutter speed slower than the 1/60 second minimum that is in force by default when you use fill flash and red-eye reduction flash. Remember, in these two exposure modes, you can't directly control shutter speed, so the camera automatically drops down the shutter speed for you.

The benefit of this longer exposure is that the camera has time to absorb more ambient light, which in turn has two effects: Background areas that are beyond the reach of the flash appear brighter, and less flash power is needed, resulting in softer lighting.

The downside of the slow shutter speed is, well, the slow shutter speed. As discussed earlier in this chapter, the longer the exposure time, the more you have to worry about blur caused by movement of your subject or your camera. A tripod is essential to a good outcome, as are subjects that can hold very, very still. I find that the best practical use for this mode is shooting nighttime still-life subjects, such as the one you see in Figure 7-29. But if you have an adult portrait subject, slow-sync can also produce good results; Chapter 9 has an example.

Normal flash   Slow-sync flash

Figure 7-29: Slow-sync flash produces softer, more even lighting than normal flash in nighttime pictures.

Some photographers, though, turn the downside of slow-sync flash to an upside, using it to purposely blur their subjects, thereby emphasizing motion.

Whatever your creative goals, if you want to use flash with a slow shutter in the S or M exposure mode, just choose the normal Flash mode (front-curtain sync) and then select the shutter speed you want to use. The flash will fire at the beginning of the exposure. Or as an alternative choice, choose rear-curtain sync, explained next.

✔ **Rear-curtain sync:** In this mode, available in P, S, A, and M exposure modes, the flash fires at the very end of the exposure, just before the shutter's second curtain draws across the frame to prevent any more light from hitting the image sensor.

The classic use of this mode is to combine the flash with a slow shutter speed to create trailing-light effects like the one you see in Figure 7-30. With rear-curtain sync, the light trails extend behind the moving object (my hand, and the match, in this case), which makes visual sense. If instead you use slow-sync flash (or front-curtain sync with a slow shutter), the light trails appear in front of the moving object.

Figure 7-30: I used rear-curtain flash and a shutter speed of about 1.5 seconds to create this candle-lighting image.

When you shoot in the P and A exposure modes, the camera actually combines slow-sync flash with rear-curtain sync when you select this Flash mode. You see the words *Slow Rear* in the Flash mode display area of the Control panel and Information display. Shutter speeds automatically drop below normal because the camera assumes that when you use rear-curtain flash, you're after the longer exposure time needed to produce the "trailing ghost" effect. (In the M and S modes, you dial in that slow shutter speed yourself.)

✔ **Slow-sync with red-eye reduction:** In P and A exposure modes, you can also combine a slow-sync flash with the red-eye reduction feature. Given the potential for blur that comes with a slow shutter, plus the potential for subjects to mistake the prelight from the AF-assist lamp for the real flash and walk out of the frame before the image is actually recorded, I vote this Flash mode as the most difficult to pull off successfully.

All these modes are somewhat tricky to use successfully, in fact. So have fun playing around, but at the same time, don't feel too badly if you don't have time right now to master these modes plus all the other exposure options presented to you in this chapter. In the meantime, do a Web search for slow-sync and rear-sync image examples if you want to get a better idea of the effects that other photographers create with these Flash modes.

Adjusting flash output

On the D7000, the way the camera calculates the necessary flash output varies depending on your exposure metering mode:

- **In matrix and center-weighted modes,** flash power is adjusted to expose the picture using a balance of ambient light and flash light. Nikon uses the term *i-TTL Balanced Fill Flash* for this technology. The *i* stands for *intelligent;* again, the *TTL* means that the camera calculates exposure by reading the light that's coming *through-the-lens.* The *balanced fill* part refers to the fact that the flash is used to fill in shadow areas, while brighter areas are exposed by the available light, resulting (usually) in a pleasing balance of the two light sources.

- **In spot metering mode,** the camera assumes that you're primarily interested in a single area of the frame. So it calculates flash power on the same single area it uses to calculate overall exposure, without much regard for the background. This mode is called *Standard i-TTL Flash.* (See the earlier discussion of metering modes to find out how the specific metering spot, which is based on a single autofocus point, is chosen.)

Regardless of your metering mode, if you want a little more or less flash light than the camera thinks is appropriate, you can adjust the flash output by using *Flash Compensation.*

Available only when you set the exposure mode to P, S, A, or M, this feature works just like Exposure Compensation, discussed earlier in the chapter, except that it enables you to tweak flash power instead of the overall exposure. As with Exposure Compensation, the Flash Compensation settings are stated in terms of EV *(exposure value)* numbers. A setting of 0.0 indicates no flash adjustment; you can increase the flash power to EV +1.0 or decrease it to EV –3.0.

As an example of the benefit of this feature, look at the carousel images in Figure 7-31. The first image shows you a flash-free shot. Clearly, I needed a flash to compensate for the fact that the horses were shadowed by the roof of the carousel. But at normal flash power, as shown in the same image, the flash was too strong, creating glare in some spots on the horse's neck, as shown in the middle image. By dialing the flash power down to EV –0.7, I got a softer flash that straddled the line perfectly between no flash and too much flash.

No flash

Flash EV 0.0

Flash EV –0.7

Figure 7-31: When normal flash output is too strong, dial in a lower Flash Compensation setting.

As for boosting the flash output, well, you may find it necessary on some occasions, but don't expect the built-in flash to work miracles even at a Flash Compensation of +1.0. Any built-in flash has a limited range, and you simply can't expect the flash light to reach faraway objects. In other words, don't even try taking flash pictures of a darkened recital hall from your seat in the balcony — all you'll wind up doing is annoying everyone.

With that preface in mind, you adjust flash power by pressing the Flash button while rotating the Sub-command dial. (Rotating the Main command dial adjusts the Flash mode.) As long as you hold the button, the Flash Compensation setting appears in the Control panel and Information display (see Figure 7-32). In the viewfinder, the current setting takes the place of the usual shots-remaining value, and a plus or minus sign also appears to indicate whether you're dialing in a positive or negative value.

Flash mode   Flash Compensation setting   Flash Compensation symbol

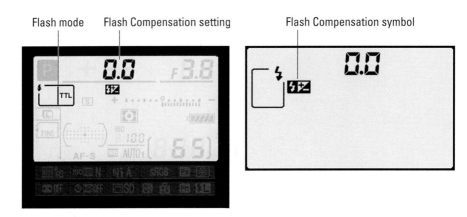

Figure 7-32: Rotate the Sub-command dial while pressing the Flash button to adjust flash power.

After you release the Flash button, you see just the Flash Compensation icon in all three displays. To check the specific compensation value, press and hold the Flash button.

As with Exposure Compensation, any flash-power adjustment you make remains in force, even if you turn off the camera, until you reset the control. So be sure to check the setting before you next use your flash.

Locking flash exposure on your subject

With *FV Lock,* or *Flash Value Lock,* you can lock flash power similar to the way you can use the AE-L/AF-L button to lock autoexposure. (Note that not all external flash units support this function; the camera manual and your flash manual provide a list of supported flash features.) This option can come in handy when you want to compose your photo so that your subject is located at the edge of the frame, for example. You frame the scene initially so the subject is at the center of the frame, lock the flash power, and then reframe. If you didn't lock the flash value, the camera would calculate flash power on your final framing, which could be inappropriate for your subject. You also can use FV Lock to maintain a consistent flash power for a series of shots.

To use FV Lock, follow these steps:

1. **Frame the shot so that your subject is in the center of the viewfinder.**

   You can adjust composition after locking the flash power if you want.

2. **Press and hold the shutter button halfway to engage the exposure meter and, if autofocusing is used, set focus.**

3. **Press and release the Fn button.**

The button is on the front left side of the camera, just below the AF-assist lamp; the letters Fn appear off to the side.

The flash fires a little preflash to determine the correct flash power. When flash power is locked, you see a little flash symbol with the letter L at the left end of the viewfinder, next to the metering mode icon. The same symbol appears in the Control panel and Information display.

4. Recompose the picture if desired and then take the shot.

To release the FV Lock, just press the Fn button again.

If you don't use FV Lock often, you can assign another task to the Fn button. You also can assign the FV Lock function to the AE-L/AF-L button or Depth-of-Field Preview button. Chapter 11 shows you how.

Exploring a few additional flash options

For most people, the flash options covered to this point in the chapter are the most useful on a regular basis. But your D7000 does offer a few other flash options that some photographers may appreciate on occasion, so the next several sections provide a quick look-see. Again, keep in mind that I am only touching on the highlights — be sure to dive into the camera manual or your flash manual, if you use an external flash unit, for all the nitty-gritty.

Enabling high-speed flash (Auto FP)

To properly expose flash pictures, the camera has to synchronize the timing of the flash output with the opening and closing of the shutter. For technical reasons that are too gnarly to get into in this book, this synchronization normally dictates a maximum shutter speed of 1/250 second when you use the built-in flash on the D7000.

Through a Nikon feature called Auto FP flash, you can bump the maximum sync speed up to 1/320 second for the built-in flash, however. Furthermore, if you attach some specific Nikon flash units, you can access the full range of shutter speeds, all the way up to 1/8000 second.

It's important to note, though, that when Auto FP flash is used, the flash fires a little differently. Instead of a single pop of light, it emits a continuous, rapid-fire burst for the entire time that the shutter is open. Although that sounds like a good thing, it actually forces a reduction of the flash power, thereby shortening the distance over which subjects remain illuminated. The faster your shutter speed, the greater the impact on the flash power. So at very high speeds, your subject needs to be pretty close to the camera to be properly exposed by the flash. You even lose a little flash effectiveness when you set the built-in flash to sync at 1/320 second.

Because of this limitation, high-speed flash is mostly useful for shooting portraits or other close-up subjects. In fact, it's very useful when you're shooting portraits outside in the daytime because it permits you to use a wider aperture to blur the background. At a shutter speed of 1/250 second, a very wide aperture would normally overexpose the picture even at ISO 100. With high-speed flash, you can increase the shutter speed enough to compensate for the large aperture.

To access the high-speed flash option, open the Bracketing/Flash section of the Custom Setting menu and select the Flash Sync Speed option, as shown in Figure 7-33. You can choose from the following settings:

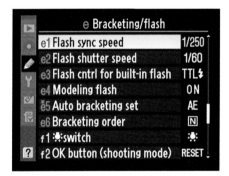 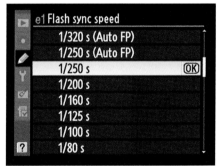

Figure 7-33: Through this option, you can enable high-speed flash, permitting a faster maximum shutter speed for flash photos.

> ✓ **1/320 s (Auto FP):** At this setting, you can use the built-in flash with speeds up to 1/320 second, but remember that using speeds over 1/250 second reduces flash power slightly. For select Nikon flash units (models SB-900, SB-800, SB-700, SB-600, and SB-R200), you can use shutter speeds up to 1/8000 second. At speeds between 1/250 and 1/320, flash power is less affected than when you use the other Auto FP setting, explained next.

> ✓ **1/250 s (Auto FP):** This setting has no effect on the built-in flash. For compatible external flash units, the high-speed flash behavior kicks in at shutter speeds over 1/250 second. As shutter speed goes up, flash power is reduced.

> ✓ **1/250 s to 1/60 s:** The other settings on the menu (see the right image in Figure 7-33) establish a fixed maximum sync speed. By default, it's set to 1/250 second. High-speed flash operation is disabled.

Enabling manual, repeating, or commander-mode flash

The Bracketing/Flash submenu of the Custom Setting menu also offers a setting called Flash Cntrl (Control) for Built-In Flash, as shown in Figure 7-34.

Normally, your flash operates in the TTL, or *through-the-lens,* mode, in which the camera automatically determines the right flash output for you, as discussed earlier in this chapter.

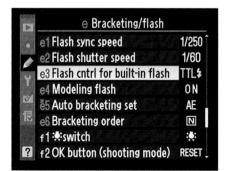

Figure 7-34: The Commander Mode option enables you to trigger off-camera flash units with your built-in flash.

However, if you're an advanced flash user, you may want to explore the other options available only when you shoot in the P, S, A, or M exposure modes:

- **Manual:** This setting enables you to select a specific flash power, with settings ranging from full power to 1/128 power. (If you're hip to rating flash power by Guide Numbers, the manual spells out the ratings for the built-in flash.)

- **Repeating Flash:** If you select this option, the camera fires the flash repeatedly as long as the shutter is open. The resulting picture looks as though it was shot with a strobe light. In other words, this is a special-effects function. You can modify certain aspects of the flash output, including how often the flash fires per second.

- **Commander Mode:** This mode enables the camera's built-in flash as a *master* to trigger (command) off-camera flash units, which are called *slaves.* (I know, but don't write me any nasty letters — I'm here to tell you what the current terminology is, no matter how politically incorrect those words may be.) You can even set the power of the external units through the Commander Mode options and specify whether you want the built-in flash to simply trigger the other flash heads or add its own flash power to the scene.

To use this feature, your external flash heads must support the Nikon Creative Lighting System, or CLS. Visit the Nikon Web site to get a better idea of how the system works. It's pretty cool, and it can provide you with some great added lighting flexibility without having to spend lots of money (although you certainly can) or rely on lots of bulky, traditional lighting equipment. In fact, I rely on this lighting option to shoot most of my product and still-life shots, using the on-board flash to trigger one Nikon SB-600 and one SB-R200 flash unit. The SB-600 also works in the camera's hot shoe, whereas the SB-R200 is a small, fist-sized flash that works only as a slave.

Firing a modeling flash

Chapter 8 introduces you to your D7000's Depth-of-Field Preview button, which enables you to preview through the viewfinder how your selected aperture setting will affect depth of field. By default, pressing the button with flash enabled also causes the flash to emit a *modeling flash* when you shoot in the P, S, A, or M exposure modes.

When the modeling flash feature is turned on, the flash emits a repeating, strobelike series of flash light while you press the button. The idea is to enable you to preview how the light will fall on your subject. However, living subjects aren't likely to appreciate the feature — it's a bit blinding to have the flash going off repeatedly in your face. And obviously, using the feature drains the camera battery or, if you're using an external flash, its battery.

If you want to disable it, you can do so through the Modeling Flash option, found on the Bracketing/Flash submenu of the Custom Setting menu. Changing the function of the Depth-of-Field Preview button, which I show you how to do in Chapter 11, also disables the modeling flash. The feature works only when you set the button to its default function, Preview.

Bracketing Exposures

Many photographers use *exposure bracketing* to ensure that at least one shot of a subject is properly exposed. Bracketing simply means to shoot the same subject multiple times, slightly varying the exposure settings for each image.

In the P, S, A, and M exposure modes, your D7000 offers *automatic bracketing.* When you enable this feature, your only job is to press the shutter button to record the shots; the camera automatically adjusts the exposure settings between each image. The D7000, however, takes things one step further than most cameras that offer automatic bracketing, enabling you to bracket not just basic exposure, but also flash power, Active D-Lighting, and white balance.

Aside from cover-your, uh, "bases" shooting, bracketing is useful for *HDR imaging. HDR* stands for *high dynamic range,* with *dynamic range* referring to the spectrum of brightness values in a photograph. The idea behind HDR is to capture the same shot multiple times, using different exposure settings for each image. You then use special imaging software, called *tone mapping software,* to combine the exposures in a way that uses specific brightness values from each shot. By using this process, you get a shot that contains more detail in both the highlights and shadows that a camera could ever record in a single image.

Figure 7-35 shows an example. The first two images show you the brightest and darkest exposures; the bottom image shows the HDR composite.

Figure 7-35: Using HDR software tools, I merged the brightest and darkest exposures (top) along with several intermediate exposures, to produce the composite image (bottom).

When applied to its extreme limits, HDR produces images that have something of a graphic-novel look. My example is pretty tame; some people might not even realize that any digital trickery has been involved. To me, it has the look of a hand-tinted photo.

Whether you're interested in HDR or just want to give yourself an exposure safety net, the next section explains how to bracket exposure and flash. Following that, you can find details about bracketing Active D-Lighting. Chapter 8 walks you through the process of bracketing white balance.

Bracketing exposure and flash

After setting the Mode dial to P, S, A, or M follow these steps to bracket exposure only, flash only, or both together. (Don't be put off by the length of these steps; although describing the features takes quite a few words, actually using them isn't all that complicated.)

1. **Specify what you want to bracket through the Auto Bracketing Set option, located in the Bracketing/Flash section of the Custom Setting menu.**

   Shown in Figure 7-36, this option determines what aspect of your picture you want to vary between shots. For exposure and flash bracketing, you have three choices:

 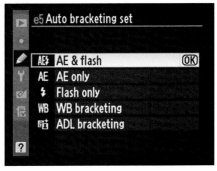

Figure 7-36: Use this option to select the setting you want the camera to adjust between shots.

   • *AE & Flash:* Brackets exposure settings and flash power between shots.

   • *AE Only:* Brackets exposure settings only.

   In P mode, the camera may vary shutter speed, aperture, or both between shots to produce the different exposures. In S mode, it adjusts aperture only; in A and M modes, it changes shutter speed only. In all modes, ISO may also be adjusted between shots if you enable ISO Sensitivity Auto Control, as outlined earlier in this chapter.

   • *Flash Only:* Brackets flash power only.

2. **Choose the order in which you want the bracketed shots recorded.**

   Make the call via the Bracketing Order option, found with the other bracketing options on the Custom Setting menu. As shown in Figure 7-37, you have two options:

   • *MTR>Under>Over:* This setting is the default. For a three-shot exposure bracketing series, your first shot is captured at your original settings. (MTR stands for *metered* and designates the initial settings suggested by the camera's exposure meter.) The second image is captured at settings that produce a darker image, and the third, at settings that produce a brighter image.

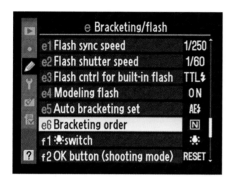 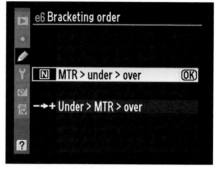

Figure 7-37: You can choose the order in which you want the bracketed shots to be captured.

This sequence can vary slightly depending on how many frames you include in your bracketed series; if you're a detail nut, you can find out the specific order used in every scenario in the camera manual.

- *Under>MTR>Over:* The darkest image is captured first, then the metered image, and then the brightest image.

BKT

3. **Select the number of frames in each series by pressing the BKT button while rotating the Main command dial.**

   As soon as you press the button, you see the current bracketing settings in the Control panel and Information display, as shown in Figure 7-38. You also see an exposure meter with some symbols related to bracketing; more on how to interpret the bracketing information a little later.

   With the BKT button pressed, rotate the Main command dial to cycle to through the available settings. Here's what you can accomplish at each of the frame-count settings:

   - *Disable bracketing:* Set the frame count to 0.
   - *Capture your original plus one darker and one lighter frame:* Choose 3 frames.
   - *Capture your original plus a brighter frame only:* Choose +2.
   - *Capture your original plus a darker frame only:* Select –2.

4. **Set the level of adjustment between frames by pressing the BKT button while rotating the Sub-command dial.**

   By default, you can adjust exposures by as much as two stops, in one-third stop (0.3) increments. If you change the setting of the EV Steps for Exposure Control to the 1/2 step setting, bracketing settings are instead presented in half-stop (0.5) increments. See the earlier sidebar

"Exposure stops: How many do you want to see?" for details on this menu option and an explanation of stops.

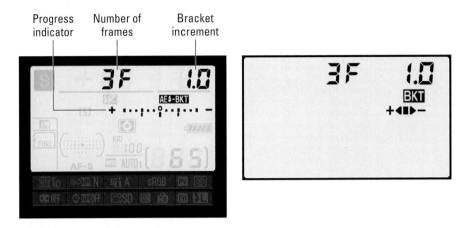

Progress indicator   Number of frames   Bracket increment

Figure 7-38: Rotate the Main command dial while pressing the BKT button to adjust the number of bracketed frames; press the button and rotate the Sub-command dial to adjust the bracketing increment.

Now for the promised decoder guide to the bracketing information displayed with the meter: In the Information display, the meter serves as a bracketing progress indicator and appears as shown on the left in Figure 7-38 when you enable the three-frame bracketing option. The markings near the meter indicate the following:

- The symbol above the meter tells you what you're bracketing — AE+Flash, in the figure.

- The notches under the meter show you how many frames are enabled and the amount of adjustment between frames. For example, in the figure, the notch at the zero point represents the neutral shot — the one that will be recorded with no adjustment. The notches to the left and right show that the other two shots will be recorded at settings that produce a one-stop increase and a one-stop decrease in exposure.

The Control panel shows a miniaturized version of the progress indicator; for a three-shot series, you see a little notch bordered by two triangles, with a plus and minus at each end, as shown on the right in the figure. Frankly, the indicator is so miniaturized that I can't make it out even with my strongest reading glasses on, but that's the price of living past your 20s, I guess.

5. Release the BKT button to return to shooting mode.

The bracketing frame and increment settings then disappear from the Control panel and Shooting Information display; the bracketing indicators remain.

6. **Take your first shot.**

   After you take the picture, the indicator representing the shot you just took disappears from under the meter in the Information display. For example, if you're bracketing three frames, the notch at the 0 position disappears after your first shot. Likewise, the middle bar of the indicator in the Control panel goes away.

7. **Take the remaining shots in the series.**

   When the series is done, the indicator scale returns to its original appearance, and you can then begin shooting the next series of bracketed shots.

8. **To disable bracketing, press the BKT button and rotate the Main command dial until the number of frames returns to 0.**

Three frames may not be enough to produce a good HDR image, even if you set the bracketing increment to two stops. So if HDR is your goal, you may want to shoot two or even three series of bracketed shots but use a smaller increment of adjustment between each shot. Just select different initial exposure starting points for each series: Choose settings that underexpose the photo for the first series, settings that more properly expose the image for the second series, and settings that overexpose the image for the final series. If you want to record a huge series of bracketed shots, you may find it easier to simply set the exposure mode dial to M and then simply change the shutter speed between each shot rather than using autobracketing. (Don't change the aperture, or depth of field will change from image to image.)

Bracketing Active-D Lighting

Active D-Lighting, as explained earlier in this chapter, adjusts exposure in a way that brightens shadows without blowing out highlights in the process. In the P, S, A, or M exposure modes, you can set up a bracketed series that applies different levels of the adjustment to each shot.

The process varies slightly from the steps in the preceding section, so instead of repeating it all here, I'll just hit the highlights:

1. **Set the Auto Bracketing Set option to ADL Bracketing, as shown in Figure 7-39.**

   This option is located in the Bracketing/Flash section of the Custom Setting menu.

Figure 7-39: You can capture a series of up to three shots, each with a different amount of Active D-Lighting applied.

The Bracketing Order option discussed in Step 2 in the preceding section doesn't matter for Active D-Lighting bracketing; the camera always uses the default setting.

BKT

2. **Press the BKT button while rotating the Main command dial to set up the bracketed series.**

When you press the BKT button, the Information display and Control panel display the data shown in Figure 7-40. Notice that instead of the bracket increment that appears for exposure and flash bracketing, you see just the frame count, the symbol ADL (to let you know that Active D-Lighting bracketing is enabled), and a progress indicator. With Active D-Lighting bracketing, you don't set the frame count and level of shot-to-shot adjustment as you do for exposure and flash bracketing. Instead, the number of frames you select determines what Active D-Lighting setting is used for each frame.

Number of frames   Progress indicator

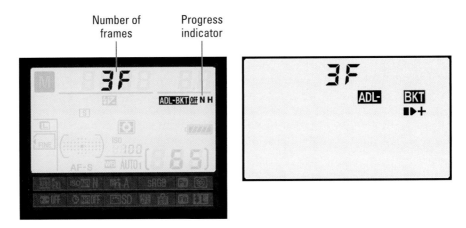

Figure 7-40: With Active D-Lighting, a single value controls both the frame count and the level of Active D-Lighting adjustment.

Here are your options:

- *2 Frames:* Records one image with Active D-Lighting turned off and another at the value currently selected for Active D-Lighting. (You set that value via the Shooting menu or the Information panel control strip; see the earlier section "Expanding Tonal Range with Active D-Lighting" for help.) If Active D-Lighting happens to be set to Off, the second shot is recorded using the Auto setting.

- *3:* Records one shot with Active D-Lighting off, one at the Normal setting, and one at the High setting.

Notice that in the Information display, the labels next to the progress indicator tell you which settings are used for the different frame counts. For example, in Figure 7-40, the labels display the settings associated with recording three frames: Off, N (Normal), and H (High). The Control panel shows — er, wait, I have to go find a stronger pair of glasses — two bars and a plus sign for three frames, and two bars for two frames.

3. Release the BKT button and take your shots.

As with exposure and flash bracketing, each little bar under the meter represents one frame in the series. After you capture a shot, the bar representing that frame disappears. When you've captured all shots in the series, the meter indicators return to their "starting position."

Manipulating Focus and Color

*T*o many people, the word *focus* has just one interpretation when applied to a photograph: Either the subject is in focus or it's blurry. And it's true — this characteristic of your photographs is an important one. There's not much to appreciate about an image that's so blurry that you can't make out whether you're looking at Peru or Peoria.

But an artful photographer knows that there's more to focus than simply getting a sharp image of a subject. You also need to consider *depth of field,* or the distance over which objects remain sharply focused. This chapter explains all the ways to control depth of field as well as how to take best advantage of the myriad focusing options on your camera.

In addition, this chapter dives into the topic of color, explaining your camera's white balance control, which compensates for the varying color casts created by different light sources. You also can get my take on the other color features, including the Color Space option and Picture Controls, in this chapter.

Mastering the Autofocusing System

One of the most important advantages you gain from stepping up to a powerhouse camera like the D7000 is access to an amazing array of autofocusing features, all designed to help you achieve tack-sharp focus with just a half-press of the shutter button.

REMEMBER

The first step in putting the autofocus system to work is to set the Focus-mode selector on the front of the camera to AF, as shown in Figure 8-1. With a lens like the 18–105mm kit lens, also set the switch on the lens to the A position, as shown in the figure. For other lenses, check the lens instruction manual for details on this setting.

Pressing the AF-mode button, also labeled in the figure, gives you access to the two most critical auto-focusing options:

Lens focus-mode switch

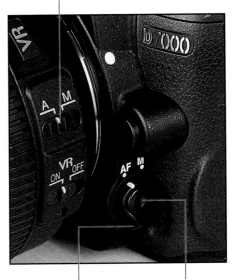

Focus-mode selector   AF-mode button

Figure 8-1: These switches control whether the camera uses autofocusing or manual focusing.

- **Autofocus mode:** This setting determines whether the camera locks focus when you press the shutter button halfway or continues to adjust focus up to the time you take the picture.

- **AF-area mode:** This setting tells the camera what area of the frame to analyze when establishing focus. You can ask the camera to consider all 39 of its autofocusing points, a single point, or something in between.

You can view the current Autofocus mode and AF-area mode settings in the Information display and Control panel, in the areas labeled in Figure 8-2.

For all but a few of the Scene exposure modes, both options are set by default to produce the most automatic settings: AF-A for the Autofocus mode and Auto Area for the AF-area mode. At these settings, the camera decides what focusing point to use and when (or if) to lock focus. If you want to stick with this setup, Chapter 3 provides the specific steps to follow to set focus and take a picture. That chapter also details the autofocusing steps for the aforementioned Scene modes that deviate from the defaults.

But as with most camera options, you can get more reliable results by abandoning the default settings and choosing other Autofocus and AF-area mode settings. The next several sections detail each option individually; following that, you can find step-by-step instructions for using the combinations of Autofocus and AF-area mode settings that I recommend for shooting stationary subjects and for moving subjects.

AF-area mode

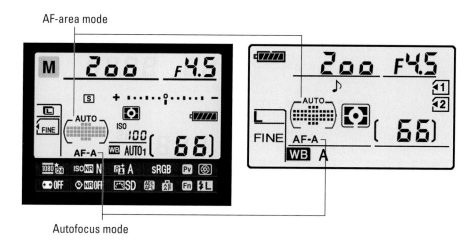

Autofocus mode

Figure 8-2: You can see the current Autofocus mode and AF-area mode settings here.

One note before you dig in: Information in this chapter assumes that you haven't changed the default functions of camera buttons (such as OK and the shutter button). I detail those customization options in Chapter 11, but leave the buttons at their default settings until you're fully acquainted with the camera — otherwise, instructions here (and those you find in the camera manual) aren't going to work. Also note that the settings and techniques described here relate to normal, through-the-viewfinder photography. Autofocusing works differently in Live View mode; Chapter 4 covers that topic as well as all other Live View and movie-making information.

Choosing an Autofocus mode

When you use autofocusing, you press the shutter button halfway to kick-start the autofocusing system. Whether the camera locks focus at that point or continually adjusts focus until you press the button the rest of the way depends on the Autofocus mode.

You can choose from three options, which work as follows:

- ✔ **AF-S (single-servo autofocus):** With this option, the camera locks focus when you depress the shutter button halfway. It's designed for shooting stationary subjects. (Think *S* for *still, stationary.*)

- ✔ **AF-C (continuous-servo autofocus):** In this mode, which is designed for moving subjects, the camera focuses continuously for the entire time you hold the shutter button halfway down. (Think *C* for *continuous motion.*)

✔ **AF-A (auto-servo autofocus):** This mode is the default setting. The camera analyzes the scene and, if it detects motion, automatically selects continuous-servo mode (AF-C). If the camera instead believes you're shooting a stationary object, it selects single-servo mode (AF-S).

This mode works pretty well, but it can get confused sometimes. For example, if your subject is motionless but other people are moving in the background, the camera may mistakenly switch to continuous autofocus. By the same token, if the subject is moving only slightly, the camera may not make the switch. So my best advice is to choose either AF-S or AF-C instead.

To change the Autofocus setting, press the AF-mode button (refer to Figure 8-1) while rotating the Main command dial.

While the button is pressed, all data disappears from the Information screen and Control panel except the Autofocus mode setting and an icon representing the AF-area mode, as shown in Figure 8-3. The viewfinder display also changes, with the Autofocus mode and AF-area mode settings appearing in the areas labeled in Figure 8-4. The viewfinder also shows the autofocus brackets, which indicate the area of the frame that contain the 39 autofocus points, and rectangles representing the active points. Which points appear depend on the AF-area mode, as outlined in the next section. Figures 8-3 and 8-4 show the default Autofocus mode and AF-area mode settings: AF-A and Auto Area, respectively. (Note that the viewfinder doesn't show all 39 autofocus points at the Auto Area setting — only the points around the perimeter of the autofocusing brackets appear, as shown in the figure. All 39 are active in Auto Area mode just the same.)

 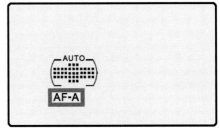

Figure 8-3: Press the AF-mode button while rotating the Main command dial to change the Autofocus mode setting.

When you release the button, the viewfinder display returns to normal, but the Information display and Control panel show the selected setting along with all the other usual data. (Refer to Figure 8-2.)

One other critical thing to know about this setting: By default, the camera refuses to take a picture in AF-S mode if it can't achieve focus. No way, no how, it's not going to take an out-of-focus picture no matter how hard you press the shutter button. With AF-C mode, the opposite occurs. The camera assumes that because this mode is designed for shooting action, you want to capture the shot at the instant you fully depress the shutter button, regardless of whether it had time to set focus.

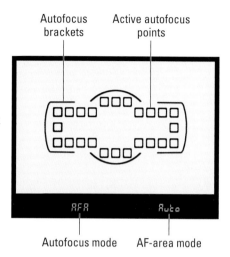

Autofocus brackets   Active autofocus points

Autofocus mode   AF-area mode

Figure 8-4: The viewfinder also shows the current setting while you press the AF-mode button.

Because Nikon figures you didn't buy a camera as advanced as the D7000 to be limited to only one way of doing things, though, you can adjust this behavior through the Custom Setting menu. The relevant options are the two AF Priority Selection options at the top of the Autofocus section of the menu, shown in Figure 8-5.

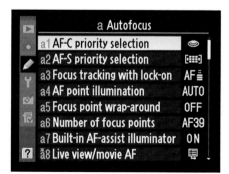

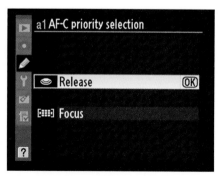

Figure 8-5: You can tell the camera whether to go ahead and take the picture even if focus hasn't been achieved.

The first option affects how things work in AF-C mode; the second, AF-S mode. For both options, you can choose from the two settings shown on the right in the figure:

- ✓ **Release:** This setting is the default for the AF-C mode and enables you to take the picture regardless of whether focus is achieved.

- ✓ **Focus:** You can't take the picture until focus is achieved. This setting is the default for the AF-S mode.

To decide which option is right for you, you have to consider whether you'd rather have any shot, even if it's out of focus, or capture only those that are in focus. I prefer the latter, so I set both options to Focus. Why waste battery power, memory card space, and inevitable time deleting out-of-focus pictures, after all? Yes, if you're shooting rapid action, you may miss a few shots waiting for the focus to occur, but if they're going to be lousy shots, who cares?

Sports shooters who regularly fire off hundreds of shots while covering an event, though, may want to "unlock" the shutter release for AF-C mode. Again, you may wind up with lots of wasted shots, but you increase the odds that you'll capture that split-second "highlight reel" moment. If it's slightly out of focus, you can probably retouch it enough to make it passable, especially if the picture content is truly special. And by using camera settings that produce a large *depth of field* (zone of sharp focus), your subject may appear in focus even if the actual focusing point the camera used wasn't dead on. Later sections in this chapter discuss depth of field.

Choosing an AF-area mode: One focus point or many?

The AF-area mode setting determines how the camera decides which of its 39 autofocus points to use as the focusing target. To adjust the setting, press the AF-mode button while rotating the Sub-command dial.

When the button is pressed, all data except the current setting and the Autofocus mode setting disappear from the Information screen and Control panel (refer to Figure 8-3). If you're looking through the viewfinder, the display updates to show you which autofocus points are active, and the current AF-area mode setting appears at the right end of the display, as shown in Figure 8-4. After you release the button, the displays return to normal.

You have the following AF-area mode choices:

- ✓ **Single Point:** This mode is designed to help you quickly and easily lock focus on a still subject. You select a single focus point, and the camera bases focus on that point only. This option is best paired with the single-servo (AF-S) autofocus mode, which is also geared to still subjects.

In the Control panel, the icon representing this mode appears as it does in the margin here. In the Information display, the icon for this mode and the other AF-area mode settings is similar but tells you a bit more information: Active autofocus points are represented by gray squares, inactive points appear as small dots, and the selected point is a black square. You can also determine the active point by simply looking through the viewfinder; see the next section for more details on selecting an autofocus point.

✔ **Dynamic Area:** The Dynamic Area autofocusing technology is designed for focusing on a moving subject. You select an initial focus point, but if your subject moves out of that point before you snap the picture, the camera looks to surrounding points for focusing information.

On the D7000, you can choose from three Dynamic Area settings, represented in the Control panel by the icons you see here:

- *9-point Dynamic Area:* Instead of looking at all 39 autofocus points, the camera takes focusing cues from your selected point plus the 8 surrounding points. If you choose the center focus point, for example, the points shown on the left in Figure 8-6 are active. This setting is ideal when you have a moment or two to compose your shot and your subject is moving in a predictable way, making it easy to reframe as needed to keep the subject within the 9-point area.

  This setting also provides the fastest Dynamic Area autofocusing because the camera has to analyze the fewest number of autofocusing points.

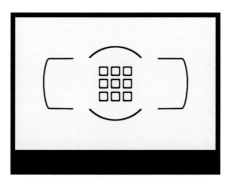 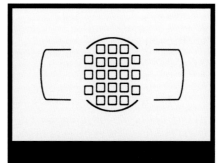

Figure 8-6: The 9- and 21-point Dynamic Area options sometimes offer faster autofocusing because fewer points are considered.

- *21-point Dynamic Area:* This mode uses your selected point plus the 20 surrounding points. The right screen in Figure 8-6 shows you which points are active if you select the center point.

Obviously, this setting enables your subject to move a little farther afield from your selected focus point and still remain in the target zone. So it works better than 9-point mode when you can't quite predict the path your subject is going to take.

- *39-point Dynamic Area:* The camera makes use of the full complement of autofocus points. (Figure 8-7 shows you how the points are laid out within the autofocus brackets.) This mode is designed for subjects that are moving so rapidly that it's hard to keep them within the framing area of the 21-point or 9-point setting — a flock of birds, for example. The drawback to this setting is focusing time: With all 39 points on deck, the camera has to work a little harder to find a focus target.

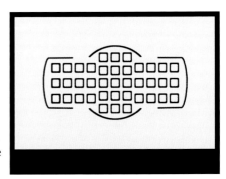

Figure 8-7: At the 39-point Dynamic Area setting, all autofocus points are active.

To use Dynamic Area autofocusing, you must set the Autofocus mode to AF-C or AF-A. In fact, the Dynamic Area options don't even appear when the Autofocus mode is set to AF-S. Again, I prefer to use AF-C mode instead of relying on the camera to sense motion and shift to continuous autofocusing, as it does in AF-A mode.

✔ **3D Tracking:** This one is a variation of the 39-point Dynamic Area autofocusing — well, sort of. As in that mode, you start by selecting a single focus point and then press the shutter button halfway to set focus. But the goal of the 3D Tracking mode is to maintain focus on your subject if you recompose the shot after you press the shutter button halfway to lock focus.

The only problem with 3D Tracking is that the way the camera detects your subject is by analyzing the colors of the object under your selected focus point. So if not much difference exists between the subject and other objects in the frame, the camera can get fooled. And if your subject moves out of the frame, you must release the shutter button and reset focus by pressing it halfway again.

If you want to try 3D Tracking autofocus, set the Autofocus mode to AF-C or AF-A; you can't access this AF-area mode when the Autofocus mode is set to AF-S.

✔ **Auto Area:** At this setting, the camera automatically chooses which of the 39 focus points to use. Focus priority is typically assigned to the object closest to the camera.

Although Auto Area mode requires the least input from you, it's also typically the slowest option because of the technology it must use to set focus. First, the camera analyzes all 39 focus points. Then it consults an internal database to try to match the information reported by those points to a huge collection of reference photographs. From that analysis, it makes an educated guess about which focus points are most appropriate for your scene. Although it's still amazingly fast considering what's happening in the camera's brain, it's slower than the other AF-area options.

Frankly, I don't use Auto Area mode very often unless I'm handing the camera over to someone who's inexperienced and wouldn't know how to use the other two modes. And with a camera that costs as much as the D7000, I can think of only a few people who I'd even trust to hand it over *to*. ("Oh, I'm sorry, but I'm borrowing this from my boss and I *swore* I wouldn't let anyone else use it.") So I keep things nice and simple and stick with Single Point for still subjects and one of the Dynamic Area modes for moving subjects.

If you do use Auto Area mode, remember that all 39 autofocus points are active, even though the viewfinder display appears as shown in Figure 8-4, showing only autofocus points around the perimeter of the autofocus brackets when you press the AF-mode button and rotate the Sub-command dial to adjust the AF-area mode.

Choosing the right autofocus combo

You'll get the best autofocus results if you pair your chosen Autofocus mode with the most appropriate AF-area mode because the two settings work in tandem. Here are the combinations that I suggest for the maximum autofocus control:

✔ **For still subjects: AF-S and Single Point.** You then select a specific focus point, and the camera locks focus on that point when you press the shutter button halfway. Focus remains locked on your subject even if you reframe the shot after you press the button halfway. (It helps to remember the *s* factor: For *s*till subjects, *S*ingle Point and AF-*S.*)

✔ **For moving subjects: AF-C and 39-point Dynamic Area.** You still begin by selecting a focus point, but the camera adjusts focus as needed if your subject moves within the frame after you press the shutter button halfway to establish focus. (Think *motion, dynamic, continuous.*) Remember to reframe as needed to keep your subject within the boundaries of the autofocus points, though. And if you want speedier autofocusing, consider switching to 21-point or 9-point Dynamic Area mode — just remember that you need to keep your subject within that smaller portion of the frame for the focus adjustment to work properly.

Upcoming sections in this chapter spell out the exact steps you use to set focus with these autofocus pairings. First, though, I need to take a slight detour to explain how you select a specific focus point when you use Single Point, Dynamic Area, or 3D Tracking mode or focus manually.

Selecting (and locking) an autofocus point

When you use any AF-area mode but Auto Area, you see a single autofocus point in the viewfinder. That point is the *selected autofocus point* — the one the camera will use to set focus in the Single Point mode and to choose the starting focusing distance in the Dynamic Area and 3D Tracking modes. By default, the center point is selected, as shown in Figure 8-8.

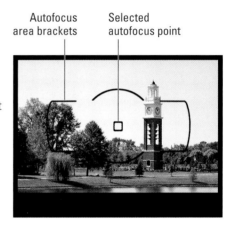

Autofocus area brackets   Selected autofocus point

To choose a different focus point, first make sure that the Focus Selector Lock switch is set to the position shown in Figure 8-9. Then just press the Multi Selector right, left, up, or down to cycle through the available focus points, which are all located within the area surrounded by the autofocus brackets (labeled in Figure 8-8). I moved the focus point over the clock tower, for example, in the second image in Figure 8-9.

Figure 8-8: By default, the center focus point is selected.

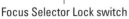

Focus Selector Lock switch

Figure 8-9: When the Focus Selector Lock switch is set to this position, you can press the Multi Selector to select a different focus point.

If nothing happens when you press the Multi Selector, press the shutter button halfway to activate the metering system. Then release the button and try again.

A couple additional tips:

✔ **You can reduce the number of available focus points available for the Single Point AF-area mode from 39 to 11.** Why would you do this? Because it enables you to choose a focus point more quickly — you don't have to keep pressing the Multi Selector zillions of times to get to the one you want to use. Make the change via the Number of Focus Points option, found on the Autofocus section of the Custom Setting menu, as shown on the left in Figure 8-10. The right half of the figure shows you which autofocus points are available at the reduced setting.

If you do change the setting, the AF-area icon in the Information display changes to show the reduced number of points. But your setting doesn't affect the Dynamic Area, 3D Tracking, or Auto Area AF-area modes; the camera always uses the normal number of points for those modes.

✔ **The nine autofocus points at the center of the frame are more capable than others.** These points use *cross-type sensors,* which evaluate focus by analyzing both horizontal and vertical lines in the scene. The other points assess only horizontal lines. Cross-type sensors typically work better, especially in dim lighting, so if you're having trouble getting the camera to focus, select one of these focus points and try again.

✔ **You can quickly select the center focus point at any time by pressing OK.** Again, this assumes that you haven't changed the function of that button, an option you can explore in Chapter 11.

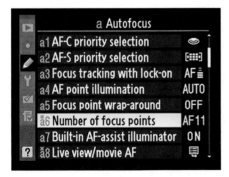
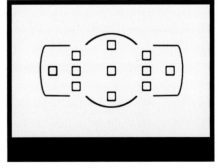

Figure 8-10: You can choose to limit the number of available focus points to the 11 shown here.

- ✔ **If you want to use a certain focus point for a while, you can "lock in" that point by moving the Focus Selector Lock switch to the L position.** This feature ensures that an errant press of the Multi Selector doesn't accidentally change your selected point.

- ✔ **The selected focus point is also used to meter exposure when you use spot metering.** The point you choose affects the way the camera calculates flash exposure as overall exposure. See Chapter 7 for details about the metering mode setting.

- ✔ **Focus-point wraparound is disabled by default.** What's focus-point wraparound, you ask? Well, by default, you hit a "wall" when you reach the top, bottom, left, or right focus point in the group. So if the leftmost point is selected, for example, pressing left again gets you nowhere. But if you turn on the Focus Point Wrap-Around option, found with the other autofocus options on the Custom Setting menu, you instead jump to the rightmost point. I like this option, but it's totally a personal preference.

Autofocusing with still subjects: AF-S + Single Point

For stationary subjects, the fastest, most precise autofocus option is to pair the AF-S (single-servo) Autofocus mode with the Single Point AF-area mode. With this combination, the autofocus system can quickly home in on your subject.

To adjust both settings, press and hold the AF-mode button (refer to Figure 8-1). Then rotate the Main command dial to change the Autofocus mode; rotate the Sub-command dial to change the AF-area mode. While the button is pressed, the Information screen, Control panel, and viewfinder displays show just these two settings, as shown in Figure 8-11.

Autofocus
mode   AF-area mode

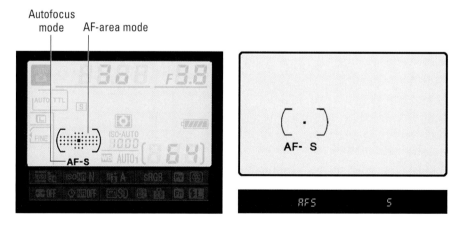

Figure 8-11: Select these autofocus settings for stationary subjects.

Shutter speed and blurry photos

A poorly focused photo isn't always related to the issues discussed in this chapter. Any movement of the camera or subject can also cause blur. Both of these problems are related to shutter speed, an exposure control that I cover in Chapter 7. Be sure to also visit Chapter 7, which provides some additional tips for capturing moving objects without blur.

After selecting these options, follow these steps to focus:

1. **Looking through the viewfinder, use the Multi Selector to position the focus point over your subject.**

   If the focus point doesn't respond, press the shutter button halfway and release it to jog the camera awake. Then try again. Also be sure that the Focus Selector Lock switch is set to the position shown in Figure 8-9.

2. **Press the shutter button halfway to set focus.**

   The camera displays a green focus lamp in the viewfinder, as shown in Figure 8-12, and emits a beep to let you know that focus was achieved. The beep doesn't sound, however, if you set the AF-S Priority option, discussed earlier, to Release. You also can disable the beep through the Custom Setting menu, as covered in Chapter 1, or by setting the Release mode to Quiet.

Selected focus point

Focus indicator

Figure 8-12: By default, the camera won't take the picture until focus is achieved and the green focus indicator lights.

   Focus remains locked as long as you keep the shutter button pressed halfway. If you're using autoexposure (any exposure mode but M), the initial exposure settings are also chosen at the moment you press the shutter button halfway, but they're adjusted as needed up to the time you take the shot.

3. **Press the shutter button the rest of the way to take the shot.**

   Don't forget that at the default AF-S Priority setting (Focus), the camera doesn't let you take the picture when focus isn't set. To modify that behavior, see the earlier section "Choosing an Autofocus mode."

Now for a few nuances of this autofocusing process:

- ✏ **A triangle on either side of the green focus dot indicates incorrect focusing.** I cover this issue in the part of Chapter 3 that shows you how to take a picture in the Auto and Auto Flash Off exposure modes, but what the heck, the illustrations are small, so Figure 8-13 shows you what the triangles look like again so you don't have to tromp back to Chapter 3. An arrow to the left of the dot means that focus is set in front of the object under the focus point; an arrow to the right means that focus is set behind the object. Typically, you see one or both of the triangles while the camera is hunting for the correct focusing distance. If the triangles don't go away, the subject is confusing the autofocus system — your best bet is to switch to manual focusing in that situation. You also may simply be too close to your subject, so try backing away a little to see whether that helps.

- ✏ **You can position your subject outside a focus point if needed.** Just compose the scene initially so that your subject is under a point, press the shutter button halfway to lock focus, and then reframe. However, note that if you're using autoexposure, you may want to lock focus and exposure together using the AE-L/AF-L button, as covered in Chapter 7. Otherwise, exposure is adjusted to match your new framing, which may not work well for your subject. In fact, the Chapter 7 technique for locking exposure is designed to work when teamed up with the AF-S/Single Point autofocus settings.

- ✏ **Which focus points you can select depend on the setting of the Number of Focus Points option on the Custom Setting menu.** Normally, you can choose from all 39 points; but if you change the menu setting to 11, you're limited to the points shown in Figure 8-10. See the preceding section for details on this topic.

Focus in front of subject   Focus behind subject

Figure 8-13: The triangles indicate that focus isn't accurately set on the object under the selected focus point.

Focusing on moving subjects: AF-C + Dynamic Area

When you need to autofocus on a moving target, whether it's a fast-paced subject or just a child playing, select AF-C for the Autofocus mode and choose one of the three Dynamic Area options for the AF-area mode. The section "Choosing an AF-area mode: One focus point or many?" earlier in this chapter, provides some information to help you decide whether to use the 9-, 21-, or 39-point Dynamic Area setting.

The focusing process is the same as just outlined, with a couple exceptions:

- ✔ **When you press the shutter button halfway, the camera sets the initial focusing distance based on your selected autofocus point.** But if your subject moves from that point, the camera checks surrounding points for focus information.

- ✔ **Focus is adjusted continually up to when you take the picture.** You see the green focus indicator light in the viewfinder, but it may flash on and off as focus is adjusted. The beep that you hear when using the AF-S Autofocus mode doesn't sound in AF-C mode however, which is a Good Thing — otherwise, things could get pretty noisy because the beep would sound every time the camera adjusted focus.

- ✔ **Try to keep the subject under the selected focus point to increase the odds of good focus.** But as long as the subject falls within one of the other focus points (9, 21, or 39, depending on which Dynamic Area mode you selected), focus should be adjusted accordingly. Note that you don't see the focus point actually move in the viewfinder, but the focus tweak happens just the same. (You can hear the focus motor doing its thing.)

- ✔ **By default, the camera lets you take the picture regardless of whether focus has been achieved.** To change this behavior, head for the AF-C Priority Selection option on the Custom Setting menu; see the earlier section "Choosing an Autofocus mode" for details.

Getting comfortable with continuous autofocusing takes some time, so it's a good idea to practice before you need to photograph an important event. After you get the hang of the AF-C/Dynamic Area system, though, I think you'll really like it. When you're up to speed on the basics, explore these related options:

- ✔ **Using autofocus lock:** Should you want to "freeze" the focus adjustment at any time so that focus remains set at a specific distance, press and hold the AE-L/AF-L button. Remember, though, that the default setup for this button freezes both focus and exposure. If you use this option a lot, you may want to decouple the two functions by the button customization options covered in Chapter 11. You can use the button to lock focus only, for example, and select another button to lock exposure only.

- ✔ **Preventing focusing miscues with tracking lock-on:** So you're shooting your friend's volleyball game, practicing your action-autofocusing skills. You've set the initial focus, and the camera's doing its part by adjusting focus to accommodate her pre-serve moves. Then all of a sudden, some clueless interloper walks in front of the camera. Okay, it *was* the referee, who probably did have a right to be there, but *still*.

The good news is that as long as the ref gets out of the way before the action happens, you're probably okay. A feature called *focus tracking with lock-on,* designed for just this scenario, tells the camera to ignore objects that appear temporarily in the scene after you begin focusing. Instead of resetting focus on the newcomer, the camera continues focusing on the original subject.

You can vary the length of time the camera waits before starting to refocus through the Focus Tracking with Lock-On option, found on the Custom Setting menu and shown in Figure 8-14. Normal (3 seconds) is the default setting. You can choose a longer or shorter delay or turn off the lock-on altogether. If you do turn off the lock-on, the camera starts refocusing on any object that appears in the frame between you and your original subject.

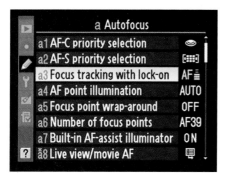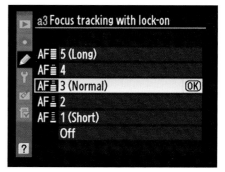

Figure 8-14: This option controls how the autofocus system deals with objects that come between the lens and the subject after you initiate focusing.

Exploring a few last autofocus tweaks

All these autofocus options making your brain hurt? Hang in there — just a few more to go, and they're of the no-brainer type. Well, easy-brainer types, at least.

The Autofocus section of the Custom Setting menu (refer to the left screen in Figure 8-14) offers the following options:

✔ **AF Point Illumination:** It happens so fast that you might not notice it unless you pay close attention, but when you press the shutter button halfway, the selected focus point in the viewfinder flashes red and then goes back to black. At the default setting for this option (Auto), the red highlights are displayed only when the background is dark, which would make the black focus points difficult to see. You can choose the On setting to force the highlights no matter whether the background is dark. Or you can choose Off to disable the highlights altogether.

✔ **Built-in AF-Assist Illuminator:** In dim lighting, the camera may emit a beam of light from the little lamp just below the Control panel, on the front of the camera. If you're in a situation where that light could be distracting to others in the room, you can disable it by setting this option to Off. You may need to focus manually, though, because without the light to help it find its target, the autofocus system may have trouble.

Additionally, the Setup menu offers an AF Fine Tune option, which is provided to enable you to create custom focusing adjustments for specific lenses. This feature is one for the experts, though; Nikon doesn't recommend that you use the fine-tuning tool unless it's unavoidable. If you consistently have focusing trouble with a lens, I recommend that you start by having your local camera tech inspect the lens to be sure it doesn't need repair. If everything checks out and you want to try the fine-tuning feature, the D7000 camera manual provides instructions.

And now for the very last (I promise) autofocus customization option: Through settings on the Controls section of the Custom Setting menu, you can set the Function (Fn) button, AE-L/AF-L button, and Depth-of-Field Preview button to lock focus or lock focus and exposure together. And you can set the OK button to highlight the active autofocus point instead of selecting the center point. But what say I leave that discussion for Chapter 11, okay?

Focusing Manually

Some subjects confuse even the most sophisticated autofocusing systems, causing the camera's autofocus motor to spend a long time "hunting" for its focus point. Animals behind fences, reflective objects, water, and low-contrast subjects are just some of the autofocus troublemakers. Autofocus systems also struggle in dim lighting, although that difficulty is often offset on the D7000 by the AF-assist lamp, which shoots out a beam of light to help the camera find its focusing target.

When you encounter situations that cause an autofocus hangup, you can try adjusting the autofocus options discussed earlier in this chapter. But often, it's simply easier and faster to switch to manual focusing. For best results, follow these manual-focusing steps:

1. **Adjust the viewfinder to your eyesight.**

   Chapter 1 shows you how to take this critical step. If you don't adjust the viewfinder, scenes that are in focus may appear blurry and vice versa.

2. **Set the camera and the lens-focusing switches to the manual focusing positions, as shown in Figure 8-15.**

3. **Select a focus point.**

   Use the same technique as when selecting a point during autofocusing: Looking through the viewfinder, press the Multi Selector right, left, up, or down until the point you want to use flashes red.

Focusing ring

Figure 8-15: On the kit lens, the focusing ring is behind the zoom ring.

During autofocusing, the selected focus point tells the camera what part of the frame to use when establishing focus. And technically speaking, you don't *have* to choose a focus point for manual focusing — the camera will set the focus according to the position that you set by turning the focusing ring. However, choosing a focus point is still a good idea, for two reasons: First, even though you're focusing manually, the camera provides some feedback to let you know if focus is correct, and that feedback is based on your selected focus point. Second, if you use spot metering, an exposure option covered in Chapter 7, exposure is based on the selected focus point.

4. **Frame the shot so that your subject is under your selected focus point.**

5. **Twist the lens focusing ring to focus.**

Figure 8-15 shows you where to find the focusing ring on the kit lens.

When the camera thinks focus is set on the object under your focus point, the green focus lamp in the lower-left corner of the viewfinder lights, just as it does during autofocusing. Little triangles on either side of the green dot indicate that focus is set in front of or behind the object in the focus point. (Refer to Figure 8-13.)

6. **Press the shutter button halfway to initiate exposure metering.**

   Adjust exposure as needed; see Chapter 7 for help.

7. **Press the shutter button the rest of the way to take the shot.**

Correcting lens distortion

If you take a lot of pictures with wide-angle lenses, you may notice that vertical structures in the scene sometimes appear to bend outward from the center of the image. This is known as *barrel distortion*. On the flip side of the coin, shooting with a long telephoto lens sometimes causes those verticals to bow inward, creating an effect called *pincushion distortion*.

The Retouch menu on your camera has a post-capture filter you can apply to try to correct both problems. (See Chapter 10 for help.) But the D7000 also has an Auto Distortion Control feature that attempts to correct the image as you're shooting. It only works with certain types of lenses (specifically, those that Nikon

classifies as type G and D), but is worth trying if your lens is compatible. You can turn the feature on and off via the Shooting menu or the Information display control strip, as shown in the figures here.

When you use this feature, understand that some of the area you see in your viewfinder may not be visible in the final photo because the anti-distortion manipulation requires some cropping of the scene. So after activating the feature, take some test shots and examine the pictures carefully. If you're not happy with the results, return to the menu and change the setting back to Off.

Manipulating Depth of Field

Getting familiar with the concept of *depth of field* is one of the biggest steps you can take to becoming a more artful photographer. I introduce you to depth of field in Chapters 3 and 7, but here's a quick recap just to hammer home the lesson:

- *Depth of field* refers to the distance over which objects in a photograph appear sharply focused.

- With a shallow, or small, depth of field, distant objects appear more softly focused than the main subject (assuming that you set focus on the main subject, of course).

- With a large depth of field, the zone of sharp focus extends to include objects at a distance from your subject.

Which arrangement works best depends entirely on your creative vision and your subject. In portraits, for example, a classic technique is to use a short depth of field, as I did for the photo in Figure 8-16. This approach increases emphasis on the subject while diminishing the impact of the background. But for the photo shown in Figure 8-17, I wanted to emphasize that the foreground figures were in St. Peter's Square, at the Vatican, so I used a large depth of field, which kept the background buildings sharply focused and gave them equal weight in the scene.

Aperture, f/5.6; Focal length, 90mm

Figure 8-16: A shallow depth of field blurs the background and draws added attention to the subject.

So exactly how do you adjust depth of field? You have three points of control: aperture, focal length, and camera-to-subject distance, as spelled out in the following list:

✔ **Aperture setting (f-stop):** The aperture is one of three exposure settings, all explained fully in Chapter 7. Depth of field increases as you stop down the aperture (by choosing a higher f-stop number). For shallow depth of field, open the aperture (by choosing a lower f-stop number). Figure 8-18 offers an example; in the f/22 version, focus is sharp all the way through the frame; in the f/13 version, focus softens as the distance from the center lure increases. I snapped both images using the same focal length and camera-to-subject distance, setting focus on the front of the center lure.

✔ **Lens focal length:** In lay terms, *focal length* determines what the lens "sees." As you increase focal length, measured in millimeters, the angle of view narrows, objects appear larger in the frame, and —

Aperture, f/14; Focal length, 42mm

Figure 8-17: A large depth of field keeps both foreground and background subjects in focus.

the important point for this discussion — depth of field decreases. Additionally, the spatial relationship of objects changes as you adjust focal length. As an example, Figure 8-19 compares the same scene shot at a focal length of 127mm and 183mm. I used the same aperture, f/5.6, for both examples.

Whether you have any focal length flexibility depends on your lens: If you have a zoom lens, you can adjust the focal length — just zoom in or out. (The Nikon lens shown with the camera in this book, for example, offers a focal range of 18–105mm.) If you don't have a zoom lens, the focal length is fixed, so scratch this means of manipulating depth of field.

For more technical details about focal length and your camera, flip to Chapter 1 and explore the section related to choosing lenses.

✔ **Camera-to-subject distance:** As you move the lens closer to your subject, depth of field decreases. This assumes that you don't zoom in or out to reframe the picture, thereby changing the focal length. If you do, depth of field is affected by both the camera position and focal length.

Aperture, f/22; Focal length, 92mm

Aperture, f/13; Focal length, 92mm

Figure 8-18: A lower f-stop number (wider aperture) decreases depth of field.

Aperture, f/5.6; Focal length, 127mm

Aperture, f/5.6; Focal length, 183mm

Figure 8-19: Zooming to a longer focal length also reduces depth of field.

Together, these three factors determine the maximum and minimum depth of field that you can achieve, as illustrated by my clever artwork in Figure 8-20 and summed up in the following list:

- **To produce the shallowest depth of field:** Open the aperture as wide as possible (the lowest f-stop number), zoom in to the maximum focal length of your lens, and get as close as possible to your subject.

- **To produce maximum depth of field:** Stop down the aperture to the highest possible f-stop number, zoom out to the shortest focal length your lens offers, and move farther from your subject.

Greater depth of field:
Select higher f-stop
Decrease focal length (zoom out)
Move farther from subject

Shorter depth of field:
Select lower f-stop
Increase focal length (zoom in)
Move closer to subject

Figure 8-20: Your f-stop, focal length, and shooting distance determine depth of field.

Here are a few additional tips and tricks related to depth of field:

✏ **Aperture-priority autoexposure mode (A) enables you to easily control depth of field while enjoying exposure assistance from the camera.** In this mode, detailed fully in Chapter 7, you set the f-stop, and the camera selects the appropriate shutter speed to produce a good exposure. The range of aperture settings you can access depends on your lens.

Even in aperture-priority mode, keep an eye on shutter speed as well. To maintain the same exposure, shutter speed must change in tandem with aperture, and you may encounter a situation where the shutter speed is too slow to permit hand-holding of the camera.

✏ **Press the Depth-of-Field Preview button to get an idea of how your f-stop will affect depth of field.** When you look through your viewfinder and press the shutter button halfway, you can get only a partial indication of the depth of field that your current camera settings will produce. You can see the effect of focal length and the camera-to-subject distance, but not how your selected f-stop will affect depth of field.

By using the Depth-of-Field Preview button, however, you can preview the f-stop's impact. Almost hidden away on the front of your camera, the button is highlighted in Figure 8-21. When you press the button, the camera temporarily sets the aperture to your selected f-stop so that you can preview depth of field. At small apertures (high f-stop settings), the viewfinder display may become quite dark, but this doesn't indicate a problem with exposure — it's just a function of how the preview works.

By default, the camera also emits a modeling flash when you preview depth-of-field and have flash enabled. If you want to experiment with this feature, visit the flash discussion in Chapter 7 for details. Turn the feature off via the Modeling Flash option on the Custom Setting menu. And if you don't use the Depth-of-Field Preview button often, see Chapter 11 to find out how to assign the button a different role in life.

Depth-of-Field Preview button

Figure 8-21: Press this button to get a preview of the effect of aperture on depth of field.

✔ **For greater background blurring, move the subject farther from the background.** The extent to which background focus shifts as you adjust depth of field also is affected by the distance between the subject and the background. For increased background blurring, move the subject farther in front of the background.

Controlling Color

Compared with understanding some aspects of digital photography — resolution, aperture and shutter speed, depth of field, and so on — making sense of your camera's color options is easy-breezy. First, color problems aren't all that common, and when they are, they're usually simple to fix with a quick shift of your camera's white balance control. And getting a grip on color requires learning only a couple of new terms, an unusual state of affairs for an endeavor that often seems more like high-tech science than art.

The rest of this chapter explains the aforementioned white balance control, plus a couple of menu options that enable you to fine-tune the way your camera renders colors. For information on how to use the Retouch menu's color options to alter colors of existing pictures, see Chapter 10.

Correcting colors with white balance

Every light source emits a particular color cast. If you think that your beloved looks especially attractive by candlelight, you aren't imagining things: Candlelight casts a warm, yellow-red glow that is flattering to the skin.

Science-y types measure the color of light, officially known as *color temperature,* on the Kelvin scale, which is named after its creator. You can see the Kelvin scale in Figure 8-22.

When photographers talk about "warm light" and "cool light," though, they aren't referring to the position on the Kelvin scale — or at least not in the way we usually think of temperatures, with a higher number meaning hotter. Instead, the terms describe the visual appearance of the light. Warm light, produced by candles and incandescent lights, falls in the red-yellow spectrum you see at the bottom of the Kelvin scale in Figure 8-22; cool light, in the blue-green spectrum, appears at the top of the Kelvin scale.

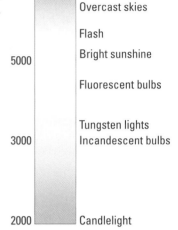

8000 — Snow, water, shade

Overcast skies

Flash

5000 — Bright sunshine

Fluorescent bulbs

Tungsten lights
3000 — Incandescent bulbs

2000 — Candlelight

Figure 8-22: Each light source emits a specific color.

At any rate, most people don't notice these fluctuating colors of light because our eyes automatically compensate for them. Except in very extreme lighting conditions, a white tablecloth appears white no matter whether we view it by candlelight, fluorescent light, or regular houselights.

Similarly, a digital camera compensates for different colors of light through *white balancing.* Simply put, white balancing neutralizes light so that whites are always white, which in turn ensures that other colors are rendered accurately. If the camera senses warm light, it shifts colors slightly to the cool side of the color spectrum; in cool light, the camera shifts colors the opposite direction.

The good news is that, as with your eyes, your camera's Auto White Balance setting tackles this process remarkably well in most situations, which means that you can usually ignore it and concentrate on other aspects of your picture. But if your scene is lit by two or more light sources that cast different colors, the white balance sensor can get confused, producing an unwanted color cast.

For example, when shooting the pencil image shown in Figure 8-23, I lit the scene with photo lights that use tungsten bulbs, which produce light with a color temperature similar to regular household incandescent bulbs. But some strong daylight was filtering in through nearby windows. In Auto White Balance mode, the camera reacted to that daylight — which has a cool color cast — and applied too much warming, giving my original image a yellow tint. No problem: I just switched the White Balance mode from Auto to the Incandescent setting. The right image in Figure 8-23 shows the corrected colors.

Figure 8-23: Multiple light sources resulted in a yellow color cast in Auto White Balance mode (left); switching to the Incandescent setting solved the problem (right).

The next section explains precisely how to make a simple white balance correction; following that, you can explore some advanced white balance options.

Changing the White Balance setting

You can adjust the White Balance setting only in the P, S, A, and M exposure modes. So if you have a color issue and want to use the other exposure modes, you're out of luck. See Chapter 7 to find out how to step up from the fully automatic exposure modes to one of these advanced exposure modes.

The current White Balance setting appears in the Control panel and Information display, as shown in Figure 8-24. The figures show the symbols that represent the Auto setting; other settings are represented by the icons you see in Table 8-1.

Table 8-1	Manual White Balance Settings
Symbol	*Light Source*
☀	Incandescent
≋	Fluorescent
☀	Direct sunlight
⚡	Flash
☁	Cloudy
🏠	Shade
K	Choose color temperature
PRE	Custom preset

WB

The quickest way to change the setting is to press and hold the WB button as you rotate the Main command dial. But you also can change the setting from the Shooting menu, as shown in Figure 8-25. If you go through the menu, you have access to some additional options. After highlighting the setting you want to use, press OK. For all settings except Auto, PRE (Preset Manual), K, and Fluorescent, you're taken to a screen where you can fine-tune the amount of adjustment the camera applies to colors. See the next section for details. If you don't want to make any adjustment, just press OK.

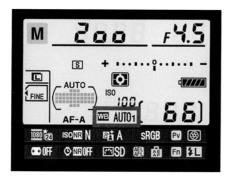
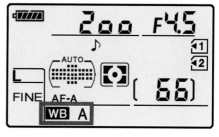

Figure 8-24: These icons represent the current White Balance setting.

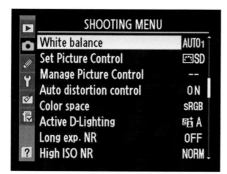
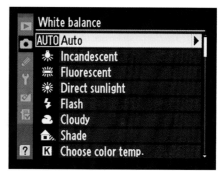

Figure 8-25: The White Balance option on the Shooting menu gives you access to some fine-tuning options.

A few other white balance factoids of note:

✔ **Modifying the Auto setting:** I know what you're thinking: "For heaven's sake, even the Auto setting is complicated?" Yep — but just a little. You can choose from two Auto White Balance settings. At the default setting, Normal, things happen as you'd expect: The camera analyzes the color temperature of the light and adjusts colors to render the scene accurately. If you use the other setting, Keep Warm Lighting Colors, the warm hues produced by incandescent lighting are left intact. I prefer the default but if you want to choose the other setting, open the Shooting menu, choose White Balance, and then choose Auto and press the Multi Selector right. You see the screen shown in Figure 8-26; make your choice and press OK. You then see the aforementioned fine-tuning screen; just press OK to move on.

You can tell which Auto setting is selected by looking at the Shooting menu and Information display; a little 1 appears next to the word *Auto* when the Normal option is active, as shown in the left screens in Figure 8-24 and 8-25. A 2 appears when the other setting is in force.

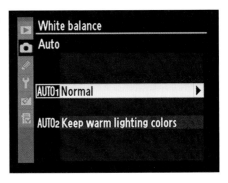

Figure 8-26: The Auto 2 setting preserves some of the warm hues that incandescent lighting lends to a scene.

✔ **Specifying a color temperature through the K White Balance setting:** If you know the exact color temperature of your light source — perhaps you're using some special studio bulbs, for example — you can tell the camera to balance colors for that precise temperature. (Well, technically, you have to choose from a preset list of temperatures, but you should be able to get close to the temperature you have in mind.) First, select the K White Balance setting. (*K* for *Kelvin,* get it?) Then, while pressing the WB button, rotate the Sub-command dial to set the color temperature, which appears at the top of the Control panel and Information display, as shown in Figure 8-27.

You also can set the temperature through the White Balance option on the Shooting menu. If you do, you see the fine-tuning screen after you select the temperature and press OK. Again, just press OK to exit the screen without making any adjustment.

✔ **Specifying a fluorescent bulb type:** For the Fluorescent setting, you can select a specific type of bulb. To do so, you must go through the Shooting menu. Select Fluorescent as the White Balance setting and then press OK to display the list of bulbs, as shown in Figure 8-28. Select the option that most closely matches your bulbs and then press OK. Press OK again, and you're taken to the fine-tuning screen. If you don't want to make any further adjustment, just press OK once more to return to the Shooting menu.

After you select a fluorescent bulb type, that option is always used when you use the WB button to select the Fluorescent White Balance setting. Again, you can change the bulb type only through the Shooting menu.

✔ **Creating a custom White Balance preset:** The PRE (Preset Manual) option enables you to create and store a precise, customized White Balance setting, as explained in the upcoming "Creating White Balance presets" section. This setting is the fastest way to achieve accurate colors when your scene is lit by multiple light sources that have differing color temperatures.

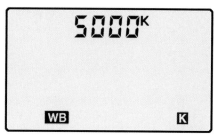

Figure 8-27: Set the White Balance option to K to select a specific color temperature.

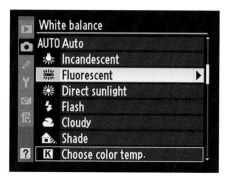
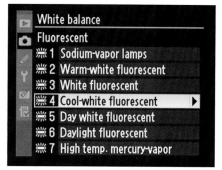

Figure 8-28: You can select a specific type of fluorescent bulb.

Your selected White Balance setting remains in force for the P, S, A, and M exposure modes until you change it. So you may want to get in the habit of resetting the option to the Auto setting after you finish shooting whatever subject it was that caused you to switch to manual White Balance mode.

Fine-tuning White Balance settings

You can fine-tune any White Balance setting (Incandescent, Cloudy, and so on). For the greatest amount of control, make the adjustment as spelled out in these steps:

1. **Set the Mode dial to P, S, A, or M.**

   Again, you can modify white balance in these exposure modes only.

2. **Display the Shooting menu, highlight White Balance, and press OK.**

3. **Highlight the White Balance setting you want to adjust, as shown on the left in Figure 8-29, and press the Multi Selector right.**

   You're taken to a screen where you can do your fine-tuning, as shown on the right in Figure 8-29.

   If you select Auto, Fluorescent, or K (Choose Color Temp.), you first go to a screen where you select the Auto setting you want to use, the specific type of bulb, or Kelvin color temperature, as covered in the preceding section. After you take that step, press OK to get to the fine-tuning screen. For custom presets that you create, you must select the preset you want to use and press OK. (See the next section for an explanation of presets.)

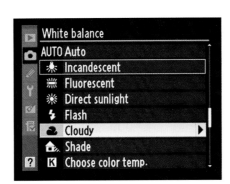
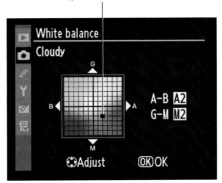

Adjustment marker

Figure 8-29: You can fine-tune the White Balance settings via the Shooting menu.

4. **Fine-tune the setting by using the Multi Selector to move the adjustment marker in the color grid.**

   The grid is set up around two color pairs: Green and Magenta, represented by G and M; and Blue and Amber, represented by B and A. By pressing the Multi Selector, you can move the adjustment marker around the grid. (The adjustment marker is labeled in Figure 8-29.)

   As you move the marker, the A–B and G–M boxes on the right side of the screen show you the current amount of color shift. A value of 0 indicates the default amount of color compensation applied by the selected White Balance setting. In Figure 8-29, for example, I moved the marker two levels toward amber and two levels toward magenta to specify that I wanted colors to be a tad warmer.

   If you're familiar with traditional colored lens filters, you may know that the density of a filter, which determines the degree of color correction it provides, is measured in *mireds* (pronounced *my-redds*). The white balance grid is designed around this system: Moving the marker one level is the equivalent of adding a filter with a density of five mireds.

5. Press OK to complete the adjustment.

After you adjust a White Balance setting, an asterisk appears next to that setting in the White Balance menu, Information display, and Control panel.

 If you want to apply a white balance shift on only the blue-to-amber axis, you don't have to go through the Shooting menu. Instead, press and hold the WB button and then rotate the Sub-command dial. You see the amount of adjustment in the Control panel and Information display, as shown in Figure 8-30, while the button is pressed. An *a* value indicates a shift toward the amber direction; a *b* value, toward blue. For example, in the figure, the A2 value shows that I shifted the setting two steps toward amber (A). Note that this trick isn't available for the K (Choose Color Temp.) or PRE (Preset Manual) White Balance settings.

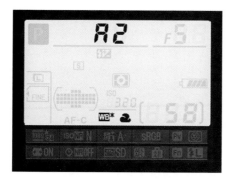 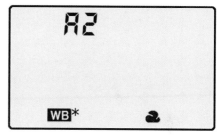

Figure 8-30: You can apply a shift along the blue/amber axis just by rotating the Sub-command dial while pressing the WB button.

Here's one other tip specifically related to shifting white balance along the blue-to-amber axis: By using a feature called *white balance bracketing,* you can automatically record your picture with and without that shift. You can even record one picture with no shift, one with an amber shift, and one with a blue shift. See the later section "Bracketing white balance" for details.

Creating White Balance presets

 If none of the standard White Balance settings do the trick and you don't want to fool with fine-tuning them, take advantage of the PRE (Preset Manual) feature. This option enables you to do two things:

✔ Base white balance on a direct measurement of the actual lighting conditions.

✔ Match white balance to an existing photo.

You can create and store up to five custom White Balance presets, which are assigned the names d-0 through d-4. The next two sections provide you with the step-by-step instructions; following that, you can find out how to select and manage your presets.

Setting white balance with direct measurement

To use this technique, you need a piece of card stock that's either neutral gray or absolute white — not eggshell white, sand white, or any other close-but-not-perfect white. (You can buy reference cards made just for this purpose in many camera stores for less than $20.)

Position the reference card so that it receives the same lighting you'll use for your photo. Then take these steps:

1. **Set the exposure mode to P, S, A, or M.**

   As with all White Balance features, you can take advantage of this one only in those exposure modes.

2. **Frame your shot so that the reference card completely fills the viewfinder.**

3. **Check exposure and adjust settings if needed.**

   This process doesn't work if the picture will be over- or underexposed.

WB

4. **Press the WB button while rotating the Main command dial to choose the PRE (Preset Manual) White Balance setting.**

   You see the letters PRE in the white balance area of the Control panel as well as in the Information display.

5. **Release the button and then immediately press and hold it again until the letters PRE begin flashing in the Control panel and viewfinder.**

6. **Release the WB button and take a picture of the gray card before the PRE warning stops flashing.**

   You have about six seconds to snap the picture.

   If the camera is successful at recording the white balance data, the letters "Gd" flash in the viewfinder. In the Control panel, the word "Good" flashes. If you instead see the message "No Gd," adjust your lighting and then try again.

When you create a preset this way, the camera automatically stores your setting as Preset d-0. (The other presets are named d-1 through d-4.) So any time you want to select and use the preset, press the WB button and rotate the Main command dial to select PRE, as in Step 4. Then rotate the Sub-command dial while pressing the button to select d-0, as shown in Figure 8-31.

(The Control panel shows the same data.) You also can select the preset through the White Balance option on the Shooting menu; see the upcoming section "Selecting a preset" for a few critical details on that method.

Figure 8-31: Preset d-0 is always used for the most recent direct-measurement preset.

Each time you go through these steps, your d-0 preset is replaced by the new white balance data you record. However, you can preserve your original preset by copying it to one of the other preset slots. See the upcoming section "Managing presets" for details on how to copy your preset as well as how to select it when you're ready to shoot.

Matching white balance to an existing photo

Suppose that you're the marketing manager for a small business, and one of your jobs is to shoot portraits of the company bigwigs for the annual report. You build a small studio just for that purpose, complete with a couple of photography lights and a nice, conservative, beige backdrop.

Of course, the bigwigs can't all come to get their pictures taken in the same month, let alone on the same day. But you have to make sure that the colors in that beige backdrop remain consistent for each shot, no matter how much time passes between photo sessions. This scenario is one possible use for an advanced white balance feature that enables you to base white balance on an existing photo.

Basing white balance on an existing photo works well only in strictly controlled lighting situations, where the color temperature of your lights is consistent from day to day. Otherwise, the White Balance setting that produces color accuracy when you shoot Big Boss Number One may add an ugly color cast to the one you snap of Big Boss Number Two.

To give this option a try, follow these steps:

1. Copy the picture that you want to use as the reference photo to a camera memory card, if it isn't already stored there.

You can copy the picture to the card using a card reader and whatever method you usually use to transfer files from one drive to another. Copy the file to the folder named DCIM, inside the main folder, named 100D7000 by default.

You can put the card containing the photo in either memory card slot.

2. **Set the exposure mode to P, S, A, or M; then open the Shooting menu, highlight White Balance, and press OK.**

3. **Select PRE (Preset Manual) and press the Multi Selector right.**

   After you press the Multi Selector right, the screen shown on the left in Figure 8-32 appears. The five thumbnails represent the five preset slots, d-0 through d-4.

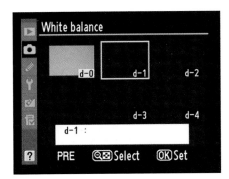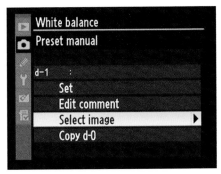

Figure 8-32: Select Preset d-1 through d-4; d-0 is reserved for direct-measurement presets.

4. **Use the Multi Selector to highlight any preset except d-0.**

   The d-0 preset is always used for White Balance settings you create by taking a picture of a reference card, as described in the preceding section.

5. **Press the ISO button.**

   You see the menu shown on the right in Figure 8-32.

6. **Highlight Select Image and press the Multi Selector right.**

   You see thumbnails of your photos.

7. **Use the Multi Selector to move the yellow highlight box over the picture you want to use as your white balance photo.**

8. **Press OK.**

   You return to the screen showing your White Balance preset thumbnails. The thumbnail for the photo you selected in Step 7 appears as the thumbnail for the preset slot you chose in Step 4.

9. **Press OK to travel to the white balance fine-tuning screen.**

   Make any adjustments to the setting that you see fit, as described in the earlier section "Fine-tuning White Balance settings."

10. **Press OK to return to the Shooting menu.**

   The White Balance setting you just created is now selected.

Selecting a preset

After creating White Balance presets, you can select the one you want to use in two ways:

✏ **Use the WB button together with the command dials.** First, select PRE as the White Balance setting by pressing the WB button as you rotate the Main command dial. Keep holding the button and rotate the Sub-command dial to cycle through the available presets (d-0 through d-4). The number of the selected preset appears in the Control panel and Information display while the button is pressed.

✏ **Use the White Balance option on the Shooting menu.** Open the Shooting menu, select White Balance, press OK, highlight PRE (Preset Manual) and press the Multi Selector right. You then see the screen that contains thumbnails for all your presets. (Refer to the left screen in Figure 8-32.) Use the Multi Selector to place the yellow highlight box over the preset you want to use and then press OK. You're taken to the fine-tuning screen that appears any time you select a White Balance setting from the menu; press OK to exit the screen without adjusting the setting.

Managing presets

Just to recap this whole White Balance preset deal:

✏ You can create up to five presets, which take the names d-0 through d-4.

✏ Preset d-0 is always used for the most recent preset you created through the direct measurement method (where you take a photo of a reference card).

✏ Presets d-1 through d-4 can be assigned to presets based on photos.

✏ If you want to create more than one preset through direct measurement, you can copy the existing d-0 setting to one of the other four preset slots before doing another direct measurement. This feature is very handy if you regularly use different studio or lighting setups, by the way. You can create one direct-measurement preset for a home studio, for example, and another for a work studio.

To copy Preset d-0 to another slot, first set the Mode dial to P, S, A, or M so that you can access the White Balance features. Then take these steps:

1. **Select the White Balance option on the Shooting menu and press OK.**

2. **Select PRE (Preset Manual) and press the Multi Selector right.**

    You see the thumbnails representing the five presets. For example, the left image in Figure 8-33 shows the d-0 position held by an existing direct-measurement preset and d-1 held by a preset based on a photo.

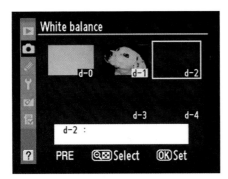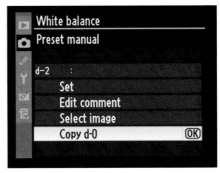

Figure 8-33: To create an additional direct-measurement preset, first copy the existing one from d-0 to another slot (d1–d4).

3. **Highlight the slot where you want to copy your d-0 preset.**

   Use the Multi Selector to place the yellow highlight box around the slot. In the figure, I selected an empty slot (d-2), but you can also copy over an existing preset. (The preset that has the yellow label — d-1 in the figure — represents your current White Balance setting.)

4. **Press the ISO button to display the menu shown on the right in the figure.**

5. **Highlight Copy D-0 and press OK.**

   You return to the preset thumbnails screen, and your original d-0 preset now occupies both d-0 and the slot you selected in Step 3. You can now create your second direct-measurement preset, which will take over the d-0 position.

Finally, you also can add a brief text comment to describe each preset. For example, you might add the label "Studio A" to one preset and "Studio B" to another to help you remember which is which. The label then appears with the preset thumbnail, as shown in Figure 8-34.

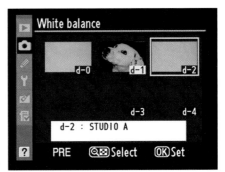

Figure 8-34: Enter text labels that describe each preset.

To enter a comment, take the exact same steps as you do to copy a preset, but instead of choosing Copy D-0 in Step 5, select Edit Comment and press the Multi Selector right. You then see a screen where you can enter your text. The specific text-entry steps are the same as you use for entering image comments, which I detail in Chapter 11, so I won't repeat them here.

Bracketing white balance

Chapter 7 introduces you to your camera's automatic bracketing feature, which enables you to easily record the same image at several different exposure settings. In addition to being able to bracket autoexposure, flash, and Active D-Lighting settings, you can use the feature to bracket white balance.

Note a couple of things about this feature:

- ✔ **You must set the Mode dial to P, S, A, or M.** You can't take advantage of auto bracketing in the other exposure modes.

- ✔ **You can bracket JPEG shots only.** You can't use white balance bracketing if you set the camera's Image Quality setting to either Raw (NEF) or any of the RAW+JPEG options. And frankly, there isn't any need to do so because you can precisely tune colors of Raw files when you process them in your Raw converter. Chapter 6 has details on Raw processing.

- ✔ **You take just one picture to record each bracketed series.** Each time you press the shutter button, the camera records a single image and then makes the bracketed copies, each at a different White Balance setting. One frame is always captured with no white balance adjustment.

- ✔ **You can apply white balance bracketing only along the blue-to-amber axis of the fine-tuning color grid.** You can't shift colors along the green-to-magenta axis, as you can when tweaking a specific White Balance setting. (For a reminder of this feature, see the earlier section "Fine-tuning White Balance settings.")

- ✔ **You can shift colors a maximum of three steps between frames.** For those familiar with traditional lens filters, each step on the axis is equivalent to a filter density of five mireds.

When you use white balance bracketing, you can request that the camera record the bracketed images so that they're progressively bluer or more amber. Or you can record one image that's pushed toward blue and another that leans toward amber. Regardless, you also get one shot that's *neutral* — that is, recorded at the current White Balance setting, without any adjustment.

I used white balance bracketing to record the three candle photos in Figure 8-35. For the blue and amber versions, I set the bracketing to shift colors the maximum three steps. As you can see, even at that max setting, the color differences between the shots are subtle. In this photo, I find the shift most noticeable in the color of the backdrop.

Neutral   Amber +3   Blue +3

Figure 8-35: I used white balance bracketing to record three variations on the subject.

To apply white balance bracketing, you first need to take these steps:

1. **Set the Mode dial to P, S, A, or M.**

2. **Set the Image Quality setting to one of the JPEG options (Fine, Normal, or Basic).**

QUAL

   Chapter 2 explains these options. To adjust the setting quickly, press the Qual button while rotating the Main command dial.

3. **Display the Custom Setting menu, select the Bracketing/Flash sub-menu, and press OK.**

4. **Select Auto Bracketing Set, as shown on the left in Figure 8-36, and press OK.**

   You see the screen shown on the right in the figure.

5. **Select WB Bracketing and press OK.**

   The bracketing feature is now set up to adjust white balance between your bracketed shots.

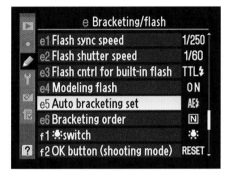 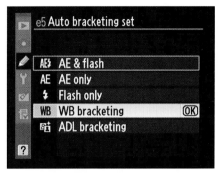

Figure 8-36: Set the Auto Bracketing Set option to WB Bracketing.

From here on, bracketing works pretty much as detailed in the steps at the end of Chapter 7. Rather than repeating everything here, I'll save some page space and provide just a quick summary of how to establish the bracketing settings.

✔ **To set the number of frames and direction of the bracketing adjustment:** Press and hold the BKT button (right-front side of the camera) while rotating the Main command dial. For white balance bracketing, the options are as follows:

- *b2F:* Records two frames, one without any adjustment and one shifted toward blue.

- *a2F:* Again, you get two frames, but the second is shifted toward amber.

- *3F:* This setting records three frames, with one neutral, one pushed toward amber, and one shifted toward blue.

- *0F:* Select this setting to turn off bracketing.

✔ **To set the amount of white-balance adjustment:** Press the BKT button and rotate the Sub-command dial. Again, you can set the bracketing amount to 1, 2, or 3.

While the BKT button is pressed, you can view both settings in the Control panel and Info display. When you release the button, you see the same BKT symbol and progress indicator that appears when you bracket exposure settings. (Again, check out Chapter 7 for details.)

After establishing the bracketing parameters, just shoot your bracketed frames. Remember, you press the shutter button just once, and the camera records the entire bracketed series. Bracketing remains in force until you disable it (by setting the frame number to 0F).

Choosing a Color Space: sRGB versus Adobe RGB

By default, your camera captures images using the *sRGB color mode,* which simply refers to an industry-standard spectrum of colors. (The *s* is for *standard,* and the RGB is for *red-green-blue,* which are the primary colors in the digital color world.) The sRGB color mode was created to help ensure color consistency as an image moves from camera (or scanner) to monitor and printer; the idea was to create a spectrum of colors that all these devices can reproduce.

However, the sRGB color spectrum leaves out some colors that *can* be reproduced in print and onscreen, at least by some devices. So as an alternative, your camera also enables you to shoot in the Adobe RGB color mode, which includes a larger spectrum (or *gamut)* of colors. Figure 8-37 offers an illustration of the two spectrums.

Some colors in the Adobe RGB spectrum can't be reproduced in print. (The printer just substitutes the closest printable color, if necessary.) Still, I usually shoot in Adobe RGB mode because I see no reason to limit myself to a smaller spectrum from the get-go.

However, just because I use Adobe RGB doesn't mean that it's right for you. First, if you plan to print and share your photos without making any adjustments in your photo editor, you're usually better off sticking with sRGB because most printers and Web browsers are designed around that color space. Second, know that to retain all your original Adobe RGB colors when you work with your photos, your editing software must support that color space — not all programs do. You also must be willing to study the whole topic of digital color a little bit because you need to use some specific settings to avoid really mucking up the color works.

If you want to go with Adobe RGB instead of sRGB, you can make the change either via the Shooting menu, as shown on the left in Figure 8-38, or via the control strip at the bottom of the Info display, as shown on the right. To use the control strip, press the Info button twice and then use the Multi Selector to highlight the Color Space option. Then press OK to access the screen where you can change the setting.

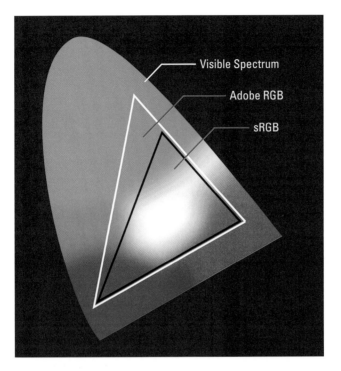

Figure 8-37: Adobe RGB includes some colors not found in the sRGB spectrum.

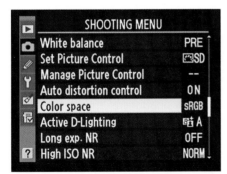 

Figure 8-38: Stick with sRGB unless you understand color management and have software that supports the Adobe RGB color space.

You can tell whether you captured an image in the Adobe RGB format by looking at its filename: Adobe RGB images start with an underscore, as in _DSC0627.jpg. For pictures captured in the sRGB color space, the underscore appears in the middle of the filename, as in DSC_0627.jpg.

Taking a Quick Look at Picture Controls

A Nikon feature called *Picture Controls* offers one more way to tweak image sharpening, color, and contrast. You can select the Picture Control setting through the Shooting menu, as shown on the left in Figure 8-39, or through the control strip option shown on the right. (Remember, press the Info button twice to activate the strip, use the Multi Selector to highlight the option, and press OK to display the relevant menu screen.)

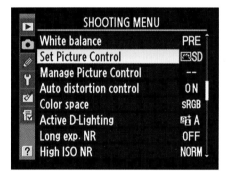 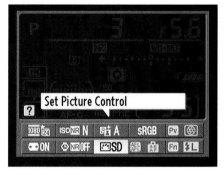

Figure 8-39: Picture Controls apply preset adjustments to color, sharpening, and other photo characteristics to images you shoot in the JPEG format.

Sharpening, in case you're new to the digital meaning of the term, refers to a software process that adjusts contrast in a way that creates the illusion of slightly sharper focus. I emphasize, "slightly sharper focus." Sharpening produces a subtle *tweak,* and it's not a fix for poor focus.

When you shoot in the advanced exposure modes — P, S, A, and M — you can choose from the following Picture Controls, represented in the menus and Information screen by the two-letter codes in parentheses. In the other exposure modes, the camera selects the Picture Control setting for you.

 ✓ **Standard (SD):** The default setting, this option captures the image normally — that is, using the characteristics that Nikon offers up as suitable for the majority of subjects.

✔ **Neutral (NL):** At this setting, the camera doesn't enhance color, contrast, and sharpening as much as in the other modes. The setting is designed for people who want to precisely manipulate these picture characteristics in a photo editor. By not overworking colors, sharpening, and so on when producing your original file, the camera delivers an original that gives you more latitude in the digital darkroom.

✔ **Vivid (VI):** In this mode, the camera amps up color saturation, contrast, and sharpening.

✔ **Monochrome (MC):** This setting produces black-and-white photos. Only in the digital world, they're called *grayscale images* because a true black-and-white image contains only black and white, with no shades of gray.

I'm not keen on creating grayscale images this way. I prefer to shoot in full color and then do my own grayscale conversion in my photo editor. That technique just gives you more control over the look of your black-and-white photos. Assuming that you work with a decent photo editor, you can control what original tones are emphasized in your grayscale version, for example. Additionally, keep in mind that you can always convert a color image to grayscale, but you can't go the other direction. You can create a black-and-white copy of your color image right in the camera, in fact; Chapter 10 shows you how.

✔ **Portrait (PT):** This mode tweaks colors and sharpening in a way that is designed to produce nice skin texture and pleasing skin tones. (If you shoot in the Portrait or Night Portrait Scene modes, the camera selects this Picture Control for you.)

✔ **Landscape (LS):** This mode emphasizes blues and greens. As you might expect, it's the mode used by the Landscape Scene mode.

The extent to which Picture Controls affect your image depends on the subject as well as the exposure settings you choose and the lighting conditions. But Figure 8-40 gives you a general idea of what to expect. As you can see, the differences between the Picture Controls are pretty subtle, with the exception of the Monochrome setting.

At least while you're new to the camera, I recommend that you stick with the Standard Picture Control setting, for two reasons. First, you have way more important camera settings to worry about — aperture, shutter speed, autofocus, and all the rest. Why add one more setting to your list, especially when the impact of changing it is minimal?

Second, if you really want to mess with the characteristics that the Picture Control options affect, you're much better off shooting in the Raw (NEF) format and then making those adjustments on a picture-by-picture basis in your Raw converter. In Nikon ViewNX 2, you can even assign any of the existing Picture Controls to your Raw files and then compare how each one affects the image. The camera does tag your Raw file with whatever Picture Control is active when you take the shot, but the image adjustments are in no way set in stone, or even in sand — you can tweak your photo at will. (The selected Picture Control does affect the JPEG preview that's used to display the Raw image thumbnails in ViewNX 2 and other browsers.)

Standard   Neutral   Vivid

Monochrome   Portrait   Landscape

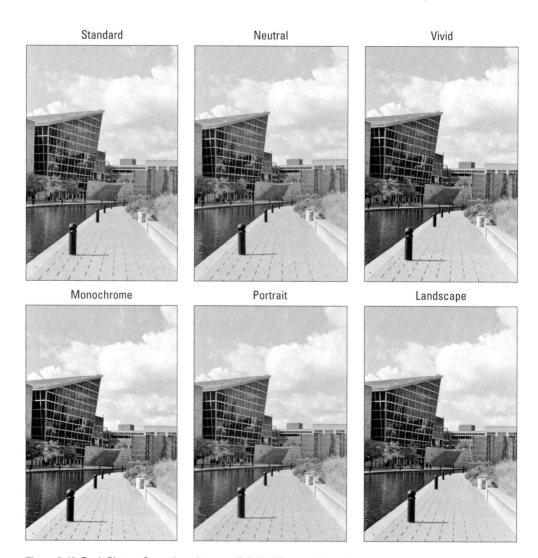

Figure 8-40: Each Picture Control produces a slightly different take on the scene.

However, in the interest of full disclosure, I should alert you to a feature that may make Picture Controls a little more useful to some people: You can modify any Picture Control to more closely render a scene the way you envision it. So, for example, if you like the bold colors of Landscape mode but don't think the effect goes far enough, you can adjust the setting to amp up colors even more.

To reserve page space in this book for functions that experience tells me will be the most useful to the most readers, I opted not to provide full details about customizing Picture Controls. But the following steps provide a quick overview of the process so that if you encounter the menu screens that contain the related options, you'll have some idea what you're seeing. So here are the basics:

1. **Set the Mode dial to P, S, A, or M.**

   These are the only modes that let you modify a Picture Control.

2. **Display the Shooting menu, choose Set Picture Control, and press OK.**

3. **Highlight the Picture Control you want to modify.**

   For example, I highlighted the Vivid setting on the left in Figure 8-41.

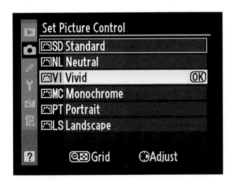 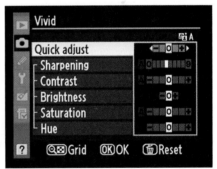

Figure 8-41: After selecting a Picture Control, press right to display options for adjusting its effect on your pictures.

4. **Press the Multi Selector right.**

   You see the screen shown on the right in Figure 8-41, containing sliders that you use to modify the Picture Control. Which options you can adjust depend on your selected Picture Control.

5. **Highlight a picture characteristic and then press the Multi Selector right or left to adjust the setting.**

A couple tips:

- Some Picture Controls offer a Quick Adjust setting, which enables you to easily increase or decrease the overall effect of the Picture Control. A positive value produces a more exaggerated effect; set the slider to 0 to return to the default setting.

- After you adjust a setting, a little line appears under the scale to mark the position of the previous setting of the option.

- The little line under the scale for each adjustment option represents the default setting for the selected Picture Control.

- Reset all the options to their defaults by pressing the Delete button.

- To display a grid that lets you see how your selected Picture Control compares with the others in terms of color saturation and contrast, as shown in Figure 8-42, press and hold the ISO button. (I vote this screen most likely to confound new camera users who stumble across it.) Note that the Standard and Portrait settings are identical in terms of contrast and saturation, so the P for Portrait doesn't appear unless you selected that Picture Style initially.

  You can't change any settings via the grid — it's for informational purposes only. However, if you display the grid from the first Set Picture Control menu (the left screen in Figure 8-41), you can press the Multi Selector up or down to select a different Picture Control. You then can press right to access the Picture Control adjustment screen.

6. **Press OK to save your changes and exit the adjustment screen.**

   As when you fine-tune a White Balance setting, an asterisk appears next to the edited Picture Style in the menu and Information screen to remind you that you have adjusted it.

Again, these steps are intended just as a starting point for those who are interested in playing with Picture Styles. Complete details on each of the Picture Control adjustment options are found in the camera manual.

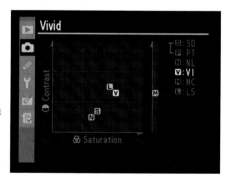

Figure 8-42: Press the ISO button to display a grid that ranks each Picture Style according to its level of saturation and contrast.

9

Putting It All Together

*E*arlier chapters of this book break down each and every picture-taking feature on your D7000, describing in detail how the various controls affect exposure, picture quality, focus, color, and the like. This chapter pulls all that information together to help you set up your camera for specific types of photography.

Keep in mind, though, that there are no hard-and-fast rules as to the "right way" to shoot a portrait, a landscape, or whatever. So feel free to wander off on your own, tweaking this exposure setting or adjusting that focus control, to discover your own creative vision. Experimentation is part of the fun of photography, after all — and thanks to your camera monitor and the Delete button, it's an easy, completely free proposition.

Recapping Basic Picture Settings

Your subject, creative goals, and lighting conditions determine which settings you should use for some picture-taking options, such as aperture and shutter speed. I offer my take on those options throughout this chapter. But for many basic options, I recommend the same settings for almost every shooting scenario. Table 9-1 shows you those recommendations and also lists the chapter where you can find details about each setting.

One key point: Instructions in this chapter assume that you set the exposure mode to P, S, A, or M, as indicated in the table. These modes, detailed in Chapter 7, are the only ones that give you access to the entire cadre of D7000 features. In most cases, I recommend using S (shutter-priority autoexposure) when controlling motion blur is important, and A (aperture-priority auto-exposure) when controlling depth of field is important. These two modes let you concentrate on one side of the exposure equation and let the camera handle the other. Of course, if you're comfortable making both the aperture and shutter speed decisions, you may prefer to work in M (manual) exposure mode instead. P (programmed autoexposure) is my last choice because it makes choosing a specific aperture or shutter speed more cumbersome.

I don't recommend the fully automated modes — Auto, Auto Flash Off, and Scene — because they don't permit you to access certain settings that can be critical to capturing good shots of certain subjects. In Portrait mode, you can't use flash in bright daylight to produce better outdoor portraits, for example. For help using the automated modes, visit Chapter 3. See Chapter 11 to find out how to use the U1 and U2 Mode dial settings to create custom exposure modes.

Finally, this chapter discusses choices for normal, through-the-viewfinder photography; Chapter 4 guides you through the options available for Live View photography and movie recording. (For Live View photography, however, most settings work the same as discussed here, with the exception of the autofocus options.)

Table 9-1	All-Purpose Picture-Taking Settings	
Option	*Recommended Setting*	*Chapter*
Exposure mode	P, S, A, or M	2
Image Quality	JPEG Fine or Raw (NEF)	2
Image Size	Large or medium	2
White Balance	Auto$_1$	8
ISO Sensitivity	100	7
Autofocus mode	Still subjects, AF-S; Moving subjects, AF-C	8
AF-area mode	Still subjects, Single Point; moving subjects, 9-, 21-, or 39-point Dynamic Area	8
Release mode	Action photos: Continuous Low or High; all others: Single Frame	2
Metering	Matrix	7
Active D-Lighting	Off	7

Shooting Still Portraits

By *still portrait,* I mean that your subject isn't moving. For subjects who aren't keen on sitting still long enough to have their picture taken, skip to the next section and use the techniques given for action photography instead.

Assuming that you do have a subject willing to pose, the classic portraiture approach is to keep the subject sharply focused while throwing the background into soft focus. This artistic choice emphasizes the subject and helps diminish the impact of any distracting background objects in cases where you can't control the setting. The following steps show you how to achieve this look:

1. **Set the Mode dial to A (aperture-priority autoexposure) and select the lowest f-stop value possible.**

   As Chapter 7 explains, a low f-stop setting opens the aperture, which not only allows more light to enter the camera but also shortens *depth of field,* or the range of sharp focus. So dialing in a low f-stop value is the first step in softening your portrait background.

   I recommend aperture-priority mode when depth of field is a primary concern because you can control the f-stop while relying on the camera to select the shutter speed that will properly expose the image. Just rotate the Sub-command dial to select your desired f-stop. (You do need to pay attention to shutter speed also, however, to make sure that it's not so slow that any movement of the subject or camera will blur the image.)

   You can monitor the current f-stop and shutter speed in the Control panel, viewfinder, and Information display, as shown in Figure 9-1.

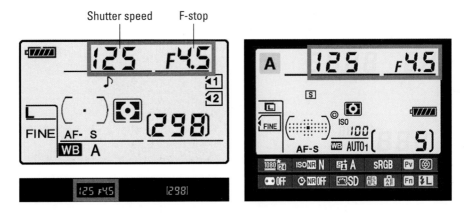

Figure 9-1: You can monitor aperture and shutter speed settings in all the displays.

2. **To further soften the background, zoom in, get closer, and put more distance between the subject and background.**

As covered in Chapter 8, zooming in to a longer focal length also reduces depth of field, as does moving physically closer to your subject. And the greater the distance between the subject and background, the more the background blurs. (A good rule is to place the subject at least an arm's length away from the background.)

A lens with a focal length of 85–120mm is ideal for a classic head-and-shoulders portrait. You should avoid using a much shorter focal length (a wider-angle lens) for portraits. They can cause features to appear distorted — sort of like how people look when you view them through a security peephole in a door. See Chapter 1 for information about calculating the effective focal lengths of lenses mounted on the D7000.

3. **For indoor portraits, shoot flash free if possible.**

Shooting by available light rather than flash produces softer illumination and avoids the problem of red-eye. To get enough light to go flash free, turn on room lights or, during daylight, pose your subject next to a sunny window, as I did for the image in Figure 9-2.

In the A exposure mode, simply keeping the built-in flash unit closed disables the flash. If flash is unavoidable, see my list of flash tips at the end of the steps to get better results.

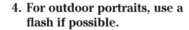
Figure 9-2: For more pleasing indoor portraits, shoot by available light instead of using flash.

4. **For outdoor portraits, use a flash if possible.**

Even in daylight, a flash adds a beneficial pop of light to subjects' faces, as illustrated in Figure 9-3. A flash is especially important when the background is brighter than the subjects, as in this example.

In the A exposure mode, press the Flash button on the side of the camera to enable the built-in flash. For daytime portraits, use the Front Curtain Flash setting. (That's the regular, basic Flash mode.) For nighttime images, try red-eye reduction or slow-sync flash; again, see the flash tips at the end of these steps to use either mode most effectively.

No flash

Fill flash

Figure 9-3: To properly illuminate the face in outdoor portraits, use fill flash.

Remember that by default, the top shutter speed for flash photography on the D7000 is 1/250 second, so in bright light, you may need to stop down the aperture a little to avoid overexposing the photo. Doing so, of course, brings the background into sharper focus. So try to move the subject into a shaded area instead. You can also use the Flash Sync Speed option on the Custom Setting menu to increase the maximum shutter speed for flash photography; see Chapter 7 for details.

5. **Press and hold the shutter button halfway to initiate exposure metering and autofocusing.**

If the camera has trouble finding the correct focusing distance, simply set your lens to manual focus mode and then twist the focusing ring to set focus. See Chapter 8 for help with focusing.

6. Press the shutter button the rest of the way to capture the image.

Again, these steps just give you a starting point for taking better portraits. A few other tips can also improve your people pics:

✔ **Pay attention to the background.** Scan the entire frame looking for intrusive objects that may distract the eye from the subject. If necessary, reposition the subject against a more flattering backdrop. Inside, a softly textured wall works well; outdoors, trees and shrubs can provide nice backdrops as long as they aren't so ornate or colorful that they diminish the subject (for example, a magnolia tree laden with blooms).

✔ **Pay attention to white balance if your subject is lit by both flash and ambient light.** If you set the White Balance setting to Auto$_1$, as I recommend in Table 9-1, enabling flash tells the camera to warm colors to compensate for the cool light of a flash. If your subject is also lit by other light sources, such as sunlight, the result may be colors that are slightly warmer or cooler (bluer) than neutral. A warming effect typically looks nice in portraits, giving the skin a subtle glow. But if you aren't happy with the result, see Chapter 8 to find out how to fine-tune white balance.

✔ **When flash is unavoidable, try these tricks to produce better results.** The following techniques can help solve flash-related issues:

• *Indoors, turn on as many room lights as possible.* With more ambient light, you reduce the flash power that's needed to expose the picture. This step also causes the pupils to constrict, further reducing the chances of red-eye. (Pay heed to my white balance warning, however.) As an added benefit, the smaller pupil allows more of the subject's iris to be visible in the portrait, so you see more eye color.

• *Try using a Flash mode that enables red-eye reduction or slow-sync flash.* If you choose the first option, warn your subject to expect both a preliminary pop of light from the AF-assist lamp, which constricts pupils, and the actual flash. And remember that slow-sync flash modes use a slower-than-normal shutter speed, which produces softer lighting and brighter backgrounds than normal flash. (Chapter 7 explains the various Flash modes.)

Take a look at Figure 9-4 for an example of how slow-sync flash can really improve an indoor portrait. When I used regular flash, the shutter speed was 1/60 second. At that speed, the camera has little time to soak up any ambient light. As a result, the scene is lit primarily by the flash. That caused two problems: The strong flash created some "hot spots" on the subject's skin, and the window frame is much more prominent because of the contrast between it and the darker bushes outside the window. Although it was daylight when I took the picture, the skies were overcast, so at 1/60 second, the exterior appears dark.

Regular fill flash, 1/60 second Slow-sync flash, 1/4 second

Figure 9-4: Slow-sync flash produces softer, more even lighting and brighter backgrounds.

In the slow-sync example, shot at 1/4 second, the exposure time was long enough to permit the ambient light to brighten the exteriors to the point that the window frame almost blends into the background. And because much less flash power was needed to expose the subject, the lighting is much more flattering. In this case, the bright background also helps to set the subject apart because of her dark hair and shirt. If the subject had been a pale blonde, this setup wouldn't have worked as well, of course. Again, too, note the warming effect that can occur when you use Auto$_1$ White Balance and shoot in a combination of flash and daylight.

Any time you use slow-sync flash, don't forget that a slower-than-normal shutter speed means an increased risk of blur due to camera shake. So always use a tripod or otherwise steady the camera. And remind your subjects to stay absolutely still, too, because they'll appear blurry if they move during the exposure. I was fortunate to have both a tripod and a cooperative subject for my examples, but I probably wouldn't try slow-sync for portraits of young children or pets.

- *For professional results, use an external flash with a rotating flash head.* Then aim the flash head upward so that the flash light bounces off the ceiling and falls softly down onto the subject. An external flash isn't cheap, but the results make the purchase worthwhile if you shoot lots of portraits. Compare the two portraits in Figure 9-5 for an illustration. In the first example, the built-in flash resulted in strong shadowing behind the subject and harsh, concentrated light. To produce the better result on the right, I used the Nikon Speedlight SB-600 and bounced the light off the ceiling. I also moved the subject a few feet farther in front of the background to create more background blur.

Figure 9-5: To eliminate harsh lighting and strong shadows (left), I used bounce flash and moved the subject farther from the background (right).

Make sure that the ceiling or other surface you use to bounce the light is white; otherwise, the flash light will pick up the color of the surface and influence the color of your subject.

- *Invest in a flash diffuser to further soften the light.* Whether you use the built-in flash or an external flash, attaching a diffuser is also a good idea. A *diffuser* is simply a piece of translucent plastic or fabric that you place over the flash to soften and spread the light — much like sheer curtains diffuse window light. Diffusers come in lots of different designs, including small, fold-flat models that fit over the built-in flash.

✔ **Frame the subject loosely to allow for later cropping to a variety of frame sizes.** Your D7000 produces images that have an aspect ratio of 3:2. That means that your portrait perfectly fits a 4-x-6-inch print size but will require cropping to print at any other proportions, such as 5 x 7 or 8 x 10. Chapter 6 talks more about this issue.

Capturing action

A fast shutter speed is the key to capturing a blur-free shot of any moving subject, whether it's a flower in the breeze, a spinning Ferris wheel, or, as in the case of Figure 9-6, a racing cyclist.

Along with the basic capture settings outlined in Table 9-1, try the techniques in the following steps to photograph a subject in motion:

1. **Set the Mode dial to S (shutter-priority autoexposure).**

   In this mode, you control the shutter speed, and the camera takes care of choosing an aperture setting that will produce a good exposure.

2. **Rotate the Main command dial to select the shutter speed.**

Figure 9-6: Use a high shutter speed to freeze motion.

(Refer to Figure 9-1 to locate shutter speed in the viewfinder and Information display.) After you select the shutter speed, the camera selects an aperture (f-stop) to match.

What shutter speed should you choose? Well, it depends on the speed at which your subject is moving, so you need to experiment. But generally speaking, 1/320 second should be plenty for all but the fastest subjects (race cars, boats, and so on). For very slow subjects, you can even go as low as 1/250 or 1/125 second. My subject in Figure 9-6 was zipping along at a pretty fast pace, so I set the shutter speed to 1/500 second. Remember, though, that when you increase shutter speed, the camera opens the aperture to maintain the same exposure. At low f-stop numbers, depth of field becomes shorter, so you have to be more careful to keep your subject within the sharp-focus zone as you compose and focus the shot.

You also can take an entirely different approach to capturing action: Instead of choosing a fast shutter speed, select a speed slow enough to blur the moving objects, which can create a heightened sense of motion and, in scenes that feature very colorful subjects, cool abstract images. I took this approach when shooting the carnival ride featured in Figure 9-7, for example. For the left image, I set the shutter speed to 1/30 second; for the right version, I slowed things down to 1/5 second. In both cases, I used a tripod, but because nearly everything in the frame was moving, the entirety of both photos is blurry — the 1/5 second version is simply more blurry because of the slower shutter.

1/30 second   1/5 second

Figure 9-7: Using a shutter speed slow enough to blur moving objects can be a fun creative choice, too.

3. In dim lighting, raise the ISO setting if necessary to allow a fast shutter speed.

Unless you're shooting in bright daylight, you may not be able to use a fast shutter speed at a low ISO, even if the camera opens the aperture as far as possible. If auto ISO override is in force, ISO may go up automatically when you increase the shutter speed — Chapter 7 has details on that feature. Raising the ISO does increase the possibility of noise, but a noisy shot is better than a blurry shot.

Why not add flash to brighten the scene? Well, adding flash is a bit tricky for action shots, unfortunately. First, the flash needs time to recycle between shots, so try to go without if you want to capture images at a fast pace. Second, the built-in flash has limited range — so don't waste your time if your subject isn't close by. And third, remember that the fastest shutter speed you can use with flash is 1/250 second by default, which may not be high enough to capture a quickly moving subject without blur.

4. **For rapid-fire shooting, set the Release mode to the Continuous Low or Continuous High setting.**

   In both modes, you can capture multiple images with a single press of the shutter button. By default, Continuous Low captures up to 3 frames per second, and Continuous High bumps the frame rate up to 6 frames per second. As long as you hold down the button, the camera continues to record images. Here again, though, you need to go flash free; you can't use these Release modes with flash.

5. **Select speed-oriented focusing options.**

   For fastest shooting, try manual focusing: It eliminates the time the camera needs to lock focus when you use autofocusing. If you do use autofocus, try these two autofocus settings for best performance:

   - Set the AF-area mode to one of the Dynamic Area settings. Chapter 7 has information to help you decide whether the 9-point, 21-point, or 39-point Dynamic Area setting is best for your subject
   - Set the Autofocus mode to AF-C (continuous-servo autofocus).

   Chapter 8 details focus options.

6. **Compose the subject to allow for movement across the frame.**

   Frame your shot a little wider than you normally might so that you lessen the risk that your subject will move out of the frame before you record the image. You can always crop to a tighter composition later. (I used this approach for my cyclist image — the original shot includes a lot of background that I later cropped away.) It's also a good idea to leave more room in front of the subject than behind it. This makes it obvious that your subject is going somewhere.

Using these techniques should give you a better chance of capturing any fast-moving subject. But action-shooting strategies also are helpful for shooting candid portraits of kids and pets. Even if they aren't currently running, leaping, or otherwise cavorting, snapping a shot before they do move or change positions is often tough. So if an interaction or scene catches your eye, set your camera into action mode and then just fire off a series of shots as fast as you can.

Capturing scenic vistas

Providing specific capture settings for landscape photography is tricky because there's no single best approach to capturing a beautiful stretch of countryside, a city skyline, or other vast subject. Take depth of field, for example: One person's idea of a super cityscape might be to keep all buildings in the scene sharply focused. But another photographer might prefer to shoot the same scene so that a foreground building is sharply focused while the others are less so, thus drawing the eye to that first building.

That said, I can offer a few tips to help you photograph a landscape the way *you* see it:

✔ **Shoot in aperture-priority autoexposure mode (A) so that you can control depth of field.** If you want extreme depth of field so that both near and distant objects are sharply focused, as in Figure 9-8, select a high f-stop value. I used an aperture of f/18 for this shot. For short depth of field, use a low value.

Figure 9-8: Use a high f-stop value to keep foreground and background sharply focused.

✔ **If the exposure requires a slow shutter, use a tripod to avoid blurring.** The downside to a high f-stop is that you need a slower shutter speed to produce a good exposure. If the shutter speed drops below what you can comfortably handhold, use a tripod to avoid picture-blurring camera shake. Remember that when you use a tripod, Nikon recommends that you turn off Vibration Reduction if you're using a kit lens.

No tripod handy? Look for any solid surface on which you can steady the camera. You can increase the ISO Sensitivity setting to allow a faster shutter, too, but that option brings with it the chances of increased image noise. See Chapter 7 for details.

✔ **For dramatic waterfall shots, consider using a slow shutter to create that "misty" look.** The slow shutter blurs the water, giving it a soft, romantic appearance, as shown in Figure 9-9. Again, use a tripod to ensure that the rest of the scene doesn't also blur due to camera shake.

TIP

In very bright light, you may overexpose the image at a very slow shutter, even if you stop the aperture all the way down and select the camera's lowest ISO setting. As a solution, consider investing in a *neutral density filter* for your lens. This type of filter works something like sunglasses for your camera: It simply reduces the amount of light that passes through the lens, without affecting image colors, so that you can use a slower shutter than would otherwise be possible.

Figure 9-9: For misty waterfalls, use a slow shutter speed and a tripod.

✔ **At sunrise or sunset, base exposure on the sky.** The foreground will be dark, but you can usually brighten it in a photo editor if needed. If you base exposure on the foreground, on the other hand, the sky will become so bright that all the color will be washed out — a problem you usually can't fix after the fact. You can also invest in a graduated neutral density filter, which is a filter that's clear on one side and dark on the other. You orient the filter so that the dark half falls over the sky and the clear side over the dimly lit portion of the scene. This setup enables you to better expose the foreground without blowing out the sky colors.

Experiment with adjusting the Active D-Lighting setting as well. Chapter 7 explains this feature, which brightens dark areas in a way that doesn't blow out highlights, leaving your sky colors intact.

✔ **For cool nighttime city pics, experiment with slow shutter.** Assuming that cars or other vehicles are moving through the scene, the result is neon trails of light like those you see in the foreground of the image in Figure 9-10. Shutter speed for this image was about ten seconds.

TIP

Instead of changing the shutter speed manually between each shot, try *bulb* mode. Available only in M (manual) exposure mode, this option records an image for as long as you hold down the shutter button. So just take a series of images, holding the button down for different lengths of time for each shot. In bulb mode, you also can exceed the standard maximum exposure time of 30 seconds.

✔ **For the best lighting, shoot during the *magic hours*.** That's the term photographers use for early morning and late afternoon, when the light cast by the sun is soft and warm, giving everything that beautiful, gently warmed look.

Can't wait for the perfect light? Tweak your camera's White Balance setting, using the instructions laid out in Chapter 8, to simulate magic-hour light.

✓ **In tricky light, bracket exposures.** *Bracketing* simply means to take the same picture at several different exposure settings to increase the odds that at least one of them will capture the scene the way you envision. Bracketing is especially a good idea in difficult lighting situations, such as sunrise and sunset. Chapter 7 shows you how to set up automatic exposure bracketing.

✓ **When shooting fireworks, use manual exposure, manual focus, and a tripod.** Fireworks require a long exposure, and trying to handhold your camera simply isn't going to work. If using a zoom lens, zoom out to the shortest focal length (widest angle). Switch to manual focusing and set focus at infinity (the farthest focus point possible on your lens). Set the exposure mode to manual, choose a relatively high f-stop setting — say, f/16 or so — and start at a shutter speed of one to five seconds. From there, it's simply a matter of experimenting with different shutter speeds. Also play with the timing of the shutter release, starting some exposures at the moment the fireworks are shot up, some at the moment they burst open, and so on. For the example featured in Figure 9-11, I used a shutter speed of about five seconds and began the exposure as the rocket was going up — that's what creates the "corkscrew" of light that rises up through the frame.

For an easy way to vary exposure time between shots, try using the Bulb shutter speed. At the Bulb setting, the shutter stays open as long as you hold down the shutter button. So you can press the button when

Figure 9-10: A slow shutter also creates neon light trails in city-street scenes.

Figure 9-11: I used a shutter speed of five seconds to capture this fireworks shot.

you hear the initial fireworks "boom" and then release the button when the exploding colors start to fade from the sky. This technique enables you to experiment with shutter speed more easily because you don't have to use the Main command dial to adjust the setting between each shot. Remember that this option is available only in the M (manual) exposure mode; it's the setting one step below the slowest shutter speed (30 seconds).

Capturing dynamic close-ups

For great close-up shots, try these techniques:

- ✔ **Check your lens manual to find out its minimum close-focusing distance.** How "up close and personal" you can get to your subject depends on your lens, not the camera body.

- ✔ **Take control over depth of field by setting the camera mode to A (aperture-priority autoexposure) mode.** Whether you want a shallow, medium, or extreme depth of field depends on the point of your photo. In classic nature photography, for example, the artistic tradition is a very shallow depth of field, as shown in Figure 9-12, and requires an open aperture (low f-stop value). But if you want the viewer to be able to clearly see all details throughout the frame — for example, if you're shooting a product shot for your company's sales catalog — you need to go the other direction, stopping down the aperture as far as possible.

Figure 9-12: Shallow depth of field is a classic technique for close-up floral images.

- ✔ **Remember that zooming in and getting close to your subject both decrease depth of field.** So back to that product shot: If you need depth of field beyond what you can achieve with the aperture setting, you may need to back away, zoom out, or both. (You can always crop your image to show just the parts of the subject that you want to feature.)

- ✔ **When shooting flowers and other nature scenes outdoors, pay attention to shutter speed, too.** Even a slight breeze may cause your subject to move, causing blurring at slow shutter speeds.

✓ **Use flash for better outdoor lighting.** Just as with portraits, a tiny bit of flash typically improves close-ups when the sun is your primary light source. Again, though, keep in mind that the maximum shutter speed possible when you use the built-in flash is 1/250 second by default. So in very bright light, you may need to use a high f-stop setting to avoid over-exposing the picture. You can also adjust the flash output via the Flash Compensation control. Chapter 7 offers details.

✓ **When shooting indoors, try not to use flash as your primary light source.** Because you're shooting at close range, the light from your flash may be too harsh even at a low Flash Compensation setting. If flash is inevitable, turn on as many room lights as possible to reduce the flash power that's needed — even a hardware-

Figure 9-13: To extend your lens's close-focus capability, you can add magnifying diopters.

store shop light can do in a pinch as a lighting source. (Remember that if you have multiple light sources, though, you may need to tweak the White Balance setting.)

✓ **To really get close to your subject, invest in a macro lens or a set of diopters.** A true macro lens, which enables you to get really, really close to your subjects, is an expensive proposition; expect to pay around $200 or more. But if you enjoy capturing the tiny details in life, it's worth the investment.

For a less expensive way to go, you can spend about $40 for a set of *diopters,* which are sort of like reading glasses that you screw onto your existing lens. Diopters come in several strengths — +1, +2, +4, and so on — with a higher number indicating a greater magnifying power. I took this approach to capture the extreme close-up in Figure 9-13, attach-ing a +2 diopter to my lens. The downfall of diopters, sadly, is that they typically produce images that are very soft around the edges, a problem that doesn't occur with a good macro lens.

Part IV
The Part of Tens

The 5th Wave   By Rich Tennant

"I've got some new image editing software, so I took the liberty of erasing some of the smudges that kept showing up around the clouds. No need to thank me."

In this part . . .

*I*n time-honored *For Dummies* tradition, this part of the book contains additional tidbits of information presented in the always popular "Top Ten" list format. Chapter 10 shows you how to do some minor picture touchups, such as cropping and adjusting exposure, by using tools on your camera's Retouch menu. Following that, Chapter 11 introduces you to ten camera functions that I consider specialty tools — bonus options that, although not at the top of the list of the features I suggest you study, are nonetheless interesting to explore when you have a free moment or two.

Ten Fun and Practical Retouch Menu Features

In This Chapter

▶ Applying Retouch menu filters

▶ Removing red-eye

▶ Correcting crooked horizon lines, lens distortion, and perspective

▶ Cropping away excess background

▶ Tweaking exposure, contrast, and color

▶ Creating a black-and-white version of a photo

▶ Having fun with special effects

*E*very photographer produces a clunker image now and then. When it happens to you, don't be too quick to reach for the Delete button because many common problems are surprisingly easy to fix. In fact, you often can repair your photos right in the camera, thanks to tools found on the Retouch menu. You can even create some special effects with certain menu options.

This chapter offers step-by-step recipes for using ten of these photo-repair and enhancement features. Additionally, I received special dispensation from the *For Dummies* folks to start off things with an additional section that summarizes tips that relate to all the Retouch menu options. In the words of Nigel Tufnel from the legendary rock band Spinal Tap, "This one goes to 11!"

Applying the Retouch Menu Filters

You can get to most of the Retouch menu features in two ways:

✔ **Display the menu, select the tool you want to use, and press OK.**
You're then presented with thumbnails of your photos. Use the Multi Selector to move the yellow highlight box over the photo you want to adjust and press OK. You next see options related to the selected tool.

The only menu item you can't access this way is Side-By-Side Comparison, explained shortly.

✔ **Switch the camera to playback mode, display your photo in single-frame view, and press OK.**
(Remember, you can shift from thumbnail display to single-frame view simply by pressing OK.) The Retouch menu then appears superimposed over your photo, as shown in Figure 10-1. Select the tool you want to use and press OK again to apply the tool to your picture. I prefer the second method so that's how I approach things in this chapter, but it's entirely a personal choice.

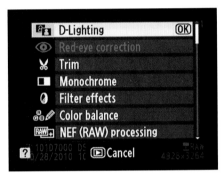

Figure 10-1: In single-frame playback view, press OK to access the Retouch menu tools.

However, you can't use this method for one Retouch menu option: Image Overlay, which combines two photos to create a third, blended image, requires you to use the first method of accessing the menu.

A few other critical factoids to note before you experiment with the Retouch menu tools:

✔ **Your originals remain intact.** When you apply a correction or enhancement from the Retouch menu, the camera creates a copy of your original photo and makes the changes to the copy only. Your original is preserved. A little icon that looks like the one that represents the Retouch menu appears with the image during playback to let you know that you're not looking at an original photo.

✔ **All menu options work with either JPEG or Raw (NEF) originals except Image Overlay.** The Image Overlay feature, which combines two pictures, works only with Raw files. See Chapter 2 for an explanation of JPEG and Raw file types.

✔ **Retouched copies for all alterations except Image Overlay are saved in the JPEG file format.** The retouched copy uses the same JPEG quality setting as the original (Fine, Normal, or Basic). For the Image Overlay option, you can choose to store the combined photo in the JPEG or Raw format.

✔ **You can apply each correction to the same picture only once.** The exception, again, is Image Overlay. If you save the composite image in the Raw format, you can combine the composite with a third Raw image. In fact, you can keep combining photos until your memory card is full, if the urge hits you.

✔ **The camera automatically assigns the next available file number to the retouched image.** Make note of the filename of the retouched version so that you can easily track it down later.

✔ **You can compare the original and the retouched version through the Side-by-Side Comparison menu option.** To use this feature, start by displaying either the original or the retouched version in full-frame playback. Then press OK, select Side-by-Side Comparison, as shown on the left in Figure 10-2, and press OK again. You see the original image on one side and the retouched version on the other, as shown in the second screen in the figure. At the top of the screen, labels indicate the Retouch tool that you applied to the photo. (I applied a Filter Effects adjustment to the after image in Figure 10-2.)

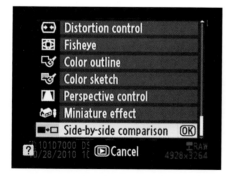 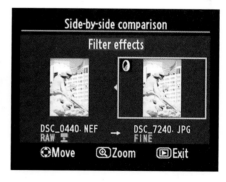

Figure 10-2: Use Side-by-Side Comparison to see whether you prefer the retouched version to the original.

These additional tricks work in Side-by-Side Comparison display:

- If you applied more than one Retouch tool to the picture, press the Multi Selector right and left to display individual thumbnails that show how each tool affected the picture.

- If you create multiple retouched versions of the same original — for example, if you create a monochrome version, save that, and then crop the original image and save that — you use a different technique to compare all the versions. First, press the Multi Selector right or left to surround the after image with the yellow highlight box. Now press the Multi Selector up and down to scroll through all the retouched versions.

QUAL

- To temporarily view the original or retouched image at full-frame view, use the Multi Selector to highlight its thumbnail and then press and hold the Qual button. Release the button to return to Side-by-Side Comparison view.

To exit Side-by-Side Comparison view and return to single-image playback, press the Playback button.

Removing Red-Eye

From my experience, red-eye isn't a major problem with the D7000. Typically, the problem occurs only in very dark lighting, which makes sense: When little ambient light is available, the pupils of the subjects' eyes widen, creating more potential for the flash light to cause red-eye reflection.

If you spot a red-eye problem, however, give the Red-Eye Correction filter a try:

1. **Display your photo in single-image view and press OK.**

   The Retouch menu appears over your photo. (Note that the Red-Eye Correction option appears dimmed in the menu for photos taken without flash.)

2. **Highlight Red-Eye Correction, as shown on the left in Figure 10-3, and press OK.**

   If the camera detects red-eye, it applies the removal filter and displays the results in the monitor. If the camera can't find any red-eye, it displays a message telling you so.

3. **Carefully inspect the repair.**

QUAL

   Press the Qual button to magnify the display so that you can check the camera's work, as shown on the right in Figure 10-3. To scroll the display, press the Multi Selector up, down, right, or left. The yellow box in the tiny navigation window in the lower-right corner of the screen indicates the area of the picture that you're currently viewing.

4. **If you approve of the correction, press OK twice.**

    The first OK returns the display to normal magnification; the second creates the retouched copy.

5. **If you're not happy with the results, press OK to return to normal magnification and then press the Playback button to cancel the repair.**

If the in-camera red-eye repair fails you, most photo-editing programs have red-eye removal tools that let you get the job done. Unfortunately, no red-eye remover works on animal eyes. Red-eye removal tools know how to detect and replace only red-eye pixels, and animal eyes typically turn yellow, white, or green in response to a flash. The easiest solution is to use the brush tool found in most photo editors to paint the proper eye colors.

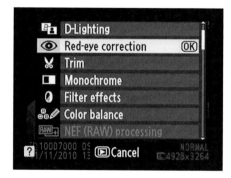
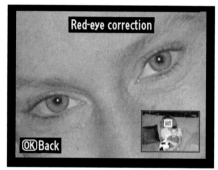

Figure 10-3: An automated red-eye remover is built right into your camera.

Straightening Tilting Horizon Lines

I seem to have a knack for shooting with the camera slightly misaligned with respect to the horizon line, which means that photos like the one on the left in Figure 10-4 often wind up crooked — in this case, everything tilts down toward the right corner of the frame. Perhaps those who say I have a skewed view of life are right? At any rate, my inability to "shoot straight" makes me especially fond of the Straighten tool on the Retouch menu. With this filter, you can rotate tilting horizons back to the proper angle, as shown in the right image in the figure.

To achieve this rotation magic, the camera must crop your image and then enlarge the remaining area — that's why the after photo in Figure 10-4 contains slightly less subject matter than the original. (The same cropping occurs if you make this kind of change in a photo editor.) The camera updates the display as you rotate the photo so that you can get an idea of how much of the original scene may be lost.

Here's how to put the tool to work:

1. **Display the photo in single-image playback mode and then press OK to get to the Retouch menu.**

2. **Highlight Straighten, as shown on the left in Figure 10-5, and press OK.**

   You see a screen similar to the one on the right in the figure, with a grid superimposed on your photo to serve as an alignment aid.

3. **To rotate the picture clockwise, press the Multi Selector right.**

   Each press spins the picture by about .25 degrees. You can achieve a maximum rotation of five degrees. The yellow pointer on the little scale under the photo shows you the current amount of rotation.

4. **To rotate in a counterclockwise direction, press the Multi Selector left.**

5. **When things are no longer off-kilter, press OK to create your retouched copy.**

Original   Straightened

Figure 10-4: You can rotate crooked photos back to a level orientation with the Straighten tool.

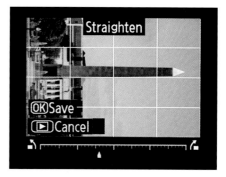

Figure 10-5: Press the Multi Selector right or left to rotate the image in increments of .25 degrees.

Removing (Or Creating) Lens Distortion

Certain types of lenses can produce a type of distortion that causes straight lines to appear curved. Wide-angle lenses, for example, often create *barrel distortion,* in which objects at the center of a picture appear to be magnified and pushed forward — as if you wrapped the photo around the outside of a barrel. The effect is perhaps easiest to spot in a rectangular subject like the oil painting in Figure 10-6. Notice that in the original image, on the left, the edges of the painting appear to bow slightly outward. *Pincushion distortion* affects the photo in the opposite way, making center objects appear smaller and farther away.

Slight barrel distortion

After Distortion Control filter

Figure 10-6: Barrel distortion makes straight lines appear to bow outward.

You can minimize the chances of distortion by researching your lens purchases carefully. Photography magazines and online photography sites regularly measure and report distortion performance in their lens reviews.

If you notice a small amount of distortion, try enabling the Auto Distortion Control option on the Shooting menu. This feature attempts to correct distortion as you take the picture. (Chapter 8 has details.) Or you may prefer to wait until after reviewing your photos and then use the Distortion Control on the Retouch menu to try to fix things. I applied the filter to create the second version of the subject in Figure 10-6, for example. Less helpful, in my opinion, is a related filter, the Fisheye filter, that actually creates distortion in an attempt to replicate the look of a photo taken with a fisheye lens.

The extent of the in-camera adjustment you can apply is fairly minimal. Additionally, I find it a little difficult to gauge my results on the camera monitor because you can't display any sort of alignment grid over the image to help you find the right degree of correction. For those reasons, I prefer to do this kind of work in my photo editor. Wherever you make the correction, understand that you lose part of your original image area as a result of the distortion correction, just as you do when you apply the Straighten tool, covered earlier in this chapter.

All that said, the first step in applying either filter is to display your photo in single-image playback mode and then press OK to display the Retouch menu. Highlight the filter you want to use (Distortion Control or Fisheye) and press OK again. From that point, the process depends on which of the two filters you're using:

- **Distortion Control:** Select Distortion Control, as shown on the left in Figure 10-7, and then press OK to see the screen shown on the right. For some lenses, an Auto option is available; as its name implies, this option attempts to automatically apply the right degree of correction. If the Auto option is dimmed or you prefer to do the correction on your own, choose Manual. You then see the screen featured in Figure 10-8. The little scale under the image represents the degree and direction of shift that you're applying. Press the Multi Selector right to reduce barrel distortion; press left to reduce pincushioning. Press OK when you're ready to make your corrected copy of the photo.

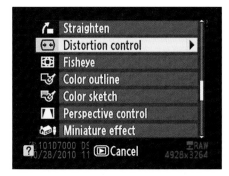 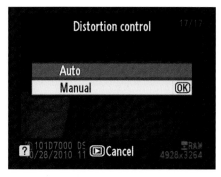

Figure 10-7: Use the Distortion Control filter to reduce barrel or pincushion distortion.

✓ **Fisheye:** After you highlight the filter name and press OK, you see a screen similar to the one in Figure 10-8, but this time, you see the word Fisheye at the top of the screen, and the scale at the bottom of the image indicates the strength of the distortion effect. Press the Multi Selector right or left to adjust the amount. Then press OK to create the fisheye copy.

Figure 10-8: Press the Multi Selector right or left to adjust the amount and type of correction.

Correcting Perspective

When you photograph a tall building and tilt the camera up to get it all in the frame, a *convergence* or *keystoning* effect occurs. This effect causes vertical structures to appear to be leaning toward the center of the frame. Buildings sometimes even appear to be falling away from you, as shown in the left image in Figure 10-9. (If the lens is tilting down, verticals instead appear to lean outward, and the building appears to be falling toward you.) Through the Retouch menu's Perspective Control feature, you can right those leaning verticals, as shown in the after photo on the right in Figure 10-9.

Original

After perspective correction

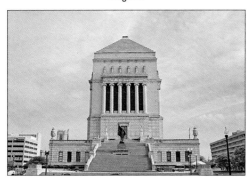

Figure 10-9: The original photo exhibited convergence (left); applying the Perspective Control filter corrected the problem (right).

Note, though, that just like the Straighten tool, you lose some area around the perimeter of your photo as part of the correction process. So when you're shooting this type of subject, frame loosely — that way, you ensure that you don't sacrifice an important part of the scene due to the correction.

To try out the feature, follow these steps:

1. **Display your photo in single-image view and press OK to bring the Retouch menu to life.**

2. **Select Perspective Control and press OK.**

   You see a grid and a horizontal and vertical scale, as shown in Figure 10-10.

3. **Press the Multi Selector left and right to move the out-of-whack object horizontally.**

4. **Press the Multi Selector up and down to rotate the object toward or away from you.**

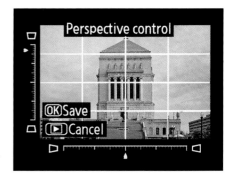

Figure 10-10: Press the Multi Selector to adjust the correction type and amount.

5. **Use the guides to get the perspective as close to normal as possible and then press OK to make a copy of the original image with your changes.**

   Depending on the scene, you may not be able to get all structures fully corrected, so just pay attention to the most prominent ones in the scene. For severe distortion problems, you may be able to get better results in your photo editor; in some programs, you can pull and push each side of the image around independently of the others, which enables you to more freely shift perspective than is possible with the type of tool provided in the camera.

Cropping (Trimming) Your Photo

To *crop* a photo simply means to trim away some of its perimeter. Cropping away excess background can often improve an image, as illustrated by Figures 10-11 and 10-12. When shooting this scene, I couldn't get close enough to the ducks to fill the frame with them, so I simply cropped it after the fact to achieve the desired composition.

Figure 10-11: The original contains too much extraneous background.

With the Trim function on the Retouch menu, you can crop a photo right in the camera. Note a few things about this feature:

✔ You can crop your photo to five different aspect ratios: 3:2, which main-tains the original proportions and matches that of a 4-x-6-inch print; 4:3, the proportions of a standard computer monitor or television (that is, not a widescreen model); 5:4, which gives you the same proportions as an 8-x-10-inch print; 1:1, which results in a square photo; and 16:9, which is the same aspect ratio as a widescreen monitor or television. If your pur-pose for cropping is to prepare your image for a frame size that doesn't match any of these aspect ratios, crop in your photo software instead.

✔ For each aspect ratio, you can choose from a variety of crop sizes, which depend on the size of your original. The sizes are stated in pixel terms, such as 3840 x 2560. If you're cropping in advance of printing the image, remember to aim for at least 200 pixels per linear inch of the print — 800 x 1200 pixels for a 4 x 6 print, for example. See Chapter 6 for more details about printing.

Figure 10-12: Cropping creates a better composition and eliminates background clutter.

✔ If you captured the original photo using the Raw or Raw+JPEG Fine Image Quality setting, the cropped version is saved as a JPEG Fine image. For other JPEG images, the crop version has the same Image Quality level as the original.

✔ After you apply the Trim function, you can't apply any other fixes from the Retouch menu. So make cropping the last of your retouching steps.

Keeping those caveats in mind, trim your image as follows:

1. **Display your photo in single-image view and press OK to launch the Retouch menu.**

2. **Select Trim and press OK.**

   You see the screen shown in Figure 10-13. The yellow highlight box indicates the current cropping frame. Anything outside the frame is set to be trimmed away.

3. **Rotate the Main command dial to change the crop aspect ratio.**

   The selected aspect ratio appears in the upper-right corner of the screen, as shown in Figure 10-13.

4. **Adjust the cropping frame size and placement as needed.**

   The current crop size appears in the upper-left corner of the screen. You can adjust the size and placement of the cropping frame like so:

ISO

- *Reduce the size of the cropping frame.* Press and release the ISO button. Each press of the button further reduces the crop size.

QUAL

- *Enlarge the cropping frame.* Press the Qual button to expand the crop boundary and leave more of your image intact.

- *Reposition the cropping frame.* Press the Multi Selector up, down, right, and left to shift the frame position.

5. **Press OK to create your cropped copy of the original image.**

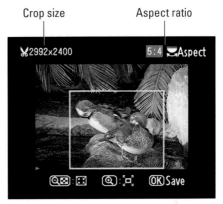

Figure 10-13: Rotate the Main command dial to change the proportions of the crop box.

Manipulating Exposure and Color

Chapters 7 and 8 discuss the bazillion exposure and color controls on the D7000. But trust me, even someone who's a pro at using all those controls sometimes produces images that are just a little off. For major problems, using a photo-editing program to make corrections is usually the answer, but for images that need just a little exposure or color tweak, try these four tools:

- **D-Lighting:** Chapter 7 explains Active D-Lighting, a Shooting menu option that brightens too-dark shadows in a way that leaves highlight details intact. You can apply a similar adjustment after you take a picture by choosing the D-Lighting filter on the Retouch menu. I used the filter on the photo in Figure 10-14, where strong backlighting left the balloon underexposed in the original image.

QUAL

When you choose the D-Lighting filter, you see before-and-after views of the image, as shown in Figure 10-15. Press the Multi Selector up or down to set the strength of the adjustment to Low, Normal, or High. I used High for the balloon image. To get a closer view of the adjusted photo, press and hold the Qual button. Release the button to return to the two-thumbnail display.

You can't apply D-Lighting to a picture taken using the Monochrome Picture Control, introduced in Chapter 8. Nor does D-Lighting work on any pictures to which you've applied the Quick Retouch filter, covered next, or the Monochrome filter, detailed a little later in this chapter.

Original image

D-Lighting, High

Figure 10-14: An underexposed photo (left) gets help from the D-Lighting filter (right).

✓ **Quick Retouch:** This filter increases contrast and color saturation and, if your subject is backlit, also applies a D-Lighting adjustment to restore some shadow detail that otherwise might be lost. In other words, Quick Retouch is sort of like D-Lighting on steroids.

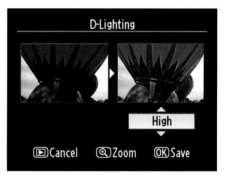

Figure 10-15: Press the Multi Selector up or down to vary the strength of the correction.

Figure 10-16 illustrates the difference between the two filters. The first example shows my original, a close-up shot of a tree bud about to emerge. I applied the D-Lighting filter to the second example, which brightened the darkest areas of the image. In the final example, I applied the Quick Retouch filter. Again, shadows got a slight bump up the brightness scale. But Quick Retouch also increased color saturation and adjusted the overall image to expand the tonal range across the entire brightness spectrum, from very dark to very bright. In this photo, the saturation change is most noticeable in the yellows and reds of the tree bud. (The sky color may initially appear to be less saturated, but in fact, it's just a lighter hue than the original, thanks to the contrast adjustment.)

As with D-Lighting, you can choose from three levels of Quick Retouch correction. And the same restrictions apply: You can't apply the filter to monochrome images or on pictures that you adjusted via D-Lighting. (However, you can create two retouched copies of your original image, applying D-Lighting to one and Quick Retouch to the other. You then can use the Side-by-Side Comparison feature, explained at the beginning of this chapter, to see which version you prefer.)

✓ **Filter Effects:** Shown in Figure 10-17, the Filter Effects option offers five color-manipulation filters that are designed to mimic the results produced by traditional lens filters. (The other two filters on the menu, Cross Screen and Soft, are special-effects filters; you can read about both later in this chapter.)

The color filters work like so:

- *Skylight filter:* This filter reduces the amount of blue in an image. The result is a very subtle warming effect.

- *Warm filter:* This one produces a warming effect that's just a bit stronger than the Skylight filter.

- *Color intensifiers:* You can boost the intensity of reds, greens, or blues individually by applying these filters. When you choose these filters, you can press the Multi Selector up or down to control the strength of the adjustment.

As an example, Figure 10-18 shows you an original image and three adjusted versions. As you can see, the Skylight and Warm filters are both very subtle; in this image, the effects are most noticeable in the sky. The fourth example shows a variation created by using the Color Balance filter, explained next, and shifting colors toward the cool (bluish) side of the color spectrum.

Original

D-Lighting

Quick Retouch

Figure 10-16: Quick Retouch adjusts saturation and contrast and, if necessary, also applies a D-Lighting correction.

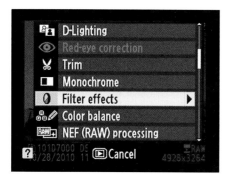
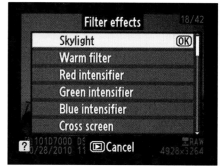

Figure 10-17: You can choose from seven effects that mimic traditional lens filters.

Original image

Skylight filter

Warm filter

Color Balance filter, shifted to blue

Figure 10-18: Here you see the results of applying two Filter Effects adjustments and a Color Balance shift.

✔ **Color Balance:** Offering more flexibility than the Filter Effects options, this filter enables you to shift colors toward any part of the color spectrum. For example, shifting colors toward the cooler — bluer — spectrum produced the fourth example in Figure 10-18.

When you choose the filter from the Retouch menu, you see the screen shown in Figure 10-19. The important control here is the color grid in the lower-left corner. You shift image colors by using the Multi Selector to move the tiny black square (labeled color shift marker in the figure) around the grid. Press up to make the image greener, press right to make it redder, and so on. In the figure, I positioned the marker to strengthen blue tones, for example.

Color shift marker

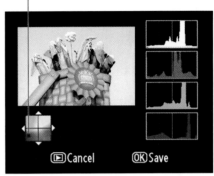

Figure 10-19: Press the Multi Selector to move the color shift marker and adjust color balance.

The histograms on the right side of the display show you the resulting impact on overall image brightness as well as on the individual red, green, and blue brightness values — a bit of information that's helpful if you're an experienced in the science of reading histograms. (Chapter 5 gives you an introduction.) But if you're not up to speed on histograms, don't sweat it — just check the image preview to monitor your results.

Creating Monochrome Photos

With the Monochrome Picture Control feature covered in Chapter 8, you can shoot black-and-white photos. Technically, the camera takes a full-color picture and then strips it of color while it records the image to the memory card, but the end result is the same.

As an alternative, you can create a black-and-white copy of an existing color photo by applying the Monochrome option on the Retouch menu. You can also create sepia and *cyanotype* (blue and white) images via the Monochrome option. Figure 10-20 shows you examples of all three effects.

Original   Black and white

Sepia   Cyanotype

Figure 10-20: You can create three monochrome effects through the Retouch menu.

I prefer to convert my color photos to monochrome images in my photo editor; going that route simply offers more control, not to mention it's easier to preview your results on a large computer monitor than on the camera monitor. Still, I know that not everyone's as much of a photo-editing geek as

I am, and there's certainly no harm in trying the in-camera filter. Just select Monochrome from the Retouch menu, as shown on the left in Figure 10-21, and then press OK to display the screen shown on the right. Select the type of monochrome image you want to create and press OK again. For the Sepia and Cyanotype options, you then see a screen that asks you to set the intensity of the tint; press the Multi Selector up and down to do so and then give OK one final tap.

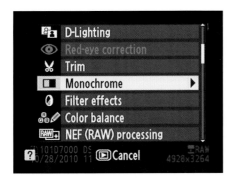 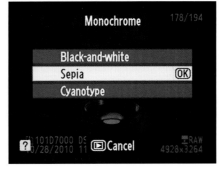

Figure 10-21: For the Sepia and Cyanotype options, you can adjust the intensity of the color tint.

Experimenting with Special Effects

Along with the practical correction tools discussed in the preceding sections, the Retouch menu also offers the following special-effects filters:

✓ **Soft:** To soften focus of an image, choose Filter Effects, select Soft, as shown in Figure 10-22, and press OK. You see a preview of your image with the filter applied at the default amount (Normal). Press the Multi Selector up or down to instead choose High for a stronger blur or Low for less blur. Figure 10-23 offers a look at how the filter alters an image at the High setting. The result is a painterly effect; squint hard enough, and you can almost see a Monet in the making.

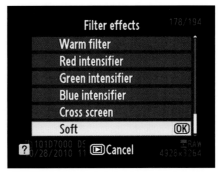

Figure 10-22: The Soft filter applies a blur to the entire image.

Original

Soft filter

Figure 10-23: I used the filter at the High setting to create the second image here.

✔ **Cross Screen:** Also accessed through the Filter Effects option, Cross Screen adds a starburst effect to the brightest part of your image, as shown in Figure 10-24. (Look for the filter just above the Soft filter, as shown in Figure 10-22.)

When you choose the Cross Screen filter, you're presented with the options shown in Figure 10-25. You can adjust the number of points on the star, the intensity of the effect, the length of the star's rays, and the angle of the effect. Just use the Multi Selector to highlight an option and then press right to display the available settings. Highlight your choice and press OK. To update the preview after changing a filter setting, highlight Confirm and press OK. When you're happy with the effect, choose Save and press OK.

Keep in mind that the number of starbursts the filter applies depends on your image. You can't change that number; the camera automatically adds the twinkle effect wherever it finds very bright objects. If you want to control the exact placement of the starbursts, forgo the in-camera filter and find out whether your photo software offers a more flexible star-filter effect. Or you can create the effect manually by painting the starburst strokes onto the image in a photo editor.

It's also important to frame your original image with a little extra "head room" around the object that will get the starburst, as I did in my examples. Otherwise, there isn't room in the picture for the effect.

✔ **Color Outline:** Select this Retouch menu option to create a black-and-white line drawing based on a photo, as I did in Figure 10-26. This is a fun project to do with kids — you can, in essence, create a custom coloring-book page that they can then fill in with watercolors, crayons, or markers.

Original   Cross Screen filter applied

Figure 10-24: The Cross Screen filter adds a starburst effect to the brightest parts of the photo.

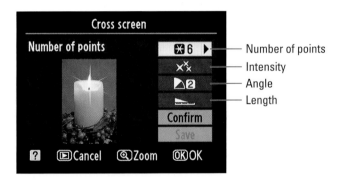

Figure 10-25: You can play with four filter settings to tweak the effect.

✓ **Color Sketch:** This filter also creates a sketch of your photo, but this time with a result similar to a drawing done in colored pencils. I used the filter on the architectural image shown in Figure 10-27, for example. When you select the effect, you see a preview like the one in Figure 10-28. You get two options: Vividness, which affects the boldness of the colors; and Outlines, which determines the thickness of outlines. Highlight an option and press the Multi Selector right or left to adjust the setting. Press OK when you create a look you like.

Figure 10-26: Use Color Outline to create a black-and-white line drawing out of a photo.

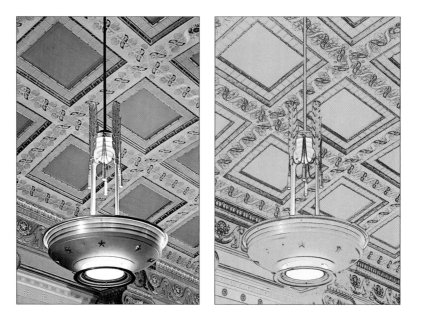

Figure 10-27: Color Sketch produces this type of effect.

Creating a Miniature Effect

Have you ever seen an architect's small-scale models of planned developments? The ones complete with tiny trees and even people? The Miniature Effect on the Retouch menu offers a tool that attempts to create a photographic equivalent by applying a strong blur to all but one portion of a landscape, as shown in Figure 10-29. The left photo is the original; the right shows the result of applying the filter. For this example, I set the focus point on the part of the street occupied by the cars.

Figure 10-28: For the Color Sketch filter, you can vary the vibrancy of the colors and the strength of the outlines.

Figure 10-29: The Miniature Effect throws all but a small portion of a scene into very soft focus.

This effect works best if you shoot your subject from a high angle — otherwise, you don't get the miniaturization result. To try it out, take these steps:

1. **Display your photo in full-frame playback and press OK to bring up the Retouch menu.**

2. **Highlight Miniature Effect, as shown on the left in Figure 10-30, and press OK.**

   You see your image in a preview similar to the one shown on the right in the figure.

3. **Use the Multi Selector to position the yellow box over the area you want to keep in sharp focus.**

QUAL

4. **To preview the effect, press the Qual button.**

   When you release the button, you return to the screen shown on the right in Figure 10-30. Keep adjusting the placement of the box and previewing the result until you're happy.

5. **To create a copy of your photo with the effect applied, press OK.**

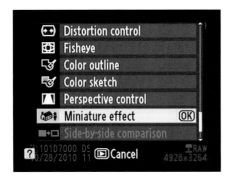 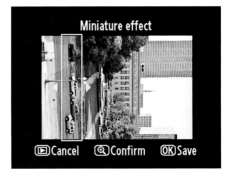

Figure 10-30: Use the Multi Selector to position the yellow rectangle over the area you want to keep in sharp focus.

Two Roads to a Multi-Image Exposure

The D7000 offers two features that enable you to combine multiple photographs into one:

- ✓ **Multiple Exposure (Shooting menu):** With this option, you can combine your next two to three shots. After you enable the option and take your shots, the camera merges them into one file. The shots used to create the composite aren't recorded and saved separately.

✓ **Image Overlay (Retouch menu):** This option enables you to merge two existing Raw images. I used this option to combine a photo of a werewolf friend, shown on the top left in Figure 10-31, with a nighttime garden scene, shown on the top right. The result is the ghostly image shown beneath the two originals. Oooh, scary!

On the surface, both options sound kind of cool. The problem is that you can't control the opacity or positioning of the individual images in the combined photo. For example, my overlay picture would have been more successful if I could move the werewolf to the left in the combined image so that he and the lantern aren't blended. And I'd also prefer to keep the background of image 2 at full opacity in the overlay image rather than getting a 50-50 mix of that background and the one in image 1, which only creates a fuzzy looking background in this particular example.

However, there is one effect that you can create successfully with either option: a "two views" composite like the one in Figure 10-32. For this image, I used Image Overlay to combine the front and rear views of the antique match striker, shown at the top of the figure, into the composite on the bottom.

Figure 10-31: Image Overlay merges two Raw (NEF) photos into one.

Figure 10-32: If you want each subject to appear solid, use a black background and position the subjects so that they don't overlap.

For this trick to work, the background in both images must be the same solid color (black seems to be best), and you must compose your photos so that the subjects don't overlap in the combined photo, as shown here. Otherwise, you get the ghostly portrait effect like what you see in Figure 10-31.

To be honest, I don't use Image Overlay or Multiple Exposure for the purpose of serious photo compositing. I prefer to do this kind of work in my photo-editing software, where I have more control over the blend. Understand, too, that neither feature is designed to produce an HDR (high dynamic range) image, which lifts different brightness ranges from different images to create the composite. For HDR, you need software that can do tone mapping, not just whole-image blending. (See the Chapter 7 section related to exposure bracketing for more about HDR.)

In the interest of reserving space in this book for features that I think you will find much more useful, I leave you to explore these two on your own. (The manual explains the steps involved in using each of them.) Again, though, I think that you'll find photo compositing much easier and much more flexible if you do the job in your photo-editing software.

11

Ten Special-Purpose Features to Explore on a Rainy Day

In This Chapter

▷ Creating your own exposure modes and menu

▷ Adding text comments and copyright notices to images

▷ Creating custom image-storage folders

▷ Changing the function of some controls

Consider this chapter the literary equivalent of the end of one of those late-night infomercial offers — the part where the host exclaims, "But wait! There's more!"

The ten features covered in these pages fit the category of "interesting bonus." They aren't the sort of features that drive people to choose one camera over another, and they may come in handy only for certain users, on certain occasions. Still, they're included at no extra charge with your camera purchase, so check 'em out when you have a few spare moments. Who knows; you may discover that one of these bonus features is actually a hidden gem that provides just the solution you need for one of your photography problems.

Creating Custom Exposure Modes (U1 and U2)

After you gain some experience with your camera, you'll probably find that you routinely use certain picture-taking options for specific types of photos. For example, you might prefer one set of options when shooting landscapes and another for shooting indoor sports. If you routinely spend a lot of time adjusting options for different scenes, here's a way to make life easier: You can store two sets of picture options as custom exposure modes: U1 and U2. Then any time you want to use those settings, you simply rotate the Mode dial to either U1 or U2, as shown in Figure 11-1.

Best of all, setting up your custom exposure modes is a quick-and-easy process:

Figure 11-1: You can create two custom exposure modes, U1 and U2.

1. **Set the Mode dial to P, S, A, or M.**

   The mode you choose determines what picture settings you can control, and thus what options you can store as part of your custom exposure mode. For example, in A mode you control the f-stop, or aperture setting, whereas in S mode you control shutter speed. (See Chapter 7 for a rundown of the P, S, A, and M exposure modes.)

2. **Select the camera settings you want to store.**

   In A mode, for example, select the initial f-stop that you want the camera to use any time you switch to the custom exposure mode. In S mode, select the initial shutter speed. Also choose settings like Image Quality, Image Size, Exposure Compensation, Flash Compensation, Flash mode, White Balance, Autofocus settings, and so on.

   Just a handful of shooting settings can't be stored: Storage Folder, File Naming, Manage Picture Control, Multiple Exposure, and Interval Timer Shooting.

3. **Display the Setup menu and choose Save User Settings, as shown on the left in Figure 11-2.**

4. **Press OK to display the right screen in Figure 11-2.**

5. **Highlight the user mode (U1 or U2) that you want to use to store your settings.**

6. **Press right to display the screen shown in Figure 11-3.**

7. **Select Save Settings and press OK.**

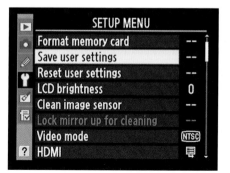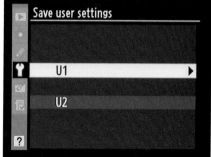

Figure 11-2: Choose the Save Settings option to store the current camera settings as custom exposure mode U1 or U2.

To use the settings you stored, just turn the Mode dial to the custom mode you created (U1 or U2). You can still adjust any settings you like while in the custom mode — you don't have to stick with your default f-stop or shutter speed, for example. The camera just starts you out with the settings that you dialed in when creating the custom mode. You can return to the stored settings at any time by rotating the Mode dial to another setting and then back to your custom mode.

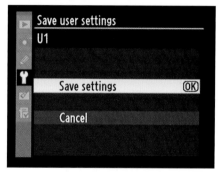

Figure 11-3: After you choose Save Settings and press OK, your custom exposure mode is ready to use.

To reset all the values in U1 or U2 to the defaults, choose the Reset User Settings option on the Setup menu. It lives just beneath the Save User Settings option. (Refer to the left screen in Figure 11-2.)

Creating Your Own Menu

In addition to creating custom exposure modes U1 and U2, you can build your very own, specialized menu that holds up to 20 of the options you use most frequently. And unlike the custom exposure modes, which can store only picture-taking options, your custom menu can contain selections from any camera menu. Check it out:

1. **Display the My Menu menu, as shown on the left in Figure 11-4.**

   The My Menu menu shares quarters with the Recent Settings menu; highlight the menu icon labeled in Figure 11-4 to access both menus. If the Recent Settings menu appears, scroll to the end of the menu, select Choose Tab, press OK, select My Menu, and press OK again. The My Menu screen then appears.

2. **Highlight Add Items and press OK.**

   You see a list of the five main camera menus, as shown on the right in Figure 11-4.

3. **Highlight a menu that contains an option you want to add to your custom menu and then press the Multi Selector right.**

   You see a list of all available options on that menu, as shown on the left in Figure 11-5. Options not available in the current exposure mode appear dimmed; remember that you can access many settings only in the P, S, A, and M modes.

   A few items can't be added to a custom menu. A little box with a slash through it appears next to those items.

4. **To add an item to your custom menu, highlight it and press OK.**

   You see the Choose Position screen, shown on the right in Figure 11-5, where you can change the order of your menu items. For now, just press OK to return to the My Menu screen; you can set up the order of your menu items later. (See the list following these steps.) The menu item you just added appears at the top of the My Menu screen.

5. **Repeat Steps 2–4 to add more items to your menu.**

   In Step 3, a check mark appears next to any item already on your menu.

My Menu/Recent Settings icon

Figure 11-4: You can create a custom menu to hold your favorite menu items.

Figure 11-5: Highlight a menu item and press OK to add it to your custom menu.

After creating your custom menu, access it by pressing the Menu button and choosing the Recent Settings/My Menu screen. (If you want to switch to the Recent Settings menu, select Choose Tab and then select Recent Settings.)

You can reorder and remove menu items as follows:

✔ **Change the order of menu options:** Display your custom menu and highlight Rank Items, as shown on the left in Figure 11-6. You see a screen that lists all your menu items in their current order. Highlight a menu item, as shown on the right in the figure, press OK, and then use the Multi Selector to move it up or down the list. Press OK to lock in the new position of the menu item. When you're happy with the order of the menu items, press the Multi Selector left to return to the My Menu screen.

 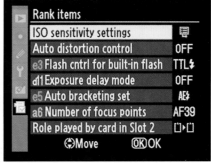

Figure 11-6: Choose Rank Items to change the order of menu items.

✔ **Remove menu items:** Again, head for the My Menu screen. Select Remove Items and press OK. You see a list of all the current menu items, with an empty box next to each item. To remove an item, highlight it and press the Multi Selector right. A check mark then appears in that item's box. After tagging all the items you want to remove, highlight Done and press OK. You see a confirmation screen asking permission to remove the item; press OK to go forward.

Annotating Your Images

Through the Image Comment feature on the Setup menu, you can add text comments to your picture files. Suppose, for example, that you're traveling on vacation and visiting a different destination every day. You can annotate all the pictures you take on a particular outing with the name of the location or attraction. You can then view the comments during playback as well as in Nikon ViewNX 2, which ships free with your camera, or Capture NX 2, which you must buy separately. The comments also appear in some other photo programs that enable you to view metadata.

Here's how the Image Comment feature works:

1. **Display the Setup menu and highlight Image Comment, as shown on the left in Figure 11-7.**

2. **Press OK to display the right screen in the figure.**

3. **Highlight Input Comment and press the Multi Selector right.**

   You see a keyboard-type screen like the one shown in Figure 11-8.

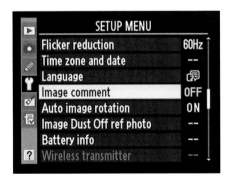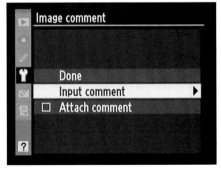

Figure 11-7: You can tag pictures with text comments that you can view in Nikon ViewNX 2.

4. **Use the Multi Selector to high-light the first letter of the text you want to add.**

   Scroll the display to access additional characters not visible on the initial screen.

5. **Press OK to enter the letter into the display box at the bottom of the screen.**

6. **Keep highlighting letters and pressing OK to enter your comment.**

   Your comment can be up to 36 characters long. Use these tricks as you enter text:

Figure 11-8: Highlight a letter and press OK to enter it into the comment box.

   - *Move the cursor:* (The cursor is the gray highlight that surrounds the active character.) Press the ISO button while pressing the Multi Selector in the direction you want to shift the cursor.

   - *Delete a character:* Move the cursor under the offending letter and then press the Delete button.

7. **To save the comment, press the Qual button.**

   The little magnifying glass symbol next to the word OK at the bottom of the menu screen reminds you to use the Qual button, which sports the same symbol.

   After you press the button, the Image Comment menu reappears.

8. **Highlight Attach Comment and press the Multi Selector right to put a check mark in the box, as shown on the left in Figure 11-9.**

   The check mark turns on the Image Comment feature.

9. **Highlight Done, as shown on the right in Figure 11-9, and press OK.**

   You're returned to the Setup menu. The Image Comment menu item should now be set to On.

The camera applies your comment to all pictures you take after turning on Image Comment. To disable the feature, revisit the Image Comment menu, highlight Attach Comment, and press the Multi Selector right to toggle off the check mark. Select Done and press OK to make your decision official.

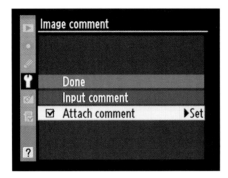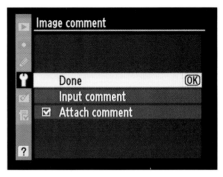

Figure 11-9: Be sure to select Done and press OK before exiting the menu.

In Nikon ViewNX 2, the comment appears as part of the file metadata, as shown in Figure 11-10. If the Metadata panel is hidden, click the arrows labeled in the figure. (See Chapter 6 for additional information about ViewNX 2.) The same area of the panel also shows copyright data that you embed using the feature explained in the next section. To view the comment during playback, enable the Shooting Data display mode; Chapter 5 has details.

Click to display Metadata panel

Figure 11-10: Comments appear with other metadata in Nikon ViewNX 2.

Embedding a Copyright Notice

By using the Copyright Information option on the Setup menu, you can load copyright data into the camera's brain. Then, whenever you shoot a picture, your copyright information is recorded with the image file. As with comments that you add through the Image Comment option, you can view the embedded copyright data during playback and in many photo programs, including Nikon ViewNX 2, as shown in Figure 11-10.

Including a copyright notice is a reasonable first step to take if you want to prevent people from using your pictures without permission. Anyone who views your picture in a program that can display *metadata* (the extra data recorded with a digital photo file) will see your copyright notice. Obviously, that won't be enough to completely prevent unauthorized use of your images. And technically speaking, you hold the copyright to your photo whether you take any steps to mark it with your name. But if you ever come to the point of pressing legal action, you can at least show that you did your due diligence in letting people know that you hold the copyright.

To enter your copyright information, take these steps:

1. **Display the Setup menu and highlight Copyright Information, as shown on the left in Figure 11-11.**

2. **Press OK to display the second screen shown in Figure 11-11.**

3. **Highlight Artist and press OK to display a text-entry screen.**

4. **Enter your name.**

    The text-entry screen works just as when you add image comments. Use the Multi Selector to highlight a letter and then press OK to enter that character. You can enter up to 36 characters.

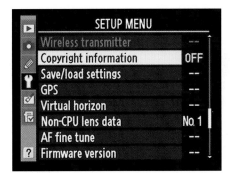
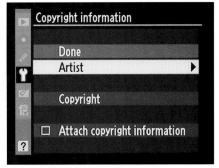

Figure 11-11: Use this feature to embed copyright information into each picture file.

To move the cursor within your text, press and hold the ISO button as you press the Multi Selector in the direction you want to move the cursor.

To delete a character, move the cursor under it and press Delete.

5. **After entering your name, press the Qual button to return to the Copyright Information screen.**

6. **Highlight Copyright, press OK, and then enter your copyright notice.**

   This time, you can enter a whopping 54 characters.

7. **Press Qual to return to the main Copyright Information screen.**

   The copyright information you entered appears on the screen, as shown on the left in Figure 11-12.

8. **Highlight Attach Copyright Information and press the Multi Selector right to place a check mark in the adjacent box, as shown on the right in Figure 11-12.**

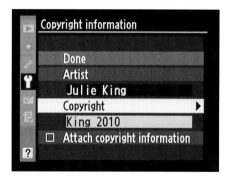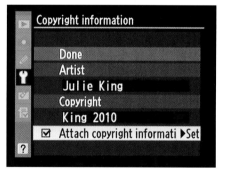

Figure 11-12: Press the Multi Selector right to toggle the Attach setting on and off.

9. **Highlight Done and press OK.**

Don't forget this step (as I always seem to do)! Otherwise, none of your changes will "stick," and you'll have to go through the whole process again. After you return to the Setup menu, the Copyright Information item on the Setup menu (left screen in Figure 11-11) should be set to On, indicating that the camera will now include your copyright text as part of the file metadata for all subsequent shots. A little copyright symbol also appears in the Information display (look for it near the Metering mode symbol).

To stop adding the copyright data, just revisit the Copyright Information screen, toggle the Attach box off, and then select Done and press OK.

Creating Custom Image Folders

By default, your camera initially stores all your images in one folder, which it names 100D7000. Folders have a storage limit of 999 images; when you exceed that number, the camera creates a new folder, assigning a name that indicates the folder number — 101D7000, 102D7000, and so on.

You can leave the folder creation and numbering completely up to the camera or, through the Storage Folder option on the Shooting menu, you can create a new folder and give it whatever three-number designation you choose. You might create a folder to store work images and assign it the name 200D7000, for example, and reserve 100-series folders for personal images. Or two photographers sharing the camera can each set up their own sets of folders.

To create a new folder, follow these steps:

1. **Display the Shooting menu and highlight Storage Folder, as shown on the left in Figure 11-13.**

2. **Press OK to display the screen shown on the right in Figure 11-13.**

3. **Choose Select Folder by Number and press the Multi Selector right.**

   You see the screen shown on the left in Figure 11-14. Just one thing to note here: A folder icon next to the current folder number indicates that the folder contains images already.

4. **Assign the folder a number.**

   Use the Multi Selector to highlight one of the three digits and then press up and down to change the number, as shown on the right in Figure 11-14. When you create a new folder, the little folder icon disappears.

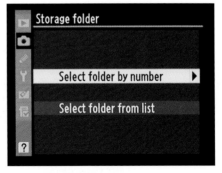

Figure 11-13: You can assign custom folder numbers to organize your images right on the camera.

Folder partially full symbol

Figure 11-14: Use this screen to create a new folder.

5. Press OK.

The camera creates your new folder and automatically selects it as the current storage folder.

If you take advantage of this option, remember to specify where you want your pictures stored each time you shoot: Select Storage Folder from the Shooting menu and then choose Select Folder by Number (if you know the folder number) or Select Folder from List (to see a list of all existing folders). Highlight your choice and press OK. If you go the first route, remember to look for the little folder icon (refer to the left screen in Figure 11-14). If the icon appears full, you can't put any more pictures in the folder.

See Chapter 5 to find out how to control which folders appear during playback.

Customizing the Fn and Preview Buttons

Earlier chapters introduce you to the Fn (Function) button and Depth-of-Field Preview button (Preview, for short), both shown in Figure 11-15. As a recap, the buttons are set by default to perform the following tasks:

- **Fn button:** Pressing the button locks the flash power at its current setting; press again to remove the lock. Chapter 7 explains FV Lock (*Flash Value Lock*).

- **Preview button:** When you look through the viewfinder and press the button, the display changes to give you an idea of how your current f-stop setting will affect depth of field. If the built-in flash is raised, it emits a modelling flash as well if the Mode dial is set to P, S, A, or M. (See Chapter 7 to find out how to disable the modelling flash.)

While learning about your camera and especially while using this book as a reference, it's a good idea to stick with these defaults — otherwise, my instructions won't work (and neither will those you find in other instructional resources). But after you gain some experience, you may want to change the functions that are performed by the buttons. Flash Value Lock, for example, isn't a function I use very often. So I set my button to enable the viewfinder grid display so that I can turn the grid on and off more quickly than going through the Custom Setting menu.

For both buttons, you can assign any function listed in Table 11-1. As you ponder the possibilities, keep in mind that the AE/AF Lock, AE Lock Only, AE Lock (Hold), AF Lock Only, and FV Lock functions also can be assigned to the AE-L/AF-L button; see the next section for details.

Fn (Function) button

Depth-of-Field Preview button

Figure 11-15: You can change the functions performed by these buttons.

You can set the function of the Fn or Preview button in two ways:

✏ **Via the Custom Setting menu:** Bring up the Controls section of the menu and then select Assign Fn Button, as shown on the left in Figure 11-16, to customize the Fn button. Choose Assign Preview Button to customize the Preview button. Then press OK to display the list of possible button assignments, as shown on the right in the figure.

Figure 11-16: Head to the Controls submenu of the Custom Setting menu to change the button functions.

✔ **Via the Information screen:** Press the Info button twice to activate the control strip at the bottom of the Information display. Then use the Multi Selector to highlight the Fn button setting, as shown on the left in Figure 11-17, or the Preview button, as shown on the right. The little symbol that appears with each button indicates its current function: For example, the little flash symbol and L that appear with the Fn button label tell you that the button is set to lock the flash value (L for lock). And the little aperture symbol next to the Preview button shows that pressing the button stops down the aperture so that you can preview depth of field in the viewfinder.

After highlighting the button you want to adjust, press OK to get to the menu screen of possible button functions. Select your choice and press OK.

Figure 11-17: You can also adjust the button functions through the control strip on the Information screen.

WB As you're exploring the menu options, you can press the WB button to display a help screen that explains what each option accomplishes. See Chapter 1 for more about using the help screens. Note that some functions work only when the exposure mode is set to P, S, A, or M.

Table 11-1	Possible Fn and Preview Button Settings
If You Choose This Setting . . .	*The Button Does This*
Preview	Default setting for the Preview button; pressing the button displays in the viewfinder a preview of how your selected aperture setting affects depth of field. Also emits modelling flash by default if flash is raised.
FV Lock	Default setting for the Fn button. Your first button press locks the flash value (FV); the second press removes the lock.

If You Choose This Setting . . .	The Button Does This
AE/AF Lock	Locks autofocus and autoexposure for as long as you hold the button.
AE Lock Only	Holding the button locks autoexposure only.
AE Lock (Hold)	Pressing the button locks autoexposure until you press the button a second time or the exposure meters turn off.
AF Lock Only	Autofocus is locked as long as you press the button.
Flash Off	Holding the button as you press the shutter button disables the flash for your next shot.
Bracketing Burst	When exposure, flash, or Active D-Lighting bracketing is enabled, pressing the button causes the camera to record all images in the bracketed series with a single press of the shutter button even if Release mode is set to Single or Quiet. In Continuous High or Continuous Low Release mode or when white-balance bracketing is enabled, the camera records multiple bracketed series as long as the shutter button is pressed.
Active D-Lighting	Press the button while rotating the Main command dial to adjust the Active D-Lighting setting.
+NEF (RAW)	When the Image Quality is set to JPEG Fine, Normal, or Basic, press the button to record a Raw (NEF) copy of the next picture you take. Keep the shutter button pressed halfway between shots to record a series of Raw+JPEG images. Press the button again to exit without recording the Raw copy.
Matrix Metering	Sets the metering mode to Matrix while the button is pressed.
Center-Weighted Metering	Sets the metering mode to center-weighted while the button is pressed.
Spot Metering	Sets the metering mode to spot metering while the button is pressed.

(continued)

Table 11-1 *(continued)*

If You Choose This Setting . . .	The Button Does This
Framing grid	Press the button while rotating the Main command dial to toggle the viewfinder framing grid on and off.
Viewfinder virtual horizon	Press the button to convert the exposure meter into a level indicator. When you see a single bar under the 0 position of the meter, the camera is level to the horizon. Bars to the left of center indicate the camera is tilted right; bars to the right indicate the camera is tilted left. Press the button again to return to the normal viewfinder display.
Access Top Item in My Menu	Displays the top item stored in a custom menu you create through the My Menu feature.
1 Step Spd/Aperture	Press the button while rotating the command dials to adjust the current f-stop or shutter speed in increments of one stop instead of using the current setting of the EV Steps for Exposure Control option (1/3 stop or 1/2 stop).
Choose Non-CPU Lens Number	Press the button while rotating the Main command dial to select a specific non-CPU lens number (relevant only if you enter data for the non-CPU lens option covered in Chapter 1). View the lens setting in the Information display.
Playback	Press the button to enter and exit playback mode.
Start movie recording	Press the button to start and stop movie recording.

Customizing the AE-L/AF-L Button

 Set just to the right of the viewfinder, the AE-L/AF-L button enables you to lock focus and exposure settings when you shoot in autoexposure and autofocus modes, as explored in Chapters 7 and 8.

Normally, autofocus and autoexposure are locked when you press the button, and they remain locked as long as you keep your finger on the button. But you can change the button's behavior via the Assign AE-L/AF-L Button option, found on the Controls section of the Custom Setting menu and shown on the left in Figure 11-18. You also can adjust the setting through the control strip on the Information display, as shown on the right in the figure. Press Info twice to access the strip, select the option, and press OK. Either way, you see a menu screen offering these choices:

Figure 11-18: You also can change the function of the AE-L/AF-L button.

- ✔ **AE/AF Lock:** This is the default setting. Focus and exposure remain locked as long as you press the button.

- ✔ **AE Lock Only:** Autoexposure is locked as long as you press the button; autofocus isn't affected. (You can still lock focus by pressing the shutter button halfway.)

- ✔ **AF Lock Only:** Focus remains locked as long as you press the button. Exposure isn't affected.

- ✔ **AE Lock (Hold):** This locks exposure only with a single press of the button. The exposure lock remains in force until you press the button again or the exposure meters turn off.

- ✔ **AF-On:** Pressing the button activates the camera's autofocus mechanism. If you choose this option, you can't lock autofocus by pressing the shutter button halfway.

- ✔ **FV Lock:** Pressing the button locks the current flash exposure value (FV). This function is assigned by default to the Fn button; see the preceding section to find out how to use that button for another purpose if you assign the AE-L/AF-L button to operate the FV Lock function.

After highlighting the option you want to use, press OK.

As another alternative, you can set the shutter button to lock focus and autoexposure together when you press it halfway — normally, the button locks focus only. To enable this feature, look for the Shutter-Release Button AE-L option, found on the Timers/AE Lock section of the Custom Setting menu and shown in Figure 11-19. If you set the option to On, your half-press of the shutter button locks exposure and focus, assuming that you use autofocus settings that permit focus locking; see Chapter 8 for details on that bit of business.

Finally (let's hope), if you attach the optional MB-D11 battery pack, it also sports an AE-L/AF-L button, and you can change the function of that button as well. The relevant option is Assign MD-D11 AE-L/AF-L Button, and it's also found on the Controls section of the Custom Setting menu. You can choose from the same settings that are available for the camera's button, or you can set the battery pack button to serve whatever purpose that you assign to the Fn button.

Whew, I'm giving myself a headache considering all these possible variations — you?

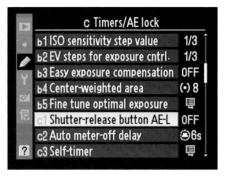

Figure 11-19: This option controls whether the shutter button can be used to lock focus and exposure.

Changing the Behavior of the Command Dials

Through the Customize Command Dials option, found on the Controls section of the Custom Setting menu and shown in Figure 11-20, you can control several aspects of how the command dials behave, as follows:

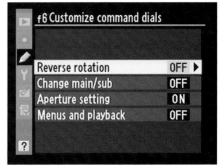

Figure 11-20: The right screen here shows the default setup for the command dials.

✔ **Reverse Rotation:** At the default setting, Off, the dials work as indicated throughout this book and the camera manual. Select Yes to reverse the direction you spin the dials to accomplish the various tasks they perform.

✔ **Change Main/Sub:** This setting controls which dial you use to adjust aperture and shutter speed. At the default setting, Off, the Main command dial adjusts shutter speed, and the Sub-command dial controls aperture. Select On to swap the dial roles.

✔ **Aperture Setting:** For this option, you have two settings:

- *Sub-Command Dial:* This is the default setting; the Sub-command dial controls aperture (assuming that you didn't alter the setting of the Change Main/Sub option just discussed). When you select this option, the Aperture Setting item on the menu appears set to On, as shown on the right in Figure 11-20.

- *Aperture Ring:* This setting relates only to lenses that have an aperture ring; if you select this option, you can adjust the f-stop only by using the aperture ring. The Aperture Setting item on the menu appears set to Off when you select this option.

✔ **Menus and Playback:** For this option, you choose from three settings: Off, On, and On (Image Review Excluded). At the default setting, Off, you use the Multi Selector to scroll through your pictures and change the data-display style during playback. And during shooting, you use the Multi Selector to navigate menus.

If you change the setting to On, you can use the command dials as follows:

- *Playback:* Use the Main command dial to scroll through pictures in single-image view and move the image-highlight box left or right during thumbnails playback. Use the Sub-command dial to adjust the data-display mode during single-image playback and move the highlight box up and down through thumbnails.

- *Menu navigation:* Rotate the Main command dial to scroll up and down through a menu. Rotate the Sub-command dial right to display the submenu for the selected item; rotate left to jump to the previous menu.

If you instead select On (Image Review Excluded), things work the same as they do when you choose the On setting, but the command dials don't work during the image-review period.

Uncoupling the Buttons and Command Dials

Under the normal camera setup, an operation that involves both a camera button and a command dial requires you to hold the button down while spinning the dial to get results. For example, to change the Flash mode, you hold down the Flash button while rotating the Main command dial.

If you find it cumbersome to keep pressing the button while you rotate the dial, you can tell the two controls that you prefer them to dance separately instead of cheek to cheek. The relevant option is located on the Controls submenu of the Custom Setting menu; it's called Release Button to Use Dial, as shown in Figure 11-21. Set the option to Yes, and you let up on the button and then rotate the command dial to adjust a camera setting. So to change Flash mode, for example, you press and release the Flash button and then rotate the Main command dial.

Figure 11-21: I think the default setting for this option is the safest way to go.

There's a little gotcha to remember if you accept this variation, however: The setting you're adjusting remains active until you press the button again, you press the shutter button halfway, or the exposure meters turn off. And if you forget and leave the setting "open," you can easily adjust the setting with the command dial when you're meaning to do something else. For this reason, I prefer to use the default setting, No.

Changing the Purpose of the OK Button

You can customize the role that OK plays during shooting through the aptly named OK Button (Shooting Mode) option, found in the Controls section of the Custom Setting menu and shown on the left in Figure 11-22. Highlight the option and press OK to display the screen on the right in the figure.

The settings work like so:

- **RESET (Select Center Focus Point):** At this setting, which is the default, the button automatically selects the center autofocus point. I think that's a pretty handy feature, so it's my choice. See Chapter 8 for help understanding autofocus points.

🖝 **Highlight Active Focus Point:** At this setting, pressing the button high-lights the active focus point in the viewfinder.

🖝 **Not Used:** This setting disables the center button during shooting altogether — although I don't know why you would unless you somehow keep pressing the button by accident.

 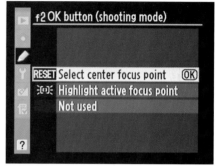

Figure 11-22: You can change the role the Multi Selector center button plays during shooting and playback.

Index

Apple & Macs

iPad For Dummies
978-0-470-58027-1

iPhone For Dummies,
4th Edition
978-0-470-87870-5

MacBook For Dummies, 3rd
Edition
978-0-470-76918-8

Mac OS X Snow Leopard For
Dummies
978-0-470-43543-4

Business

Bookkeeping For Dummies
978-0-7645-9848-7

Job Interviews
For Dummies,
3rd Edition
978-0-470-17748-8

Resumes For Dummies,
5th Edition
978-0-470-08037-5

Starting an
Online Business
For Dummies,
6th Edition
978-0-470-60210-2

Stock Investing
For Dummies,
3rd Edition
978-0-470-40114-9

Successful
Time Management
For Dummies
978-0-470-29034-7

Computer Hardware

BlackBerry
For Dummies,
4th Edition
978-0-470-60700-8

Computers For Seniors
For Dummies,
2nd Edition
978-0-470-53483-0

PCs For Dummies, Windows
7 Edition
978-0-470-46542-4

Laptops For Dummies,
4th Edition
978-0-470-57829-2

Cooking & Entertaining

Cooking Basics
For Dummies,
3rd Edition
978-0-7645-7206-7

Wine For Dummies,
4th Edition
978-0-470-04579-4

Diet & Nutrition

Dieting For Dummies,
2nd Edition
978-0-7645-4149-0

Nutrition For Dummies,
4th Edition
978-0-471-79868-2

Weight Training
For Dummies,
3rd Edition
978-0-471-76845-6

Digital Photography

Digital SLR Cameras &
Photography For Dummies,
3rd Edition
978-0-470-46606-3

Photoshop Elements 8
For Dummies
978-0-470-52967-6

Gardening

Gardening Basics
For Dummies
978-0-470-03749-2

Organic Gardening
For Dummies,
2nd Edition
978-0-470-43067-5

Green/Sustainable

Raising Chickens
For Dummies
978-0-470-46544-8

Green Cleaning
For Dummies
978-0-470-39106-8

Health

Diabetes For Dummies,
3rd Edition
978-0-470-27086-8

Food Allergies
For Dummies
978-0-470-09584-3

Living Gluten-Free
For Dummies,
2nd Edition
978-0-470-58589-4

Hobbies/General

Chess For Dummies,
2nd Edition
978-0-7645-8404-6

Drawing
Cartoons & Comics
For Dummies
978-0-470-42683-8

Knitting For Dummies,
2nd Edition
978-0-470-28747-7

Organizing
For Dummies
978-0-7645-5300-4

Su Doku For Dummies
978-0-470-01892-7

Home Improvement

Home Maintenance
For Dummies,
2nd Edition
978-0-470-43063-7

Home Theater
For Dummies,
3rd Edition
978-0-470-41189-6

Living the
Country Lifestyle
All-in-One
For Dummies
978-0-470-43061-3

Solar Power Your Home
For Dummies,
2nd Edition
978-0-470-59678-4

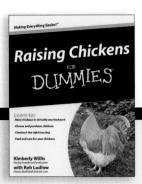

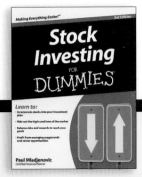

Internet

Blogging For Dummies,
3rd Edition
978-0-470-61996-4

eBay For Dummies,
6th Edition
978-0-470-49741-8

Facebook For Dummies, 3rd
Edition
978-0-470-87804-0

Web Marketing
For Dummies,
2nd Edition
978-0-470-37181-7

WordPress
For Dummies,
3rd Edition
978-0-470-59274-8

Language & Foreign Language

French For Dummies
978-0-7645-5193-2

Italian Phrases
For Dummies
978-0-7645-7203-6

Spanish For Dummies,
2nd Edition
978-0-470-87855-2

Spanish For Dummies,
Audio Set
978-0-470-09585-0

Math & Science

Algebra I For Dummies,
2nd Edition
978-0-470-55964-2

Biology For Dummies,
2nd Edition
978-0-470-59875-7

Calculus For Dummies
978-0-7645-2498-1

Chemistry For Dummies
978-0-7645-5430-8

Microsoft Office

Excel 2010 For Dummies
978-0-470-48953-6

Office 2010 All-in-One
For Dummies
978-0-470-49748-7

Office 2010 For Dummies,
Book + DVD Bundle
978-0-470-62698-6

Word 2010 For Dummies
978-0-470-48772-3

Music

Guitar For Dummies,
2nd Edition
978-0-7645-9904-0

iPod & iTunes
For Dummies,
8th Edition
978-0-470-87871-2

Piano Exercises
For Dummies
978-0-470-38765-8

Parenting & Education

Parenting For Dummies,
2nd Edition
978-0-7645-5418-6

Type 1 Diabetes
For Dummies
978-0-470-17811-9

Pets

Cats For Dummies,
2nd Edition
978-0-7645-5275-5

Dog Training For Dummies,
3rd Edition
978-0-470-60029-0

Puppies For Dummies,
2nd Edition
978-0-470-03717-1

Religion & Inspiration

The Bible For Dummies
978-0-7645-5296-0

Catholicism For Dummies
978-0-7645-5391-2

Women in the Bible
For Dummies
978-0-7645-8475-6

Self-Help & Relationship

Anger Management
For Dummies
978-0-470-03715-7

Overcoming Anxiety
For Dummies,
2nd Edition
978-0-470-57441-6

Sports

Baseball
For Dummies,
3rd Edition
978-0-7645-7537-2

Basketball
For Dummies,
2nd Edition
978-0-7645-5248-9

Golf For Dummies,
3rd Edition
978-0-471-76871-5

Web Development

Web Design
All-in-One
For Dummies
978-0-470-41796-6

Web Sites
Do-It-Yourself
For Dummies,
2nd Edition
978-0-470-56520-9

Windows 7

Windows 7
For Dummies
978-0-470-49743-2

Windows 7
For Dummies,
Book + DVD Bundle
978-0-470-52398-8

Windows 7 All-in-One
For Dummies
978-0-470-48763-1

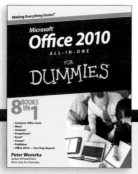

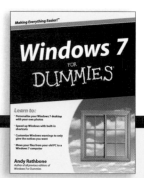